When Good Men Do Nothing

When Good
Men Do
Nothing

The Assassination of
Albert Patterson

Alan Grady

THE UNIVERSITY OF ALABAMA PRESS
Tuscaloosa and London

Typeface is New Baskerville and Birch

∞

The paper on which this book is printed meets the minimum requirements of
American National Standard for Information Science–Permanence of Paper for
Printed Library Materials, ANSI Z39.48-1984.

Library of Congress Cataloging-in-Publication Data

Grady, Alan, 1956–
When good men do nothing : the assassination of Albert Patterson / Alan Grady.
p.   cm.
Includes bibliographical references and index.
ISBN 0-8173-1141-6 (cloth : alk. paper)
1. Assassination—Investigation—Alabama—Phenix. 2. Patterson, Albert, d. 1954—
Assassination. 3. Organized crime—Alabama—Phenix City—History—20th
century. 4. Phenix City (Ala.)—History—20th century. I. Title.

HV8079.A74 G72 2003
976.1'485—dc21

2002152962

British Library Cataloguing-in-Publication Data available

Contents

Preface

Few communities have undergone an ordeal as wrenching as the one endured by Phenix City, Alabama, in the summer and fall of 1954. The murder of attorney general–nominee Albert L. Patterson on June 18 of that year set in motion what townspeople and outsiders alike refer to as "the cleanup." This term is misleading in its understatement, however, for what took place in that small southeast Alabama town was an upheaval that resulted, in less than six months, in the overthrow and replacement of the local judicial, political, and law enforcement hierarchy. Before 9:05 on that Friday night, Phenix City was a wide-open sin city that made much, if not most, of its income through illegal activities. After that single, violent action, nothing was the same. For the town's many reform-minded citizens, who for years had pursued the simple but elusive goal of basic law enforcement, it was a swift, dramatic, and, above all, glorious fight, destined to be recalled for what it truly was: the story of a citizenry who restored the will of the people, as much a triumph of liberty over tyranny as England's Glorious Revolution or America's own Revolution, the Glorious Cause.

Although Albert Patterson's murder set the Glorious Cleanup in motion, little is known about the murder investigation itself, and much of what is known is as much a myth as the up-from-the-ashes flying beast from which Phenix City takes its name. Since 1954, the biggest problem for historians has been the lack of authoritative and accurate information. Bernard Sykes, the acting attorney general who headed the probe, restricted access to the files during the investigation, and they remained restricted for years after the case was closed, even after Sykes's retirement in 1975, when he sent the twenty-one boxes of material to the state archives with strict orders that they be opened only by direct authority of the state attorney general. There, in a caged area known simply as "the vault," the Albert Patterson Case

Files gathered dust until 1994, two years after Sykes's death, when Attorney General Jimmy Evans granted access to the author.

In the meantime, the winners in the Glorious Cleanup—the Russell Betterment Association, the National Guard, and staff members from the Office of Attorney General, among others—had filled the void with conjecture, colored memories, and wishful thinking. Their story of the murder investigation, always told in its connection with the cleanup, had to be glorious too, and from the beginning there was a clear tendency for that story to become more glorious as time went on. This was not so much a conscious attempt to alter the facts as it was a natural, human tendency to remember events in the most favorable light.

Phenix City is as susceptible to gossip, embellishment, and prejudice as any other community, and those universal human foibles seem to be amplified in the former Confederacy. In his study of southern culture, *The Mind of the South,* Wilbur J. Cash said that the southern tendency toward imagination, fantasy, and romanticism led to the point where "nothing any more seems improbable save the puny inadequateness of fact, nothing incredible save the bareness of truth."[1] To put it in more familiar language, southerners are not known to let facts stand in the way of a good story. Phenix City and Russell County are about as southern as one can get, so it is not surprising that the popular tale of the Albert Patterson murder investigation closely resembles a fishing story in which, as time goes by, the fish becomes larger and the odds against the angler become greater.

Yet—no doubt because factual information about the investigation has eluded previous historians—it is precisely these folktales that, up to now, have made up much of the written histories. One example concerns Major General Walter "Crack" Hanna, the Alabama National Guard commander who was eventually put in charge of the cleanup, and his frenetic ride from Birmingham to Phenix City on the night of the murder. Within just a few weeks, Hanna told *Birmingham News* reporter Ed Strickland that the 160-mile trip, which was made with his teenage son, Private Pete Hanna, at the wheel, took about two hours. That averages out to a respectably frightening speed of 80 miles per hour—not bad for a winding two-lane highway through the Alabama countryside. When the tale of the Glorious Cleanup was rewritten about forty years later, however, the trip had been shortened to only one hour, or an average speed of 160 miles per hour, a velocity approaching qualifying speeds at Talladega. Of course, precisely how long it took General Hanna to reach Phenix City is of no direct consequence to the murder investigation, but such exaggeration speaks volumes on what is wrong with relying too heavily on personal recollections. Not that oral history has no place in the Phenix City story—I made a considerable effort over the ten years of the project to talk to anyone who could contribute, and these observations are used to the greatest extent possible—but any researcher, in determining the accuracy of these recollections, would be well advised to keep a full shaker of salt close by.

The accepted version of the Albert Patterson murder investigation, then, is as it is remembered by the victors in the Glorious Cleanup: indistinguishable from the dramatically successful anti-vice, anti-corruption crusade. But a dispassionate study of the official record, especially when isolated from the cleanup, shows that the murder investigation was more complicated and its results more ambiguous than is generally thought. These interview transcripts, interoffice memorandums, and sworn statements from both witnesses and suspects have not only remained static and free of embellishment, but they also represent a single, authoritative conduit—Bernard Sykes—through whom all official information passed. And when this information is weighed in its totality, it tells a story characterized, not by glory, but by uncertainty, internal conflict, and outside political pressure, an investigation that lost both its direction and its focus.

When Good Men Do Nothing

Crowd at crime scene following Albert Patterson's murder. At right, Albert Fuller stands beside the door of the Elite Café; at left, a cardboard box covers Patterson's blood. (Alabama Department of Archives and History, Montgomery)

1
Albert Patterson and Phenix City

Gamblers and other desperate men, here find security from their numbers . . . [the] people hold them in terror, yet dare not refuse them a hiding place.

Tyrone Power, 1833

Shortly before 9:00 on the night of June 18, 1954, Albert Patterson left his law office in Phenix City's Coulter Building and headed home. Before turning the lights off, the sixty-year-old attorney had laid a stack of signed thank-you notes on his secretary's typewriter. In the letters, about seventy-five in number, Patterson expressed his appreciation to key supporters across the state for their help in his recent nomination as Alabama attorney general. These formalities should have marked the end of a particularly hard-fought campaign, but Patterson knew better. The real battle was just beginning.[1]

Partially crippled by a World War I injury that rendered his right leg practically useless, Patterson limped down the stairs. After reaching the screen door that opened to Fifth Avenue, he turned left toward his car, which was parked in the adjoining alley. Within moments, gunshots rang out from the direction of Patterson's car, startling passersby. Those familiar with Patterson's deliberate gait were surprised to see him reeling from the alley a few seconds later without his ever-present cane. After stumbling a few steps back toward his office, he collapsed on the sidewalk and died.[2]

Phenix City, Alabama, was out of control in 1954. Although gambling and prostitution were illegal throughout the state, these very attractions drew thousands to the east Alabama town, primarily U.S. Army trainees who made the short hop across the Chattahoochee River from Fort Benning, Georgia. In *Phenix City: The Wickedest City in America,* Edwin Strickland and Gene Wortsman described the town as "an unending series of night clubs, honky tonks, clip joints, B-girl bars, whorehouses, and gambling casinos. Every highway leading into the city was lined with the institutions, and they were scattered throughout the residential districts. You could climb a tall tree, spit in any direction, and where the wind wafted the splutter, there you would find organized crime, corruption, sex and human depravity."[3] While some laughed at the dramatic description, no one, by the time the book was published in March 1955, doubted its accuracy.

Phenix City's problems had been in the making even before the area came under the authority of the United States. When Columbus, Georgia, was established in 1828, the west bank of the Chattahoochee remained part of Indian Territory. Because neither the United States nor the state of Georgia had jurisdiction in the Creek Nation, it was literally a separate country, a sanctuary for a different kind of pioneer, one on the run. From the beginning, law in Phenix City was defined by might.[4]

The village that sprang up across from Columbus had an official name, Girard, in honor of the wealthy Philadelphia philanthropist and slave dealer Stephen Girard. In late 1832, nine months after the Creeks ceded the area, the Alabama Legislature created Russell County, named after the famous Indian fighter Colonel Gilbert Christian Russell, with Girard as the first county seat.[5] As early as 1833, it was referred to by a more biblical name: Sodom. In that year, visiting Irish actor Tyrone Power gave this impression of the area: "On the Alabama side we found ourselves within a wild-looking village, scattered through the edge of the forest, bearing the unattractive name of Sodom; few of its denizens were yet stirring; they are composed chiefly of 'minions o' the moon, outlaws from the neighboring States. Gamblers and other desperate men, here find security from their numbers, and from the vicinity of a thinly inhabited Indian country, where people hold them in terror, yet dare not refuse them a hiding place."[6]

Girard lost its status as county seat in 1839 when it was transferred to Crocketsville (present-day Crawford). The county officials and lawyers left town, taking with them much of the impetus for Phenix City's early reform movement. Girard was doomed not only to retarded growth—it would not incorporate until 1890—but also to retaining its original reputation as a sin city.[7]

In 1866 the state legislature created Lee County out of the northern part of Russell County, splitting Girard as it did so. People called Girard's northern part Brownville, incorporated in 1883, but postal authorities rejected the town's application for a post office because there was already a town by that name in Tuscaloosa County. For a few years, townspeople opted for the name Lively because of the boisterous saloons frequented by the Alabama textile workers on their way home from the Columbus mills. In 1889 the legislature officially changed Lively's name to Phenix City.[8]

Unlike the more industrialized Columbus, Girard—and indeed all of Russell County—relied on farming and liquor as its principal sources of income. At the turn of the century, Girard was home to two major whiskey warehouses, shipping their stock throughout the Southeast and as far away as New York and Boston. But the whiskey interests met increasing political opposition from prohibitionists, who by 1909 were in the forefront of a move to dry up Alabama. In 1914 they gained control of the legislature, and soon afterward they passed a law prohibiting the sale of alcohol. For Girard and Russell County businessmen, this meant ignoring the law or losing everything they had.

They chose the former. Aware of the tremendous unpopularity of the law, local officials reached an unspoken agreement with the whiskey interests. Russell County grand juries routinely indicted violators, who would then pay bond. When the accused failed to show for trial, the county would pocket the forfeited surety. It seemed like a reasonable arrangement, but technically it qualified as political corruption. Whatever it was called, it was the beginning of a long history of selective law enforcement in Girard and Russell County.

Unfortunately for the Russell County distributors, local option was not an option. By the summer of 1916, prohibitionist groups were demanding state intervention in east Alabama, and the first great Russell County cleanup was under way. At the direction of the Alabama Supreme Court, Circuit Judge A. H. Alston of Clayton and the state attorney general, Logan Martin, went to Seale, the county seat since 1868, and took over the local judiciary. On August 8, Alston impaneled a new grand jury and instructed it to destroy "for once and all time" lawlessness in Russell County and to investigate collusion between bootleggers and local officials.

The resulting court proceedings were swift, merciless, and judicially questionable. Those indicted were brought to trial as soon as the grand jury voted a true bill, usually less than three hours. After the first two indictees received a hefty $2,500 fine, many of the others fled, hoping for a better day to appear before the bar. Alston declared them fugitives and confiscated their holdings.[9]

State militia entered Girard on August 10 and began hauling out bottles, kegs, and casks from the warehouses and anywhere else they could be found; these they assembled at the intersection of Seale Road and Broad Street. All day long, militiamen, special deputy sheriffs, and hired laborers destroyed some eight hundred casks of beer and an equal number of barrels of whiskey. Some workers fainted from the fumes, which could be smelled in eastern Columbus, two miles away. Eventually, more than a quarter of a million dollars' worth of illegal alcohol was destroyed during the cleanup, and several prominent citizens were ruined in the process. And as a result of the grand jury's investigation into political corruption, almost every city and county official resigned his office.[10]

The 1916 cleanup might have been longer lived had it not been for the establishment two years later of Fort Benning, the U.S. Army infantry-training school just outside Columbus. Even as the recruits were moving into the tents and thrown-together buildings, bootleg liquor was again flowing freely in Girard. Arriving doughboys quickly learned that a good time could be found on the Alabama side and crossed the Chattahoochee in droves. By the time the Roaring Twenties arrived, Martin's cleanup had completely unraveled and Girard was once again living down to its reputation.[11]

Local reformers hit upon a new idea to smooth out Girard's rough edges. They proposed to the legislature that the town be merged with Phenix City, which had grown more civilized and subdued in the half century since it was cut off from Girard. The legislature complied, and the tainted name of Girard disappeared. In 1935 a local referendum mandated that the county seat be moved from Seale to Phenix

City, which now held over half the county's population. Instead of cleaning up Girard, however, the merger fouled Phenix City. And the relocation had another unintended effect. There was now no distance between the corruption of the city and county governments. The illegal operations occurred within sight of not only city hall but the county courthouse as well.[12]

The 1930s saw another step in the consolidation of Phenix City graft and corruption. Faced with bankruptcy during the Great Depression, the city fathers, headed by Commissioner (and soon-to-be mayor) Homer D. Cobb, effected a policy of compromise with the gangsters. Confronted on the one hand by righteous citizens, who were outraged by the outright bribery of local officials, and on the other hand by Phenix City gamblers, who represented one of the few industries operating in the black, Cobb sought to keep both sides happy. To soothe the reformers, city hall routinely brought cases against the gambling establishments and brothels. The lawbreakers would either be heavily fined or, if they declined to show up in court, forfeit a hefty bond to the city. Licenses were rarely revoked outright, but if they were the standard period was only thirty days. This arrangement allowed local officials to deny that they were allowing the rackets to operate, but at the same time, it permitted the establishments to operate within a predictable system of fines and fees. In effect, the city had reached an agreement with local gangsters in which gambling, prostitution, and liquor laws would be selectively enforced in exchange for contributions to the local treasury—essentially a duplication of the system in Girard before the 1916 cleanup. Cobb's tenure also saw the establishment of the Phenix City political machine, which, having squelched his earlier runs for sheriff, now supported him for commissioner. After that, he never lost another election. Nor did anyone else who played ball.[13]

By the mid-1930s, Phenix City corruption was institutionalized. Newspapers or local reformers would occasionally make waves, but no serious scrutiny occurred on the state level. Vice continued to flourish, partly because the gangsters were shrewd businessmen who knew how to beat a retreat when the heat was turned up. When a reporter published an exposé, or when the grand jury met, or possibly during election time, the city police or the county sheriff would raid an establishment, make a few arrests, and confiscate gambling paraphernalia. Those arrested, usually warned well in advance, paid their fine or forfeited their bond. If public scrutiny was particularly intense, an establishment might even be shut down, in which case the proprietor would set up shop elsewhere, sometimes just down the street. The gambling equipment which authorities confiscated and destroyed with great fanfare was usually worn out and no longer serviceable. Oftentimes, the slot machines hauled into the city's vacant lot had been cannibalized for parts and were only ornate metal shells. The police never seemed to notice. For the reformers, this system contributed to the false impression of action. Local authorities could rightly claim they took action against gamblers whenever it was brought to their attention, and the gamblers gained a convenient way to get rid of their old equipment.[14]

Nor did the Phenix City machine have to worry about reform groups outside the county. Nationally, Prohibition had failed, and the watchdog groups that had instigated the 1916 cleanup were gone. The indifference of state authorities was demonstrated in April 1938 when an overflow crowd caused the collapse of the Ritz Café during an "Old Reliable" lottery drawing, killing twenty-four and injuring eighty-three. Governor Bibb Graves sent a detachment of National Guard troops to help keep order but took no other action, even though it was clear that Phenix City had returned to its old ways.[15]

With the outbreak of World War II, the number of recruits at Fort Benning mushroomed to nearly eighty thousand. Across the river, Phenix City's income grew proportionally. Fort Benning officials, concerned with the systematic fleecing of young infantrymen, estimated that about 80 percent of its personnel frequented Phenix City, spending more than half their pay there. Authors Strickland and Wortsman found it ironic that "the toughest soldiers in the world were trained at Fort Benning and taken for suckers in the clip joints of Phenix." Secretary of War Henry Stimson termed Phenix City the "Wickedest City in America." Another military official who confronted Phenix City was General George Patton, who, while assigned to the 2nd Armored Division at Fort Benning in 1940, proposed a drastic remedy to the problem of Phenix City: razing the town with armored weaponry.[16]

Although the flood of dollars increased the economic and political strength of the gangsters, Mayor Cobb was able to retain control of the situation and never let them forget who was boss. After Cobb, however, it was the gangsters, not the elected officials, who ran the local machine. Years later, Strickland and Wortsman would claim the influence of the Phenix City machine was "like the tentacles of a giant octopus, reach[ing] into other counties as well as the marbled halls of state office buildings in Montgomery." Despite obvious exaggeration, there is a kernel of truth here. The authors imply that Phenix City and Russell County enjoyed a political sway on state politics disproportionate to that of other local governments, but that is not a complete picture. Most states had either a two-party system or, lacking party discipline, political factions centered on single personalities, as was the case in Louisiana and Virginia. Alabama, with its monolithic Democratic Party and constitutional prohibitions against immediate succession in most political offices, had neither. As a result, the county political organizations held the real power in statewide elections. Inevitably, candidates came to the county courthouses, hat in hand, to win the blessing and influence of the local political leader. As such, Russell County was only one of sixty-seven political machines with which statewide candidates had to negotiate.[17]

Another erroneous assumption in regard to Phenix City politics is that the state government refused to interfere in Phenix City because the local political machine, primarily through vote fraud, delivered the local vote to winning gubernatorial candidates. Vote fraud was not uncommon in Alabama politics: in the 1954 Democratic primary alone, public charges of vote fraud were made in at least eleven counties, with resulting grand jury investigations in Blount, St. Clair, Escambia, and Lawrence, as well as Russell and Jefferson Counties. The concentration of political influence at the local level, precisely at the point where votes were counted and the integrity of the ballot was policed, provided an almost irresistible temptation to manipulate ballots at almost every election throughout the state, and with only the threat of a misdemeanor charge on those rare occasions where officials were caught. In addition, Russell County "voted right" only four times in the nine Democratic Party primaries for governor held from 1918 to 1954, hardly enough to maintain a consistently grateful statehouse.[18] This is not to say that Phenix City officials didn't commit vote fraud on behalf of their chosen candidates for governor—they most certainly did—but only that they weren't very good at it.[19]

What set the Russell County political community apart from the rest of Alabama was who was in charge. In most of the state's sixty-seven counties it was the popularly elected probate judge who headed the local political organization, but in Russell County the real power was John Hoyt Shepherd, the undisputed chief of Phenix City's gambling establishment. A product of the Georgia cotton mills, Shepherd had no formal schooling yet possessed a high degree of intelligence and business acumen. Over the years Shepherd and his English-born business partner, Jimmy Matthews, made a fortune running the largest of the six main lotteries in Phenix City. They also operated the famous Bama Club, one of the few gambling establishments where the games were not fixed. Unlike most of the sucker joints in Phenix City, the Bama Club was for high rollers. One was as likely to see dice throwers from New York, Chicago, Miami, and Boston as visitors from Birmingham, Montgomery, and Dothan. The Shepherd/Matthews empire also relied heavily on slot machines, and by 1951 they owned the machines in most of Phenix City's better establishments as well as those scattered among gas stations, grocery stores, cafés, and various nightspots. For fifteen years, Shepherd ruled Phenix City like a godfather. The extent of his influence became known to the general public only in July 1954, when an anonymous source sent Phenix City reformers and reporters 214 recordings of Shepherd's telephone conversations with Russell County and Phenix City officials. In them, Shepherd could be heard choosing candidates for political office, fixing juries and grand juries, and expressing concern about competing gangsters.[20]

In 1951, Shepherd and Matthews announced that they were quitting the rackets and moving into legal enterprises. Through careful investments in real estate and stocks and bonds, Shepherd increased his fortune, but he kept his hand in Phenix City gambling indirectly by renting some of his property to the racketeers who replaced him. At the time, news of Shepherd's and Matthews's retirement was cause for celebration by reformers, who predicted an end to Phenix City vice. However, the situation actually worsened because Shepherd's operations were taken over by greedy, less sophisticated men who lacked their predecessor's judgment of just how much one could get away with before the hammer came down.[21]

Phenix City is a community—one that has had more than its share of the underworld element, but a community nonetheless. This community has never been unanimous in its disregard for law and order; from the time of Tyrone Power's visit in 1833, some tolerated lawlessness and some did not. Yet there was no line through the middle of town with the gangsters on one side and the reformers on the other. As members of a community, they all sat in the same movie theaters, shopped at the same stores, sent their children to the same schools, and participated in civic affairs together.[22]

To an outside observer, the men who ran the rackets did not appear to be bad men. Many were active in their local congregations, tithing large sums weekly. It was Hoyt Shepherd and Jimmy Matthews who, over the strenuous objections of Albert Patterson, paid off the mortgage on Patterson's church; they also contributed heavily to the construction of Cobb Memorial Hospital. One Phenix City pastor joked that Matthews could be mistaken for a minister if he weren't so quiet.[23]

On the whole, then, the racketeers were not pariahs. This was less the result of a particularly open-minded attitude than of the town's long history of petty vice. Children played slot machines (illegal but found in almost every business, including the post office) with about as much guilt as the youngsters of today play video games. There were even wooden stools for those too young to reach the lever. Contributing to the community's tolerance was the fact that the gangsters' more hapless victims—those who stepped away from the crap tables penniless—were rarely fellow townsmen. And then there was the glue that holds any community together: personal relationships. The gangsters and reformers had known each other for years, as had their parents and grandparents. A reformer might find that a gangster had been in his ninth-grade civics class, that the madam of a local whorehouse was the young girl he'd had a crush on in the fifth grade, or that a local kingpin had been on the same championship basketball team during their junior year.[24]

Albert Patterson moved to this community in 1933, at the age of thirty-nine. Patterson was a Tallapoosa County native, born at New Site on January 27, 1894.[25] He came from an established family, with both grandfathers serving in the Confederate army. In some ways,

Patterson never had a childhood because he was so driven to outdo himself. Before he reached his teenage years, he had already determined that New Site was too small for him. Shortly after he finished seventh grade, he hit the road and wound up in Fairfield, Texas, taking on work on farms and in oil fields. It would have been natural to quit school, but Patterson knew that education was the key to getting ahead, and he managed to graduate from high school.[26]

By 1914 he had returned to New Site and met Agnes Benson, a teacher's daughter recently arrived from Colbert County. Although the attraction was immediate, Patterson soon returned to Texas, where he enlisted in the Third Texas Infantry on May 9, 1916. After his first tour of duty along the Mexican border in 1917, Patterson attended Officer Training School at Camp Bowie, Texas, and received a commission as second lieutenant. With the entry of the United States into World War I and the certainty that he would be shipped overseas, Patterson summoned Agnes to Texas, where they married on July 14, 1917.[27]

In July 1918, Patterson arrived in France with the 36th Infantry Division, 141st Regiment, Company B. Near St. Etienne a German machine gun shot him up so badly that his comrades left him for dead, but after two days in no-man's-land he dragged himself back to Allied lines. For his valor, Patterson won the Croix de Guerre with Gilt Star and a practically useless right leg.[28]

Discharged as a first lieutenant, Patterson underwent a lengthy convalescence at Ft. McPherson, Georgia. Eventually he learned to walk with a cane, an old man's prop on a twenty-six-year-old veteran. Undeterred by his war wounds, he returned to Alabama and took teacher certification classes at Jacksonville Normal School (now Jacksonville State University). Just as in his high school days in Texas, Patterson took on a number of odd jobs to pay his way, including farming, working in the cotton mills, and teaching school.[29]

After completing Jacksonville's two-year program in 1921, Patterson landed the job of principal at Clay County High School in Ashland and later at Coosa County High School in Rockford. According to former students, Patterson was a stern disciplinarian. Regardless of the offense, he required students to publicly own up to misdeeds and apologize to the entire student body during Monday-morning assembly. At Rockford he once expelled one of Agnes's younger sisters, who was living with them at the time, for a minor transgression. Now in her nineties, she still maintains her innocence.[30]

Agnes Patterson matched Albert's fervor for education, and she took the two-year course at Jacksonville while Albert pursued his career as principal in Clay and Coosa Counties. Even while Patterson was employed as an educator, he found time to attend the University of Alabama, graduating Phi Beta Kappa in 1924.[31] It was during this time that the Pattersons started a family, although with tragic beginnings. The first child, Albert Patterson Jr., arrived stillborn in November 1918. A second child, Sybyl Maxine, was born in 1920 with a blood disease that would kill her before she was five. Finally, in 1921, John Malcolm Patterson was born, followed by three more sons, Maurice, Jack, and Sam.[32]

Although Patterson was successful in his role of school administrator, by 1926 he decided to give up education and enter the legal profession. While Albert made his way through Cumberland Law School in Lebanon, Tennessee, Agnes and John moved to rural Morgan County in north-central Alabama, where Agnes took a job teaching at the one-room Rocky Ford School near her father's farm outside Danville.[33] Patterson received his law degree in 1927 and moved to Opelika to begin his practice.[34] A year later the family relocated to Alexander City, and in 1933 they moved again, this time to Phenix City.[35]

There is little to indicate that attorney Albert Patterson was much different from the majority of Phenix City citizens during the first twelve years or so after he moved there. As a beginning attorney, Patterson's relationship with the mob was useful, if not necessarily friendly. In 1946 he was hired, along with every other lawyer in town, to defend Hoyt Shepherd after Shepherd was charged in the murder of Fayette Leeburn, a Columbus man who had tried to muscle in on Shepherd's Phenix City operations. That trial resulted in Shepherd's acquittal. For his contribution, Patterson received the largest fee of his entire life.[36] Two years later, another Phenix City gangster, C. O. "Head" Revel, hired Patterson to fight extradition proceedings in a Florida murder case. Revel, along with fellow mobster Godwin Davis Sr., was accused of hiring two gunmen to kill Frank Stringfellow, an associate who had agreed to cooperate with federal agents in a liquor case against Revel and Davis. Instead, Stringfellow wound up in a shallow grave in Florida with a bullet hole in his head. Although prosecutors would later drop the charges when the gunmen refused to testify, Patterson lost the extradition proceeding. It was not long afterward that he began to disassociate himself from the Phenix City gang.[37]

Patterson's growing reluctance to accept cases from the gang coincided with a similar policy in his political career. Patterson had eased into politics, beginning with appointed posts on the Phenix City Board of Education in 1937 and the Russell County Draft Board in 1940, the latter as chairman. In 1942 he campaigned for political newcomer James Folsom in a run for Congress. Folsom lost that race, but already Patterson had his hands in state politics. In 1946, now as chairman of the school board, he made a run for the state senate. Although he made no promises and refused the mob's support, the Phenix City machine nevertheless gave him its blessing, and Patterson entered the statehouse with the backing of Folsom, himself swept into the governor's seat that same year on a populist platform.

During his single term in the senate, Patterson served on the Committees of Privileges and Elections, Enrolled Bills, Forestry and Conservation, Seaports, and Judiciary, in addition to chairing the Committee on Education. He was instrumental in enacting some significant legislation during this period, most notably the Wallace-Cater Act, a measure that authorized the use of state and municipal bonds to finance the construction of new industrial plants, and the Trade School Act, an appropriations bill responsible for the eventual construction of many of Alabama's trade schools.[38] In addition to this important and popular statewide legislation, Patterson also worked diligently for his constituents in Lee and Russell Counties. Locally, his most influential legislation was a bill he cosponsored in 1947 with Russell County's state representative, Jabe Brassell, to make Russell County a separate judicial circuit. Until then, Russell County had been lumped with Barbour, Bullock, and Dale Counties into Alabama's Third Circuit. The impetus for the separation came not from the area's political or judicial hierarchy but from Hoyt Shepherd, who had discovered during his close call in the Leeburn murder trial that judges and circuit solicitors outside Phenix City were more difficult to influence.[39]

In his defense of the bill, Patterson claimed that the separate circuit was necessary to "take care of the tremendous overflow of cases from Columbus and Fort Benning." With Folsom's assistance, the bill sailed through the legislature. At the recommendation of Patterson and

Brassell, Folsom appointed two of Shepherd's attorneys in the Lee-burn murder case, Julius Hicks and Arch Ferrell, as the new circuit judge and circuit solicitor, respectively.[40]

Folsom and Patterson had an irreparable falling-out in early 1949 when the governor, breaking political protocol, rejected Patterson's recommendation for a probate judge vacancy in Patterson's district and appointed his own candidate. The appointment was especially insulting because Folsom failed to inform Patterson. The governor's office made the announcement even while Patterson was expressing confidence that his selection would be appointed. After that, Patterson's voting record became increasingly anti-Folsom. For his part, Folsom never forgave the defection. In 1950, Patterson ran for the office of lieutenant governor. This time, however, the machine opposed him and he lost. The mob again opposed him two years later when he ran as a delegate to the Democratic National Convention, but this post he won.[41]

Although it was slow in developing, Patterson's stand against the gangsters was solidifying. As a result, many doubted his sincerity and chalked up his new position to political expediency. Whatever the reason, Patterson's first public move against the mob was in late 1950 when he represented Mrs. Gloria Floyd Davis, at the time seeking a divorce from William "Bubber" Davis, son of the aforementioned Godwin Davis Sr. As divorce petitions went, this one was loaded with dynamite. The Davis clan controlled a huge lottery racket and other gambling enterprises around Phenix City, netting an estimated one million dollars a year. Under Patterson's questioning, Mrs. Davis rattled off facts and figures detailing the income of the family's various clubs and businesses, backed up by financial documentation. In an environment where discretion was especially valuable, the proceedings were humiliating for the Davises. And, because the testimony was public record and could be used in criminal court, five members of the Davis organization were eventually charged and fined.[42]

Patterson's evolution from fence-sitter to reformer intensified in 1951, when his political and personal feud began with one of the Phenix City machine's most popular figures. The object of Patterson's contention was Circuit Solicitor Archer Bradford Ferrell, the same man whom Patterson had recommended for the post in 1947, when Ferrell was only thirty years old. Twenty-three years Patterson's junior,

Ferrell hailed from one of Russell County's most prominent families. His father, Henry A. Ferrell, was a well-respected attorney in the former county seat of Seale and had served as both county solicitor and state legislator. From an early age Arch showed every indication of following his father in a brilliant legal and political career. Lean and somewhat slight of build, Ferrell made up for his size in toughness. At sixteen, while attempting to run across a busy Phenix City street, he was run over by three successive cars. Despite a major head laceration and severe bruising from head to toe, Ferrell ignored his doctors and hobbled away from the hospital the next day. While a student at the University of Alabama, Ferrell was named to both the national leadership honor society Omicron Delta Kappa and the prestigious Farrah Order of Jurisprudence. In 1939, his senior year, he was elected president of his graduating class. After two years in law school, Ferrell was inducted into the army as a private, and then it was off to officer candidate school. During the last two years of World War II, Ferrell rose to the rank of captain as his unit fought through Normandy, northern France, the Ardennes, and the Rhineland. Upon his discharge in December 1945, he returned to Seale and began his law practice. That same month Ferrell joined the American Legion, a cause that would remain a lifelong passion. Over the next three years he was elected local post commander, state central area commander, state vice-commander, and, in July 1949, state commander.[43]

Ferrell was so popular as circuit solicitor that he was renominated without opposition in 1950 and 1954. He became heavily involved in Democratic Party politics and was elected chairman of the Russell County Democratic Executive Committee, a position that gave him access to the whole state political hierarchy. Through these civic and political positions, Ferrell built a network of influential friends throughout Alabama. When state politicians talked about up-and-coming governor material, Ferrell's name was often mentioned.[44]

But as Albert Patterson gravitated to the side of the reformers, Ferrell remained deeply entrenched with the status quo. In 1951 the circuit solicitor earned Patterson's animosity when he engineered Chairman Patterson's ouster from the Russell County Draft Board. Charging Patterson with engaging in "political activities" within the board, Ferrell convinced Governor Gordon Persons and Colonel J. T. Johnson, director of the Alabama Selective Service System, that Patterson had to go. Persons agreed, but it was a delicate situation. Technically, the president of the United States appointed members at the recommendation of the governor, and consequently only the president could remove a member against his will. To avoid involving President Truman in what was essentially an embarrassing local matter, Colonel Johnson, at Ferrell's urging, recommended the appointment of two of Ferrell's closest acquaintances to the board: Arch's father, H. A. Ferrell, and Jimmy Putnam, Phenix City's municipal clerk and a good friend of Ferrell's. This gave Ferrell's allies a majority, making Patterson a figurehead chairman and sending a clear message to everyone that he no longer enjoyed the confidence of the governor.[45] Persons approved the appointments, and the ploy worked as planned: Patterson chose to resign his position rather than endure the insult. From then on, Patterson was squarely on the side of the Phenix City reform movement, committed to the destruction of the Phenix City machine and the removal of Circuit Solicitor Arch Ferrell.[46]

A reform impulse had always been present in Phenix City, a fervent minority squared off against a more or less equal number of gangsters and their supporters. Since World War II, a sporting goods merchant, Hugh Bentley, had led the reform movement. In 1945, Bentley formed the Christian Laymen's Association, followed three years later by the Good Government League. Because these organizations were never more than public forums where Bentley and his associates could complain about the sorry state of affairs in Phenix City, they never had an impact on the way things were and quickly faded away.

Soon after the Good Government League folded in early 1951, Bentley organized yet another reform group, the Ministers Alliance. This time the group didn't just talk. It collected evidence of gambling and prostitution, then brought it before the Russell County Grand Jury. Jurors told Bentley and the Ministers Alliance that they should not be mixing politics with religion and dismissed them. Incensed over the reception, Bentley and another Phenix City reformer, construction superintendent Howard Pennington, formed another direct-action organization, the Russell Betterment Association (RBA). Albert Patterson joined them.[47]

A women's group, the RBA Auxiliary, helped the main organization. Patterson encouraged the group because he believed that women were sharper observers and could spot election irregularities better than men. The Auxiliary began weekly broadcasts on a Phenix City radio station that featured RBA members and other reform-minded citizens. Patterson was often the guest.[48]

The RBA was not warmly welcomed. At first the intimidation was limited to nuisances—threatening or obscene phone calls, squealing tires, poisoned pets—but in early 1952 the terrorism grew more serious. As Hugh Bentley approached his house on the night of January 9, thirty-six sticks of dynamite blew the house apart. Inside were his wife, two sons, and an infant nephew. Luckily, no one was seriously injured.[49]

The community was stunned, and the *Columbus Ledger* went so far as to call for the resignations of Phenix City's top officials. After Arch Ferrell suggested that Bentley had dynamited his own house, Bentley took a well-publicized lie detector test, which he passed easily. When RBA members openly accused Ferrell of being involved with the gamblers, he appeared at a public meeting to protest his innocence. He insisted that Phenix City was "one of the cleanest little towns in the country." Hoots of derision followed the remark, and a riot almost erupted when Ferrell's sister, Eugenia, slapped an RBA member and demanded that he "stop calling my brother a liar." Ferrell himself invited the man to step outside. Before a fistfight could erupt, a policeman escorted the man out. Composing himself, Ferrell threw down the gauntlet: "The procedure of impeachment is not nearly as complicated as your lawyer [Patterson] has advised you, and I know who he is. . . . Bring your impeachment proceedings to bar and I'll vindicate myself before the highest court of this state."[50]

As Ferrell's challenge suggested, there was no longer any doubt concerning Patterson's loyalty. As if to validate his reform credentials, a gasoline fire was set in Patterson's office in late February, charring the inside. Many, especially within the RBA, said that the fire was set to destroy evidence against the gang. And there were other indications that RBA membership would have its repercussions. In Phenix City's Trinity Methodist Church, the first church election after the RBA's formation saw not one member nominated. This included Albert Patterson, who had for years served on the church's governing body, the board of stewards.[51]

Recognizing that Phenix City would never be cleaned up as long as the gang controlled local elections, the RBA decided to give the election machinery a try. In 1952, vote fraud in Russell County was widespread and expected. Trading one's vote for a bottle of whiskey or a few dollars was neither unusual nor unacceptable. In addition to the outright purchase of votes, the local machine printed and marked its own ballots. An example of the widespread vote fraud could be found at the Palace Theater, which housed the town's largest polling place. The 721 voters registered there included 256 who had no address in Russell County; 25 who were also registered in Columbus, Georgia; and 16 who were dead. Similar proportions of illegal voters existed in the other polling places, making about one-third of Phenix City voters illegally registered.[52]

At a machine-organized mass meeting on election eve, Arch Ferrell addressed the crowd: "Fellow murderers, gangsters, rapists, and prostitutes—particularly you prostitutes." After the laughter subsided, Ferrell declared, "We want a decent election tomorrow. We want an election like the meetings we've conducted where the good women of our families can vote without being insulted and molested by noisy onlookers."[53] In the meantime, RBA members appealed to Governor Persons for help, but Persons, a solid administrator committed to the theory of limited executive power, was not apt to interfere. At the beginning of his term he told Phenix City officials that it was not his policy to interfere in local matters. He was willing to continue that policy provided they did not cause him any problems as governor. That would all change, however, if he heard "so much as a peep" from Phenix City.[54]

Persons now told the RBA delegation that it was his belief that "the people of Phenix City just want conditions like that and vote accordingly." He would not involve the governor's office in what was a local problem. The governor did, however, promise a fair election and agreed to assign state highway patrolmen to watch over polling stations. Despite the presence of state police, the gangsters proceeded to steal the election anyway. RBA poll watchers could hardly believe their eyes. At one polling place, an RBA member saw taxi after taxi unloading prostitutes, a rare sight before dark. As they got out, she overheard such questions as "What name is mine?" and "How do I vote?" At another polling place, seven goons beat poll watchers Hugh Britton, Hugh Bentley, and Bentley's sixteen-year-old son, Hughbo, along with Columbus newspaper reporters Tom Sellers and Ray Jenkins. As they were being kicked and punched, one bystander protested to a nearby patrolman, who assured her, "Hell, lady, they ain't doing no harm. They're just using their fists and feet on them." Local officials ignored RBA efforts to swear out warrants. And although Governor Persons sent fifteen more highway patrolmen to Phenix City, he flatly refused to get involved.[55]

Shortly after this debacle, the RBA decided to initiate impeachment proceedings; many were eager to meet Ferrell's recent challenge. Patterson especially urged that charges be brought against the circuit solicitor, whom Patterson believed to be particularly vulnerable. Others wanted to target Sheriff Ralph Mathews, another machine politician believed to be friendly with the gangsters. Patterson advised against it, pointing out Mathews's popularity with the voters and other state politicians. That, others argued, was precisely the point. Mathews was more visible than Ferrell and therefore the more desirable target. In June 1952 the RBA employed Opelika lawyer Roberts Brown to bring the charges before the state supreme court. Working with Patterson, Brown, who was also Speaker in the state legislature, charged Mathews with malfeasance and misfeasance in office. The case was built on the presumption that Mathews had shirked his duty as Russell County sheriff by ignoring the vice operations in Phenix City. To support the charges, the RBA documented the seemingly unrestricted gambling and prostitution in Phenix City, most of which could be observed simply by walking into the nightspots.

In his defense, Mathews brought as character witnesses nearly all of Alabama's top law enforcement officials, including Attorney General Silas Garrett, Director L. B. Sullivan of the Alabama Department of Public Safety, chief criminal investigator Joe Smelley, local Alabama Beverage Control Board officer Ben Scroggins, and even the local FBI agent. Each of them testified to Mathews's good character, denied that there was any gambling or vice in Russell County, and swore that Mathews enforced the law to the best of his ability. When the verdict was handed down, the defeat was complete and devastating. The court voted unanimously to clear Mathews. The proceedings proved that the reformers would get no help from outside Russell County.[56]

For a little while, at least, it appeared that the RBA had a chance to influence the municipal government. In the spring of 1953 it received an unexpected opportunity when the city commission dead-locked on a replacement for the recently deceased Mayor J. D. Harris. The stalemate resulted in the election of RBA supporter Otis Taff as acting mayor. Before Taff could inflict much damage, however, Circuit Judge Hicks declared Phenix City's five-man commission unconstitu-tional. As a result, Taff and another RBA supporter, Harold Coulter, were expelled. Then, for good measure, the two were charged with illegally holding public office and barred from ever holding the posi-tion in the future.[57]

As 1954 rolled around, the Phenix City reform movement had reached a standstill. The RBA continued to covertly compile informa-tion on the illegal activities in Phenix City and Russell County, but no meaningful action was being taken. Police and sheriff's deputies sent out to raid gambling establishments returned with reports that they could find nothing illegal. Early in the year, the grand jury returned a report containing only the recommendation that the screen door at the county courthouse be repaired. The RBA could make no head-way on the local level, and state politicians had turned away. There remained only one avenue for appeal: the people of Alabama.[58]

2
The 1954 Primary and Runoff

They've put in for me. There's nothing you can do about it. But if they do get me, don't let them get away with it.

Albert Patterson, June 1954

With the Russell Betterment Association dead in its tracks, Albert Patterson now argued that the reformers' efforts would be realized only if someone sympathetic to their cause were in the Office of the Alabama Attorney General. The logical choice, of course, was Patterson himself, the most politically experienced of the group.[1] As established under Alabama's 1901 constitution, the state attorney general is quite powerful. Generally speaking, he is the state's official legal representative, giving advisory opinions on points of law to state and local officials, representing them in court proceedings where the state has an interest, advising the governor on proposed legislation, preparing state contracts, and reviewing the constitutionality of all laws passed by the legislature. But in addition to his role as state legal counsel, the attorney general is empowered with significant prosecutorial duties. He possesses the authority to appear before any grand jury in the state and present evidence; in extreme cases, he may even reassign locally elected circuit solicitors and replace them with someone of his choosing, even himself.[2]

As attorney general, Patterson could march in with special prosecutors, much like Logan Martin had in 1916, and force indictments and convictions without the help of local officials. That would clear the hurdle of Russell County's reluctant circuit solicitor, Arch Ferrell. And if Ferrell gave him any trouble, Patterson could relieve him of his duties and reassign him to a circuit far from Phenix City.[3]

The current occupant of the attorney general's office was Silas Coma Garrett III. The forty-one-year-old Garrett came from a prominent Clarke County family, one of southwest Alabama's original pioneer families. Si's great-grandfather had been a Civil War casualty (on the Confederate side). His grandfather had been elected Clarke County sheriff twice, and Si's father was the current probate judge there. Like Arch Ferrell, Garrett had enjoyed a spectacular career at the University of Alabama School of Law; from there, he took a position as an assistant attorney general in 1935. Shrewd, tough, bombastic, personable, and highly intelligent, Garrett wasn't content to remain a bureaucrat and soon became involved in state politics. He announced his candidacy for attorney general in 1942 but withdrew soon after to join the Army Air Corps as a private. He entered officer candidate school and rose through the ranks at air bases in North Carolina and Virginia. Garrett wanted to run in the 1946 election, but he missed out because he still hadn't been discharged. In early 1947, having left the service with the rank of lieutenant colonel, he returned to the attorney general's office, appointed by the winner of the 1946 race, Albert Carmichael.[4]

Garrett entered the attorney general's race in 1950 as the favored candidate; to his great disappointment, however, he barely edged out his lesser-known opponent. It was a classic career-killing victory, and Garrett realized before everyone else that his chances at higher political office were in doubt. That realization contributed to bouts of depression, where he would be unexplainably absent for days at a time, followed by a manic stage in which no amount of work by his staff could satisfy his desire to get things done.[5]

Garrett had also been hampered by some unpopular actions on his part, particularly a decision to sue the federal government to stop a congressional act granting coastal states title to their oil-rich tidelands. The act, twice vetoed by President Truman but finally signed into law by Eisenhower, was widely popular in Alabama. Garrett was roundly condemned for his action and had nothing to show for it after the courts refused to hear his suit. He had made the opposite mistake in the *Brown v. Board of Education* landmark desegregation case by refusing to join other southern states in the case, although most of Alabama's voters clearly wanted him to.[6]

Garrett's probable replacement was the man he had barely beaten four years earlier. Lee "Red" Porter was a thirty-nine-year-old Gadsden attorney born in Heflin and raised in Florence. A 1939 graduate of the University of Alabama School of Law, Porter had joined the army in 1943 and served in military intelligence in the U.S. atomic bomb development program. Since 1948 he had been the U.S. commissioner for the federal courts' middle division of Alabama's northern district.[7]

This would be Porter's second run for the office. Four years earlier, the state's anti-Garrett faction had convinced him to run at the last minute, and Porter made a mad dash from Gadsden to Montgomery to qualify. During the campaign, Porter blasted Garrett, at that time first assistant attorney general, for promising to appoint his predecessor, Albert Carmichael, as first assistant should Garrett win the election. Porter received 48 percent of the vote that year, making him the heir apparent to Garrett. Despite Porter's harsh words during the previous election, Garrett now expressed his support for the Gadsden attorney.[8]

The third man in the race was forty-one-year-old Montgomery attorney George MacDonald Gallion (invariably known as "Mac"), a Birmingham native and 1937 graduate of the University of Alabama School of Law. Gallion had started at the top, as chief attorney for a major insurance company. He gave up that position in 1942 to join the U.S. Marine Corps as a private. After three years in the South Pacific he was discharged as a first lieutenant. When Gallion returned to Alabama he landed a job as an assistant attorney general assigned to the state Public Service Commission, among other duties. In that position, he worked closely with the commission's chairman, Gordon Persons. Both resigned in May 1950, Persons to run for governor, Gallion to return to private practice.[9]

Patterson was considered somewhat of a long shot. He was not well known statewide, he had no direct experience in law enforcement, and his financial resources were meager compared to those of his opponents. He mortgaged his house for startup money and relied heavily on the fervent support of RBA members, who gave their time and money generously. Because of Patterson's earlier political career, he was able to enlist dedicated campaign managers from the political alliances he had made during his four years as state senator. Closer to home, Patterson had the help of his oldest son, John, now a thirty-three-year-old lawyer and father of two.[10]

In the year following his 1939 graduation from Central High School, John joined the army as a private just as the war in Europe was heating up; before war's end he had seen action in Tunisia, Sicily, Italy, southern France, and Germany. In 1945 he was discharged with the rank of major. Patterson entered college on his return to the States, earning an undergraduate degree in political science at the University of Alabama and a law degree in 1949. He began his law practice as a partner with his father, but in 1951, at the height of the Korean conflict, he was recalled into the army and served for two years in the judge advocate department in Germany. Discharged in December 1953, John returned to Phenix City just as his father decided to enter the attorney general's race.[11]

Albert Patterson took the Phenix City vice issue and turned it into a statewide referendum on law and order. If the town was not cleaned up, Patterson argued, lawlessness and immorality would spread to other Alabama communities. A typical newspaper advertisement during the campaign claimed, "Your Vote for Albert L. Patterson Is a Vote Against Crime . . . Albert L. Patterson Pledges Himself: 1. To stamp out organized crime wherever it exists. 2. To wipe out dope-peddling, sex crimes, and protect our young people."[12]

For the Phenix City gang, of course, Patterson was out of the question. Gallion was willing to hear what the machine had to say, but he made it clear that he would make no commitments. This left Porter, who enjoyed the support of Si Garrett and especially of Arch Ferrell, a college buddy of Porter's ever since Porter had helped elect Ferrell as president of the senior class at the university.[13]

As returns filtered in on the night of May 4, Patterson began racking up a huge lead, sometimes approaching a margin of two to one over Porter. Phenix City mobsters were startled at Patterson's 70,000-vote lead and their candidate's trailing position in the three-man race. They also had another problem. Gallion was running dead even with Porter, sometimes better. It looked as if Porter might not even make the runoff race against Patterson. As the votes were still being counted, Gallion received a call at his home asking if he would play ball if victorious in a runoff. He again refused to commit himself, and as a result he received only 57 votes of the last 8,000.[14]

When all the votes were counted, Patterson had led in fifty-four of Alabama's sixty-seven counties. In the final tally, Patterson received 174,243 votes (43.4 percent), Porter 115,319 (28.7 percent), and Gallion 111,714 (27.8 percent). Porter was in the runoff, but just barely. Discouraged by his fifteen-point deficit and out of money, he seriously considered dropping out. For the Phenix City machine, that was unacceptable. Three days after the primary, Ferrell, Sheriff Mathews, and Phenix City's mayor, Elmer Reese, visited Porter and told him not to worry about the money; Phenix City stood ready to go all out against Patterson. The following day, Ferrell again met with Porter. Accompanying him was Si Garrett, who was insistent that Porter fight it out. Convinced, Porter listened as Ferrell and Garrett presented their strategy for the upcoming three-week runoff campaign.[15]

At about the same time, top members of Phenix City's gambling establishment met at the Bama Club to raise money for Porter. In addition to veterans Hoyt Shepherd and Godwin Davis Sr., the group included six up-and-coming gambling kingpins: "Shorty" Myrick, "Red" Cook, W. C. Roney, E. L. "Buck" Billingsley, J. D. Abney, and Stewart McCollister. The forty-nine-year-old McCollister was typical of this new generation of Phenix City operators. He was a partner with old-timer Clyde Yarbrough in one of Phenix City's six largest lotteries, operated out of Yarbrough's Café on Fourteenth Street. In addition to the Yarbrough-McCollister lottery, the two had teamed up with Abney and James D. "Frog" Jones to purchase the Bama Club a few years earlier when Shepherd and Matthews divested themselves of their gambling interests. Separate from Yarbrough and Jones, McCollister had a partnership with Abney in the slot machines and dice tables located in the Avalon Club and the New York Club. Although he wasn't in the same league as Shepherd or Davis, McCollister probably had as much at stake as anyone in a Patterson defeat, and perhaps even more since his investments hadn't had as much time to pay off. When the conference was over the gangsters had pledged almost $30,000, an astronomical sum in 1954.[16]

On May 11, Ferrell and Porter drove to Birmingham, where they met Shepherd, Matthews, and Davis. The subject of the meeting was campaign tactics. Since his pledge to clean up Phenix City had worked so well for Patterson during the first primary, Porter would adopt it— against Patterson. Patterson had twice defended Phenix City gangsters (including Shepherd) in court; this now would be used against him. By the end of the month, Porter's campaign would promise the voter, "You'll be voting for law & order and to defeat the Phenix City Machine." At that meeting Ferrell handed over $10,000, the first Phenix City contribution to Porter's campaign.[17]

A week later, Porter again met with Shepherd, Ferrell, and Davis in Birmingham, and this time he received $8,000. Shepherd and Davis sent another $4,600 to Porter on May 24 and $4,000 on May 26. On May 28, the Friday before the June 1 runoff, Porter's plane touched down in Montgomery on the way to Birmingham. There, Garrett and Ferrell handed him an envelope with $1,800. The day after, a Russell County sheriff's deputy delivered another $230 from Garrett and Ferrell; this was specifically earmarked for Porter to telegraph all circuit solicitors in Alabama, telling them that their help in Porter's election was appreciated. The telegrams went out over Garrett's signature on official stationery.[18]

Garrett did his own campaigning, engaging in some questionable activities along the way. He summoned all circuit solicitors to a Montgomery meeting, the purpose of which was to discuss Alabama's reaction to the recent U.S. Supreme Court decision in *Brown v. Board of Education*. Although the morning session was indeed taken up with the subject of segregation, the afternoon session, led by Ferrell, was a three-hour political pep rally for Porter. At one point Ferrell declared, "That goddamned son of a bitch Albert Patterson is not going to take the attorney general's office." Garrett also violated state ethics rules when he assigned two employees to the Porter campaign.[19]

Porter also received some hefty support from Jim Folsom, who, in his bid for a second term as governor, chalked up a majority of votes in the May primary and thus avoided the June runoff. Despite an earlier agreement with Patterson to remain neutral in the attorney general's race, Folsom's advisers now convinced him to come out publicly for Porter.[20]

The Patterson campaign picked up a major endorsement on May 14 when MacDonald Gallion declared his support. It came in exchange for his appointment as first assistant attorney general should Patterson win. With this guarantee, Gallion stumped the state to urge his former supporters to vote for Patterson.

When the polls closed on the evening of June 1, early returns again showed Porter trailing Patterson. The only thing that could save him was time. Garrett was on the telephone all evening, telling local election officials that there was no need to rush certifying the results of such an important election; too much was at stake. Over the next few days, as the vote in the attorney general's race teetered back and forth, the word went out: do whatever it takes to put Porter over the top.[21]

In business as well as in gambling, there comes a time to hold up or fold up. With Porter so close to victory, the Phenix City gang went all out. On Wednesday, the day after the runoff, Stewart McCollister and two companions pulled into Tuskegee, the county seat of Macon, and tracked down Frank Porter, Red Porter's younger brother. McCollister inquired about the whereabouts of the sheriff and the local Democratic Committee members, explaining that the folks in Phenix City had dispatched eleven cars throughout Alabama to get some more votes for Frank's older brother. Frank referred him to Sheriff Preston Hornsby. McCollister told Hornsby the same story, and Hornsby told him to forget it; the votes had already been counted and turned in to the probate judge. McCollister thanked him for his time and drove on. The trio eventually showed up in at least five other counties looking for votes.[22]

Birmingham attorney Amos Lamar Reid was not only one of Birmingham's more successful lawyers; he was also a rising star on the state political scene. In January 1954 he had taken office as chairman of the Democratic Executive Committee in Jefferson County, becoming the head of the state's majority party in Alabama's most populous county. Reid's most important job was the certification of results for the local party primaries and runoffs. It could sometimes be a difficult position because party officials served as both the (supposedly) neutral official overseers of the voting results in their county and as partisan political operatives. Although he had openly supported Red Porter during the recent primary and runoff—he had even made a television endorsement on Porter's behalf—Reid took his responsibility seriously.[23]

As the returns began coming in on the night of June 1–2, Reid was in high demand. At 4:30 A.M. he received a call from Garrett, who wanted to know the Jefferson County results for attorney general. Reid said the figures were not yet available, and he gave the same response when Garrett called again at 10:30 that morning. Finally, around 4:00 P.M., Reid went before reporters and announced the Jefferson County results: Patterson, 23,858; Porter, 23,060. After a few of the newsmen checked over the tally sheets, Reid took the three official copies to his office. When he finally called Garrett to give him the results, Garrett said it didn't make any difference; Porter had won the race statewide and would make a victory announcement shortly.[24]

Garrett called Reid again the following night, June 3, with some rather distressing news. Patterson had claimed victory on the basis of unofficial returns. Garrett was certain that Patterson's supporters had pulled this off by switching 1,700 votes in Randolph and Tallapoosa Counties. If Patterson got away with that, Porter would most certainly challenge the outcome. Garrett planned to be in Birmingham the next day and wanted to hear Reid's opinion on an election contest. The next day, June 4, Garrett's secretary called Reid to tell him that the attorney general would like to meet with him in Room 802 of the Molton Hotel; and, she added, if it wasn't too much trouble, he should bring along the official Jefferson County primary runoff recapitulation sheets.[25]

When Reid arrived at the Molton, the first thing Garrett asked for was the tally sheets, which Reid spread out on a nearby coffee table. As Garrett studied the figures, Ferrell walked in. The three then discussed some of the box totals in Tallapoosa and Randolph Counties, particularly some returns in Randolph that had reported in late and showed a tremendous increase in Patterson's vote. Garrett looked somberly at Reid and said matter-of-factly, "Patterson's crowd's stolen the election, Lamar. We've got to steal it back."[26]

Much has been said and written about what transpired over the next few days among Reid, Garrett, and Ferrell. There is no dispute that Garrett, or Ferrell, or both, persuaded Reid to go along with a number of alterations on the recapitulation sheets that resulted in an

addition of exactly 600 votes to Porter's total in Jefferson County. Part
of the argument used to convince Reid, he would later tell investigators, was Ferrell's assertion that Reid's role was part of a statewide
effort to keep Patterson out of office, an effort supported by the political hierarchy of the entire state.[27]

When Garrett and Ferrell were ready to leave Birmingham, Reid
took the tally sheets back to his office and prepared the certificate of
results for the state committee; these he left for his secretary to send
on to Montgomery. Early the next morning he headed off to his summer home in Laguna Beach, Florida, for a long-awaited vacation.[28]

No one was more interested in the final certificate of results than Birmingham attorney Albert Rosenthal, Patterson's campaign manager
for Jefferson County. Rosenthal was already on guard because of Gallion's suspicious drop in votes during the May 4 primary, and it was
with no little surprise that he discovered that Reid's final tally for
Patterson was exactly 600 votes less than what Reid had reported on
June 2. On Monday, June 7, Rosenthal contacted Jefferson County
circuit solicitor Emmett Perry, who invited him to voice his suspicions
before the grand jury, then nearing the end of its regular session. The
following day, *Birmingham News* reporter Ed Strickland was hanging
around the sheriff's office at the Jefferson County Courthouse when
he received a call. A woman whom he would later identify as a secretary for the local Democratic Executive Committee told him that Porter's official Jefferson County total had been raised from 23,060 to
23,660. Strickland didn't understand what she meant until she warned,
"You'd better watch the vote, they're stealing it." "How is that being
done?" asked Strickland. "On the sheets," she answered.[29]

Strickland knew she was referring to the official recapitulation
sheets, a chart recording the votes from individual voting boxes
throughout the county, a copy of which Sheriff Holt McDowell would
have on hand. Strickland asked to see it. He didn't see anything unusual at first. A closer look, however, showed that a number of alterations had been carefully made. Strickland then went upstairs and
tracked down Solicitor Perry to show him the changes. Perry responded with a curt "Explain it to the grand jury." Strickland did.
After Rosenthal's and Strickland's testimony, grand jurors began issuing subpoenas for newsmen and election officials to determine exactly

what had happened to the Jefferson County returns in the Alabama attorney general's race. It was at this point that the plan of the Phenix City machine started to become unglued.[30]

The official canvass on June 10 looked like a certainty for Patterson, but no one would be sure until the winner was announced. The day before, Porter charged Patterson's supporters with "gross irregularities and fraud" in Chambers, Houston, Lawrence, Lee, Mobile, Randolph, Russell, and Tallapoosa Counties and said he would have more to say about it in Montgomery the following day, a clear indication of an election contest. But when the time came, Porter said nothing, and the committee certified Patterson as the nominee. Porter had apparently given up, but Garrett hadn't. Contacting state senator Neil Metcalf, a Folsom lieutenant, Garrett argued that with all the allegations of vote fraud on both sides, maybe the committee should consider disqualifying both Patterson and Porter and naming a third candidate. Metcalf begged off, claiming that an illness in his family would not allow him to pursue the matter. Then he called Jim Folsom.[31]

As if the vote fraud investigation in Birmingham wasn't bad enough for the Phenix City machine, trouble was brewing in its own backyard. Russell County's two state legislators, Jabe Brassell and Ben Cole, generally regarded as machine politicians themselves ever since their first election eight years earlier, had been passed over by the machine in the May 4 primary in favor of two other candidates, V. Cecil Curtis and William Belcher. As soon as the votes were in, Brassell and Cole filed an election contest with the state Democratic Committee, claiming that the machine had defeated their reelection bids through vote fraud. The hearings were delayed for eleven days while Circuit Judge Hicks issued a writ of prohibition and the state supreme court overruled him. Beginning on June 14 in Phenix City, the election subcommittee hearing provided the RBA with a public forum to reveal all aspects of local corruption. RBA president Howard Pennington said that Hoyt Shepherd and Arch Ferrell headed the mobster-backed Phenix City political machine. Other witnesses testified about specific violations during the May 5 polling, such as voters pocketing five-dollar bills as they exited the polling places and Chief Deputy Albert Fuller marking ballots for unregistered voters and escorting groups of prostitutes to the voting booths. One witness estimated that at least

30 percent of Russell County votes were purchased outright during the primary. The allegations were sensational, and the subcommittee retired to deliberate, promising action in the near future.[32]

On the Gulf coast, Lamar Reid had hardly begun his vacation when his attorney/brother-in-law Bruce White called to let him know what was going on. On June 10, Reid received another jolt when the state-wide results in the attorney general's race were announced in Montgomery. Despite all of Garrett's and Ferrell's assurances about the ultimate outcome of the primary runoff, and despite Reid's risky involvement in the vote fraud, Patterson squeaked by Porter with just 854 votes. Now Reid was really worried. He tried to contact Ferrell and Garrett but couldn't get through. When the grand jury summoned him to testify and bring his election records with him, panic set in. Finally contacting Garrett, he arranged a meeting in Selma on June 12. Reid again expressed his concerns, noting that the grand jury was looking into the vote fraud. What did Garrett intend to do about it? Garrett seemed offended. Everything would be taken care of. If the grand jury went out of control, Garrett would use his powers as attorney general to dissolve it. And if Emmett Perry caused any trouble, Garrett would simply send him to north Alabama "on a five-dollar cow-stealing case" and take over the grand jury himself. That would stop the investigation in its tracks. Garrett told Reid to stop worrying, go back to Florida, and let him take care of everything. But Reid didn't feel reassured. He decided to go to Birmingham and set things straight himself.[33]

Appearing before the grand jury on June 13, Reid told members that on June 4 Garrett and Ferrell had summoned him from his office and asked to see the official returns, which Reid provided. While he was discussing the returns with them, the local garage called to say that his car, which was being serviced for the upcoming vacation to Florida, was ready. Reid left the documents with Garrett and Ferrell. When he came back about twenty minutes later, Ferrell and Garrett thanked him for his time and left. Therefore, Reid speculated, any changes to the documents must have been made while he was away.[34]

With that chore completed, Reid called a meeting of the Jefferson County Democratic Executive Committee and invited Solicitor Perry to join them. He told the other six committee members the same story he had told the grand jury, that someone had changed the vote totals on the tally sheets while he was gone. He knew *he* didn't do it, but he strongly suspected Garrett and Ferrell. To show how outraged he was, Reid suggested employing Birmingham detective Fred Bodecker to investigate the discrepancies on the returns, and the committee readily agreed. Reid then signed an amended copy of the returns, this time with Porter's illegal 600 votes removed, and sent it to the state committee.[35]

When the meeting was over, Reid went with Perry to the solicitor's office, where Perry called Bodecker, a gruff private investigator who bore a striking resemblance to FBI director J. Edgar Hoover. Perry outlined the vote fraud case to the detective and emphasized the importance of the grand jury's investigation. Reid even took the phone and helped convince him. Bodecker got right on the case. To his surprise, he discovered that Reid's story did not add up. Telephone records indicated that Reid had been contacted several times by Garrett and Ferrell on June 4, yet Reid had told the grand jury that he had heard from them only once on that date.[36]

While Bodecker checked phone records and interviewed hotel employees, the grand jury continued to hear testimony. A skittish Lee Porter was summoned and, against the express wishes of Godwin Davis Sr., told jurors about the meetings he had had with Phenix City machine representatives and the campaign funds he had received from them. A few nights later, Davis visited Porter and had him answer a series of questions written by Ferrell concerning exactly what he had told the grand jury.[37]

Worried about Garrett's rumblings of an election contest, Neil Metcalf called Jim Folsom and sized up the situation. The Folsom camp didn't want Patterson as attorney general, but it was time to deal with reality. Maybe Garrett had a case, maybe he didn't, but Patterson had made it clear that if the election was contested, he would in turn expose the statewide effort to steal the election from him. Did Folsom really want that to happen? Besides, maybe Patterson wouldn't be that bad. As a politician, Patterson had to realize that compromises were in order. Folsom could act as a peacemaker, using Garrett's threats to cut a deal. On June 15, Sheriff Mathews told Patterson that Folsom wanted to talk to him. In a telephone call later that afternoon, Folsom promised Patterson that Porter would drop any plans to contest the election and that he, as governor, would help Patterson get the legislative funding to clean up Phenix City. For his part, Patterson agreed to try and stop the Jefferson County Grand Jury's vote fraud investigation.[38]

But if Patterson was ever serious about trying to stop the grand jury, he soon changed his mind. After his conversation with Folsom, he dutifully called Albert Rosenthal and asked if there was any way the Birmingham investigation could be stopped. Surprised, Rosenthal remarked, "Hell, no!" Patterson replied with a chuckle, "I didn't think so. But I had to ask, just like I said I would." Patterson, then, had given up nothing. He would continue his drive to clean up Phenix City, which included the Jefferson County vote fraud investigation, but now he had the support of the next governor and did not have to worry about an election contest. Not only was his halfhearted attempt to call off the grand jury unsuccessful, as he no doubt expected it would be, but Patterson grew even bolder. In the same conversation with Rosenthal, Patterson said that he planned to come to Birmingham the following Monday and testify before the grand jury. By this time, Patterson had plenty to talk about.[39]

Despite his determination to begin the Phenix City cleanup right away, Patterson exhibited a peculiar fatalism. Although he refused to show any fear, he had been constantly threatened ever since he announced his candidacy. On the morning of June 17, real estate agent Grace Oliver was sitting with Patterson in his office when the telephone rang. Soon after he answered, Patterson's face showed shock, then anger, then nonchalance: "I haven't heard that was what they were going to do to me." He then handed the receiver to Grace and indicated that she should listen. She heard a man say, "If you don't change before the end of the week you won't be here." She handed the receiver back to Patterson. He was still listening to the threats as she went out the door. That evening he spoke before the Men's Club of the Phenix City First Methodist Church. In contrast to his usual precise speaking style, Patterson appeared worried and stumbled through his talk. He then startled the group by predicting he had only a one-in-a-hundred chance of ever taking office as attorney general. A few days earlier, at an open house celebrating his recent certification as attorney general nominee, Patterson joked darkly as photographers snapped his picture: "This week they shoot at me with cameras; next week, they'll shoot at me with bullets." And about the same time, he told Howard Pennington, "They've put in for me. There's nothing you can do about it. But if they do get me, don't let them get away with it."[40]

3
June 18, 1954,
Part 1

I am going before the grand jury Monday and I am going to
ruin them.

Albert Patterson, June 18, 1954

On the last morning of his life, Albert Patterson started out from his
home at a little after 7:00. His first stop was Cobb Barber Shop, where
both barbers noticed that Patterson was unusually quiet and appeared
worried. While Patterson was in the barber's chair, attorney Roy Smith
stopped by and invited him to Montgomery to attend disbarment
hearings for Reuben Newton, a Jasper attorney recently nominated to
the state senate. Newton had been accused of unethical conduct—
specifically, the solicitation of business. It was a serious matter for the
legal community, and many of the state's more prominent judges and
attorneys would be there. Patterson declined, saying he had too much
work.[1]

When Patterson's secretary, Lucille Smith, arrived at the law office
at 8:45, Patterson immediately began dictating letters. Around 9:30
Newton himself called and personally asked Patterson to appear as a
character witness on his behalf. Again Patterson begged off, explaining that he had three appointments that day, all with people from out
of town who were probably already en route. He finally promised Newton that if he could find a way to cancel the appointments and come
to Montgomery, he would. But as soon as he hung up the telephone

he grabbed his hat and cane and explained to Lucille, "When a friend calls that is in trouble, there is nothing to do but go to his assistance." On his way out, Patterson stuck his head in next door and informed his son, John, that he was headed to Montgomery.[2]

Patterson arrived in Montgomery at about 10:45 CST.[3] Entering the hearing room in the Montgomery County Courthouse, he found Newton and took a seat between him and his legal counsel, Roderick Beddow Sr. of Birmingham. He explained that he had changed his mind because the same people who had brought Newton before the bar were trying to overturn Patterson's election. But it wouldn't work, Patterson continued, because he "had the goods" on Garrett and Ferrell and was going before the Jefferson County Grand Jury on Monday to tell what he knew.[4]

Patterson stayed until the lunch recess. In the corridor, John Shaeffer, clerk of the Montgomery County Board of Revenue, saw Patterson and invited him to his home for lunch, but Patterson declined. Before he left Shaeffer, Patterson told him he would be going before the Jefferson County Grand Jury the following week. He then headed up Dexter Avenue to Walker Printing Company to discuss a bill incurred during the campaign. While there, he explained to Mrs. Ruth Avenger how the vote fraud had been carried out in Birmingham. Taking a slip of paper, Patterson illustrated how a 6 could be made from a 0 and how a 9 could be made from a 1.[5]

Shortly after 1:00 CST, Jabe Brassell, the Russell County legislator who had set the ball rolling with his election contest a few weeks earlier, ran into Patterson in the lobby of the Exchange Hotel. Brassell had just come from the governor's office, where he had urged Persons's executive secretary, Vernon Merritt, to order a raid on Phenix City gambling joints that night. Merritt was agreeable and promised to discuss it with the governor and Public Safety Director L. B. Sullivan. Patterson thought the raid was a fine idea and revealed to Brassell his plans to appear before the grand jury. Remembering something, Patterson excused himself and entered one of the lobby's telephone booths. He made a call to Albert Rosenthal, confirming his trip to Birmingham the next day to attend the wedding of Rosenthal's daughter and testify before the grand jury on Monday. Since his telephone call the evening before, Patterson explained, he had received even more information of vote fraud, this time in south Alabama and in

Walker County. Rosenthal cautioned him not to provide any specifics on the telephone.[6]

When Patterson returned, Jabe took his leave. Almost as soon as he was out of sight, "Mac" Brassell, Jabe's brother, walked in and struck up a conversation, punctuated by a sudden thunderstorm that kept Patterson from leaving. Mac brought up the possibility that Porter would contest the election because of alleged vote fraud on Patterson's behalf. Patterson said he welcomed a public forum and would use the same tactics Jabe had recently employed so well at the subcommittee hearings in Phenix City. The countercharges and supporting evidence would ruin Porter forever. He swore to Mac, "If God lets me live, I am going to clean it up," but as he did the evening before, he gave himself only a one-in-a-hundred chance of ever taking office. Mac asked why. Patterson replied, "Because they are threatening me now and I am going before the grand jury Monday and I am going to ruin them." By this time the rain had let up and Patterson offered Brassell a ride to his hotel. As they made their way down Commerce Street, Brassell noticed that Patterson seemed worried and urged him to be careful.[7]

Around 2:00 CST, Patterson stopped at the State Judicial Building, where he visited Clerk Charles Bricken and Justice R. B. Carr of the Alabama Court of Appeals. Judge Carr asked if Porter planned to contest the election. Patterson said he didn't think so, adding that he would counter with his own accusations if Porter did contest it. Carr then asked Patterson if he thought Garrett was involved in the vote fraud, and Patterson answered in the affirmative, vaguely alluding to Jefferson County. Leaving the judge's chambers, Patterson talked with Carr's secretary for a few minutes, saying that he was on his way to the state capitol.[8]

Patterson parked in the west driveway of the capitol shortly after 4:00 CST. Joe Durden of the state auditor's office stopped Patterson in the corridor to congratulate him on his nomination. Proceeding through the statehouse, Patterson dropped in on Secretary of State Agnes Baggett and reminded her to record the corrected Jefferson County figures in the statewide vote totals. He left Baggett's office about 4:25. Five minutes later he was on his way home.[9]

On his way out of Montgomery, Patterson stopped at the Parkmore

Drive-in on U.S. Highway 80 and ordered one of his favorite summer-time treats, a vanilla milkshake. According to waitress Theresa Edmondson, whom Patterson normally kidded because of her British accent, Patterson seemed uncharacteristically preoccupied and only stayed long enough to finish the milkshake, about ten minutes.[10] In Tuskegee, Patterson stopped at Scott Filling Station to gas up. While there, he had a soft drink and talked politics with the attendant. Passing back into the eastern time zone and losing the hour he had gained that morning, Patterson entered Phenix City.[11]

Albert Frederick Fuller, Sheriff Mathews's chief deputy, was a Phenix City native. After graduating from Central High School in 1937 he drove a bread delivery truck for a while, but soon he landed a job as the Russell County jailer. Not long after that, he became a $200-a-month deputy with Chief Deputy Ralph Mathews as his partner. Fuller joined the navy when World War II broke out, signing up for Shore Patrol. He saw his war years in Orange, Texas, keeping sailors in line. After the war, Fuller returned to his deputy job, now with a Texas-style attraction to big hats, big guns, and a big walk. He was again part-nered with Mathews, who had gained popularity as acting sheriff during the war. When Mathews won election as sheriff in 1946, Fuller moved into the number two spot.[12]

Like most things in Phenix City, Fuller's reputation depended on whom you talked to. His defenders judged him an effective and competent law enforcement officer, a civic-minded man who coached Little League and was heavily involved in the American Legion. He succeeded Ferrell as commander of the Fletcher-McCollister Post in Phenix City and served three straight years, once winning the legion's award for most outstanding post commander of the year. But Phenix City reformers painted a different picture of a gun-toting bully who took in as much as six thousand dollars weekly from gambling and prostitution protection.[13]

June 18 had been a routine day for Chief Deputy Fuller. He arrived at his courthouse office about 9:00, caught up on some paperwork, had lunch with his wife, and returned to his office. Late in the afternoon, he walked into the circuit clerk's office to check on court records. While there, he chatted with John Patterson about going to work for John's father as an investigator after the elder Patterson took office. At 5:00 he drove to the Columbus YMCA for heat treatments and a steam bath to ease the stiffness in his right leg that resulted from two fractures in earlier years.[14]

Upon his return to Phenix City, Fuller stopped at the Sunny Lane Café, where he had a bottle or two of beer and talked with other patrons for about twenty minutes. As he left the café, a motorist headed to Texas asked him the best route through Alabama. Fuller pulled a road map out of his car, and the two went over it. He then went home to put on a clean shirt, comb his hair, and brush his teeth, getting ready for Phenix City on a Friday night.[15]

Fuller had dinner at the Steak House Café with Mrs. James Carpenter, the wife of the owner, and one of her friends. As he paid his check, he noticed that it was a few minutes before 8:30. From there he went to the county jail, located behind the courthouse. As he drove up, he saw Sheriff Mathews entering the jail with a prisoner in tow. Close behind Mathews were Robert E. Lee Smith, the brother of Deputy Aaron Smith, and Curtis Deason, an agent for Alabama Beverage Control (ABC).[16]

When Fuller entered the jail office, the Smith brothers, Deason, and Mathews were talking with assistant jailer Johnny Dees and George Phillips, a state highway patrolman from Centreville who was currently in town to give driver's license examinations. Mathews had just returned from Seale after arresting a man for writing a worthless check, and Fuller joked, "Boss, it looks like you're the first one to score tonight." Chief jailer Ben Clark arrived and joined in the banter for a while before ABC agent Deason reminded Deputy Aaron Smith that they were due to raid some local establishments. The two left the jail, accompanied by Dees and Robert Lee Smith, who were headed to Smitty's Grill for ice cream. Fuller and Mathews excused themselves from Phillips's company and slipped into Clark's private quarters to discuss a personal matter.[17]

June 18 began bright and early for Circuit Solicitor Arch Ferrell. As was his custom, he arose shortly after sunup, let his daughter's puppy out, had a bite to eat, and then took a walk around his property just off the Seale Highway. He had intended to do some yard work on this day, but now, as he looked over two garden plots overgrown with weeds, he didn't feel up to it. It had been a hard seventeen days since the June 1 primary runoff, and it was getting worse. Although he was not a party to the Brassell-Cole election contest, the RBA had trashed him anyway during the election subcommittee hearings in Phenix City. RBA president Howard Pennington accused Ferrell of being the brains behind the so-called Phenix City machine. Publicly, Ferrell had laughed it off, saying that the only political organization he was in charge of was the Russell County Democratic Executive Committee and that Pennington was "certainly over-enthusiastic in his estimate of my amount of brains." But his biggest problem was the Jefferson County Grand Jury's investigation of the 600-vote switch that took place the same day he and Garrett had visited Lamar Reid in Birmingham.[18]

Ferrell had put everything he had into Porter's campaign, but Patterson had been declared the winner one week before. There was still the possibility that Porter would challenge the result, based on allegations of vote fraud favoring Patterson in east Alabama. Garrett kept assuring him that that would be the case, but Si had his hands full with the grand jury in Birmingham.[19]

Ferrell had been operating on about three hours' sleep over the past week, and he needed a rest. During the past few months he had hardly seen his wife, Madeline, six months pregnant with their second child, or his ten-year-old daughter, Madeline Fay. Today he planned to just hang around. He skipped lunch, opting for a late-afternoon snack instead. A little later a local sawmill owner named Perdue came by and said he might be interested in buying some timber if he could look it over first. Ferrell pulled on some coveralls and boots and went with him to inspect the trees, which were scattered over some 140 acres. About an hour and a half later, Perdue dropped Ferrell off at home, where he fell asleep reading the newspaper.[20]

Rousing himself in the early evening, Ferrell decided to go to his office to catch up on paperwork. By 8:15 he was on his way. He parked his 1953 Ford at the northeast corner of the courthouse square, walked across Fourteenth Street to retrieve his mail from the post office, and then moved his car to the rear of the courthouse, the south side. Once inside, Ferrell bought a soft drink from a hallway vending machine, climbed upstairs to the circuit solicitor's office, and began going through a pile of unanswered mail. He decided to call Garrett to see how the vote contest plan was going, but Garrett was in Bir-

mingham and Ferrell didn't know where to reach him. He called
Garrett's house in Montgomery a little after 8:30 and asked his wife,
Electra, where Garrett was staying. She didn't know but said Frank
Long was with him. Ferrell wasn't surprised. Long, a young lawyer
who headed the Alabama Young Democrats, was a strong Folsom ally
and one of the fastest-rising stars in the state Democratic Party. Ferrell
called the long-distance operator and told her to begin looking for
Long in the leading hotels in Birmingham, starting with the Redmont. At exactly 8:57, Long picked up the telephone in Room 718 of
the Redmont Hotel. Ferrell asked if he knew where Garrett was. Long
said that Garrett was in the next room and asked Ferrell to hold the
line. While Ferrell waited, he could hear quite a few people in the
background, evidently having a good time. When Long returned, he
suggested that Ferrell call Garrett in Room 720. Because of the noise
level in 718, Ferrell agreed. He flashed the operator and made the
second call. At 9:02 Garrett answered.[21]

Garrett's biggest problem, like Ferrell's, was the Jefferson County
Grand Jury. Emmett Perry had called him on Tuesday night to inform
him that Lamar Reid had mentioned his name in connection with the
vote fraud and to extend an invitation to Garrett to appear as a witness. Three days later, Garrett set about to do just that. He met Frank
Long on the morning of June 18 in Montgomery at a local café; from
there, they went to the attorney general's office. After Garrett retrieved some materials he thought he might need in Birmingham, he,
Long, and Kenneth Horne (a law student at the University of Alabama
whom Garrett had recently hired as a research assistant but who actually served as his driver and gofer) started out for Birmingham.
Garrett opened that morning's edition of the *Birmingham Post-Herald*
to see a front-page article recounting Reid's supposedly secret grand
jury testimony. The article all but gave Garrett's and Ferrell's names
and addresses, referring to them as "out-of-county officials." Clearly
agitated, Garrett ordered Horne to pull in at the Stockyards Café on
the edge of town. From there he called his secretary, Dorothy Johnson, and asked that she bring some more legal material. After Garrett
ticked off a number of law books and files, Ms. Johnson informed him
that Red Porter had been trying to contact him. Garrett suggested

that she tell Porter to meet him at the café. Soon Ms. Johnson arrived with the files.[22]

Porter arrived by cab shortly after. The evening before, Folsom had informed him of the deal he had made with Patterson. There would be no vote contest. As a consolation prize, Folsom offered to supply Porter with state legal business in north Alabama. Porter had wanted to tell Garrett about the agreement, to tell him he wasn't interested in an election contest, and to ask Garrett to please stop bringing it up, but he didn't get the chance. Garrett was in one of his animated moods and only wanted to talk about the newspaper article and what he was going to tell the grand jury. Before Porter knew it, Garrett, Long, and Horne were leaving. Garrett told Porter to stay in Montgomery and promised to contact him late that afternoon.[23]

When Garrett arrived at the Jefferson County Courthouse, local newsmen were waiting, hot on the vote fraud story. Gene Wortsman of the *Birmingham Post-Herald* asked Garrett if he was going before the grand jury. Garrett simply pulled the *Post-Herald* from his briefcase and read it to Wortsman. Garrett dropped the paper and said clearly and deliberately that he had nothing to hide but that others had apparently besmirched his good name. He was going to testify before the grand jury and dispel any adverse notions the members might have. Later that evening, Wortsman telephoned Ferrell in Phenix City and asked about the solicitor's actions in Birmingham on June 4 and 5. When Wortsman refused to go off the record, Ferrell, clearly shaken, hung up.[24]

If Garrett was worried about the grand jury, he didn't show it. Circuit Solicitor Perry wanted Garrett to answer some very specific questions about his activities in Birmingham on June 4 and 5; Garrett read from the state constitution and Alabama statutes relating to his power as attorney general, pointedly providing the example of his predecessor, Albert Carmichael, who had dismissed a Mobile grand jury under similar circumstances—a thinly disguised suggestion that Perry and the grand jury were begging for trouble.[25]

After an entire afternoon of this, Perry called it quits for the day. Garrett checked into the Redmont Hotel, where he met Long. While Garrett was in the grand jury room, Long had gathered up Birming-

ham lawyers James Jolly and Victor Gold, their wives, and local news-
paperman Leo Willett. Garrett invited them to the Governor's Suite
for dinner and drinks. The party rose in volume throughout the early
evening. A little before 8:00 CST, Long answered the telephone. It
was Ferrell, wanting to speak to Si. Long could barely hear him. Garrett was in the adjoining room, where he had escaped the noise to
take another phone call minutes earlier. Long suggested that Ferrell
call the hotel again and ask for Room 720. In less than five minutes,
the phone rang in the adjoining room. This time, Garrett answered
it. As the party in Birmingham reached full swing, Garrett began talking on the telephone, and Albert Patterson, 160 miles away in Phenix
City, left the Coulter Building and walked into history.[26]

Downtown Phenix City was a busy place on a Friday night, catering
to a city population of twenty-four thousand, residents from the surrounding rural areas, and a fair proportion of Fort Benning. The area
around the Coulter Building was especially well traveled, with Fourteenth Street, the main thoroughfare between Phenix City and Columbus, just around the corner. North of the Coulter Building, across
a wide alleyway that doubled as a parking lot for about five cars, stood
the Elite (rhymes with *delight*) Café, which closed at 9:00. Two doors
down from the Elite was Smitty's Grill, a popular round-the-clock
hangout, enjoying its usual Friday-night business. Further down Fifth
Avenue was the Palace Theater, which was showing a double feature:
The Paratrooper, starring Alan Ladd, and *Back to God's Country,* with
Rock Hudson. On the other side of the Coulter Building, toward Fourteenth Street, a small service driveway separated the south side of the
two-story brick structure from the rear of the post office. The cus-
tomer entrance faced Fourteenth Street and saw a constant stream of
traffic well into the night. Across from the post office stood the Russell
County Courthouse, an imposing structure which dominated the
small hill that rose gradually from the west before sloping down again
toward the Chattahoochee River. On this night, a Boy Scout honor
hearing was under way in the main courtroom. It was serious business,
with Probate Judge Shannon Burch presiding and a large number of
scouts and scoutmasters in attendance.[27]

On his return from Montgomery, Patterson drove straight to the
Coulter Building, pulling into the alleyway/parking lot at about 8:00

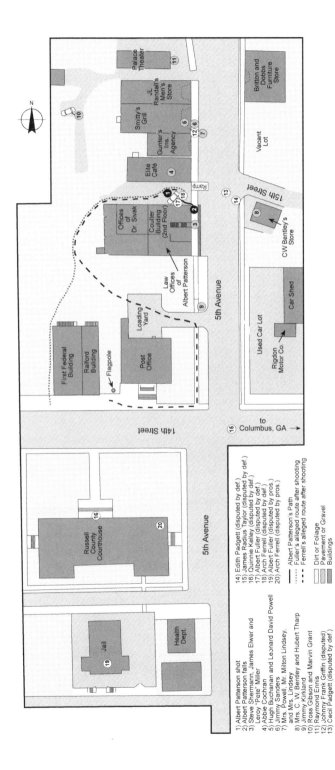

1) Albert Patterson shot
2) Albert Patterson falls
3) Steve Shermann, James Elwer and
   Leroy "Pete" Miller
4) Abbie Cochran
5) Hugh Buchanan and Leonard David Powell
6) Jimmy Sanders
7) Mrs. Powell, Mr. Milton Lindsey,
   and Mrs. Lindsey
8) Mrs. C. W. Bentley and Hubert Tharp
9) Jimmy Kirkland
10) Ross Gibson and Marvin Grant
11) Raymond Ennis
12) Johnny Frank Griffin (disputed)
13) Cecil Padgett (disputed by def.)

14) Edith Padgett (disputed by def.)
15) James Radius Taylor (disputed by def.)
16) Qunnie Kelley (disputed by def.)
17) Albert Fuller (disputed by def.)
18) Arch Ferrell (disputed by def.)
19) Albert Fuller (disputed by pros.)
20) Arch Ferrell (disputed by pros.)

········· Albert Patterson's Path
——— Fuller's alleged route after shooting
--- Ferrell's alleged route after shooting

Dirt or Foliage
Pavement or Gravel
Buildings

Area around Fourteenth Street and Fifth Avenue, Phenix City, showing major witnesses and suspects, June 18, 1954.

and parking headfirst into his reserved spot, the closest to the street. About fifteen minutes later, Mr. and Mrs. Leland Jones, two of Patterson's local supporters, were on their way to dinner and noticed that the lights were on in Patterson's office. Mrs. Jones suggested to her husband that they invite Patterson to accompany them. They parked in front of Seymour's Dress Shop, located on the Coulter Building's ground floor. While Leland went upstairs, Mrs. Jones stayed in the car and thumbed through a catalog by the light of the show windows.

As Leland walked into Patterson's law office, he noticed a pile of opened envelopes strewn around the wastebasket behind Patterson. Jones knew that this was Patterson's way: as he opened mail, he threw the envelopes over his shoulder toward the trash can; if they made it in, fine; if not, that was OK too. Patterson was signing thank-you notes to supporters in the recent runoff election. Already there was a stack sitting on top of the typewriter waiting to be mailed. Patterson asked Jones if he had read that day's editorial in the *Columbus Ledger,* a reprint from one of the Birmingham papers on the Russell County vote fraud hearings. Jones said no, and Patterson handed it to him without comment. As Jones was reading, he noticed that Patterson's attention had wandered off. "You ain't paying a damn bit of attention to me," Jones complained. Patterson looked up and replied, "Yes I am, just read on." The opinion piece recounted the allegations made during the recent election subcommittee hearings and urged state intervention. The two men discussed the editorial briefly. When Patterson declined the dinner invitation, Jones left.[28]

Sometime between 8:15 and 8:30, Woodie Pope, a local mechanic, parked in front of the post office in Phenix City. As he opened the door he met Albert Patterson heading out. Pope held the door for him. When Pope walked out a short time later, Patterson had just turned the corner headed back toward the Coulter Building. Looking across Fourteenth Street, Pope noticed a parked Chrysler. Two men were inside the car, and both appeared to be watching the post office intently. The car began backing out. Suddenly, a Buick topped the hill and locked its brakes to avoid the Chrysler. The driver of the Buick stuck his head out and shouted an obscenity. Pope thought this would certainly cause an altercation, but instead the driver of the Chrysler pulled back to the curb and cut the engine. Pope saw the passenger get out, pull the brim of his hat over his eyes, and walk toward Fifth Avenue.[29]

At the Elite Café, proprietors John and Abbie Cochran were closing up for the night. Forty-eight-year-old Margaret Sanks, who had only last Monday moved from the Russell County countryside to take a job as the Elite's night cook, was terrified of walking around alone in Phenix City. All week long, Abbie had humored her by walking her to the front door and waiting until she had crossed the adjoining alley. Tonight, Abbie again stood with the screen door open while Margaret began walking toward Fourteenth Street. From their position, both she and Margaret could see Patterson's car in the alley and, a little further up, two men at the other end of the Coulter Building, standing close and talking. Both wore light-colored shirts and hats. Margaret paused on the sidewalk and turned toward Abbie for reassurance. Abbie called out, "Ain't nothing going to bother you. I'll watch you until you get across the alley." When Margaret turned back around and began walking south again, the two men had moved up Fifth Avenue toward Fourteenth Street. Before she made it to the intersection, they had disappeared.[30]

Around 8:45, Maggie Thaxton and her ten-year-old son, Billy, set out from their apartment on Fifth Avenue and began walking south. They were headed toward the city jail to visit Mr. Thaxton, an inmate. Stopping at Bentley's Grocery, Maggie sat on a retaining wall while Billy went in to buy his father a pack of cigarettes and a box of matches. While she waited, Maggie noticed a heavy-set man in light clothes walking down the street, his head dropped as if he were watching where he stepped. Maggie didn't pay much attention to him and began walking again as soon as Billy reappeared with the cigarettes.[31]

Eighteen-year-old James Elwer was finally getting around to a job he had promised to do the previous Saturday. He had told Dr. Sivak, a Phenix City practitioner, that he would pick up some used office furniture on Wednesday and refinish it. Elwer had put the job off on Wednesday, and again on Thursday. Tonight he went to see Bill Miller, the owner of the Tropical Trailer Court, where Elwer worked during the day. He wanted to borrow Bill's pickup truck to transport the furniture. Miller agreed. Elwer also needed some help loading the furniture. Luckily, Miller's fifteen-year-old son, Pete, was agreeable to the idea of going downtown, as was twenty-two-year-old Steve Schermann, a neighbor. The three stopped by Dr. Sivak's house and picked up the office key.[32]

Sivak's office was on the second floor of the Coulter Building, directly above Seymour's Dress Shop and down the hall from Patterson's law offices. A little before 9:00, Elwer, Miller, and Schermann pulled up in front of the Coulter Building, taking the last parking space to the north, the one closest to the door. As they reached the top of the stairs, they could see that the lights were on in Patterson's office. While Schermann and Miller inspected one of Dr. Sivak's microscopes, Elwer located the furniture in a back room. The first item was an examination table, and the three cleared a path and removed the drawers. Just as Elwer and Schermann lifted the piece to take it downstairs, they heard the distinct sound of someone with a cane carefully making his way down the stairwell.[33] After maneuvering the table through the doors and down the stairs, they reached the front door of the Coulter Building probably less than two minutes later.[34]

Teenager Jimmy Sanders met his friend Hugh Buchanan on Fifth Avenue as Hugh was coming around the corner from the pool hall on Sixteenth Street. Both of them had a transportation problem. Buchanan was looking for a ride to Auburn, where his girlfriend would be attending a dance; Sanders was to meet a friend at a Columbus movie theater. Together they shuffled up the street, toward Smitty's, to find a ride. While they were still a few doors north of Smitty's, Sanders looked up Fifth Avenue and saw Albert Patterson in front of the Coulter Building. It looked as if he had dropped his keys and was bending down, awkwardly, to pick them up. Just then, Sanders felt a tap on his shoulder.[35]

Around Phenix City, seventeen-year-old Jimmy Kirkland was already a high school legend in track and boxing. The kind of athlete who was always looking for an opportunity to work out, Kirkland never rode in a car or bus if his feet would get him there in a reasonable time. On this Friday night, he was diligently jogging north up Fifth Avenue looking for Jack Remfro, who worked at the used-car lot owned by Jimmy's father. As he breezed by Randall's Clothing Store, Kirkland asked Jimmy Sanders and Hugh Buchanan if they had seen Jack. They shook their heads, and Kirkland kept jogging toward the Palace Theater, where he scanned the street for Remfro's car. Not finding it, he headed back south toward his father's used-car lot at the corner of Fourteenth Street. In the distance he could see Sanders and Buchanan, slowly walking toward Smitty's; beyond the Elite Café, he saw Albert Patterson. Patterson was stooped over picking up something off the sidewalk—a ring of keys, Kirkland judged. By this time, he had caught up with Sanders and Buchanan, and Kirkland playfully tapped Sanders on the shoulder as he passed him again. A few steps later he was in front of the Elite, and with a few steps more he was in front of the Coulter Building. Kirkland finally stopped at the Fifth Avenue service entrance to the post office to catch his breath and consider where to go next.[36]

Leonard David Powell and his wife had driven to Columbus with Powell's brother-in-law, Milton Lindsey, and his family. As they crossed the bridge back into Phenix City, Lindsey suggested that they stop at Smitty's and get some sandwiches to go. After they parked in front of the restaurant, Powell got out from the front passenger side, stepped up on the sidewalk, and reached for the door just as Hugh Buchanan arrived. Hugh let Powell enter first. While Buchanan held the door from the outside, Powell took one step inside. Before he could take a second, the sound of gunshots came from the direction of the Coulter Building.[37]

The furniture movers heard the shots just as they reached the bottom of the stairs. Schermann, the first out the door, thought someone was shooting firecrackers. He had been startled by the noise but was totally unprepared for what he saw next: former state senator Albert Patterson reeling from the alley. For a brief second, Schermann thought Phenix City's most prominent citizen was rip-roaring drunk. Patterson was gesturing at his chest and trying desperately to say something, but the only sounds coming out were gurgling and wheezing noises. Then Schermann noticed the blood. As he and Elwer watched, incredulous, Patterson sank to his hands and knees, then to his stomach. The youths took a few steps back, one of them suggesting, "Let's get the hell out of here." The other said, "No, we'd better call the law." Coming to their senses, they ran upstairs to call the police.[38]

At the Elite Café's lunch counter, Mrs. Cochran was refilling sugar dispensers when she and everyone else in the restaurant heard a sharp banging on the south wall. Her first thought was that teenagers were hitting the large metal Dr. Pepper sign with rocks. Her husband, John, said it sounded like gunshots. Abbie cautiously stepped to the back door that opened into the alley and peeked out. She saw nothing except Albert Patterson's car, parked in its usual spot, close to the street. Everything was dead quiet. She walked the length of the building toward the sidewalk. Across Fifth Avenue, in front of Bentley's Grocery, she could see the owner, Mrs. Ida Bentley; her hired hand, Hubert Tharp; and a local boy, Jimmy Burnside. They seemed just as puzzled as she was, their gazes fixed on the sidewalk in front of the Coulter Building. Finally, Abbie reached the sidewalk and saw what the others were staring at: a man lying in front of Seymour's Dress Shop. He was twitching as if he were having a seizure. Suddenly, she realized two things as Burnside crossed the street: the man was Albert Patterson and he had been shot. Things became disjointed for her at this point. She hollered across the street to Bentley and Tharp to call the police, then ran to the Elite's front door, but she had locked it from the inside just moments before and had to yell for her husband to open it. By the time he unlocked it, Abbie had completely forgotten that she had told Mrs. Bentley to call the police and hurried in to do it herself. Burnside went with her, looking up the numbers for her to dial. In quick succession, she called the Phenix City police (although Mrs. Bentley had just beaten her to it), Mrs. Patterson, and Charles Gunter, an RBA member and good friend of Albert Patterson's.[39]

In the doorway of Smitty's Grill, the shots stopped Hugh Buchanan and Leonard Powell in their tracks. Jimmy Sanders remained in front, hanging on a parking meter. Powell turned to Buchanan and asked, "What's all that?" Buchanan shrugged and said he didn't know. Powell then stepped to the sidewalk next to Sanders and looked toward Fourteenth Street. An older man staggered out of the alley beyond the Elite Café, took two steps to the right, and fell to the sidewalk. Powell remarked to no one in particular, "That man is drunk." Sanders also thought for a brief moment that the man was intoxicated. Then he recognized him. By the time he got Buchanan's attention, Patterson was already face down on the sidewalk. Sanders ran to him, asking, "Who shot you, Mr. Patterson? Who shot you?" Patterson could only respond with choking, gasping sounds. Up the street, Jimmy Kirkland heard gunshots ring out directly behind him. He, too, saw Patterson come from the alley Kirkland had just passed and collapse on the sidewalk. He reached Patterson almost simultaneously with Sanders. Powell's wife and brother-in-law had also looked toward the alley when the shots were fired and had seen Patterson come around the corner and fall. They both got out of the car to stand with Powell. In a few minutes they heard Abbie Cochran standing over Patterson, bellowing, "Call the law! Call the law!"[40]

Behind Smitty's Grill, night manager Marvin Grant and short-order cook Ross Gibson were headed to the Seale Road Curb Market to buy restaurant supplies. They had just seated themselves in Grant's car when they heard several shots. Grant didn't see the shooter, but as Gibson looked toward the sound of the gunshots he saw a medium-sized man, wearing light brown clothes and hat, run from the direction of Fifth Avenue and disappear among the bushes behind the Coulter Building.[41]

After Margaret Sanks turned west on Fourteenth Street, she noticed a black pickup truck and, directly behind it, a large black car parked in front of the Federal Savings and Loan Building. A man got out of the car and began walking toward the post office and the Fifth Avenue intersection. He was between thirty and thirty-five years old and dressed in khaki work clothes and some sort of hat or cap. At about the same time, Floyd Waites, headed in the same direction as Sanks but about a block behind, saw the man turn north on Fifth Avenue. A few minutes later, as Sanks crossed the west driveway of the courthouse, she heard the gunshots. Her first thought was that it was a car backfiring. She stopped for a minute to look back, but she didn't see any cars.[42]

Nineteen-year-old Raymond Ennis drove downtown and parked in front of the Elite Café at about 9:00. He walked to Smitty's and looked inside for a friend of his, Charlie McGuire. Charlie wasn't there, but he must have been nearby because his car was parked directly across the street. The only other place McGuire could be was the Palace Theater. Ennis walked to the ticket window and asked when the show would be over. Before the cashier could answer, Ennis heard what he thought were firecrackers. He turned and looked across the street, but he saw nothing. When he turned back to the ticket window, she answered: 9:18. He turned around again, this time looking up Fifth Avenue. A man was lying on the sidewalk beyond Smitty's Grill. Standing in the street between the Coulter Building and Bentley's Grocery was another man, in his late twenties or early thirties, heavily built, wearing khaki work clothes and a brown leather cap. He was looking over his shoulder as he walked away from the body, toward the vacant lot north of Bentley's Grocery. Ennis trotted toward the scene and got within a few feet of Patterson's body; already there were seven or eight people gathered, but the workman was gone.[43]

One block toward the river, on Third Avenue (Fourth Avenue faded out a few blocks to the north), neighbors David Mobley and James Tucker were talking as Tucker waxed his car. A little after 9:00 they both turned in the direction of a car suddenly taking off and heading toward Fourteenth Street. The car had been parked in front of a retaining wall on the west side of the street toward Fifth Avenue. Tucker said, "Look at that car, how fast it's taking off." Mobley replied, "He's probably drunk." Whatever the reason, the driver was in a hurry.[44]

Tucker and Mobley weren't the only ones in the area to notice a car in a hurry. Close to the same time, about two blocks away, Mrs. Hortense Tiller and a friend were sitting in the swing on her front porch on Fifth Avenue, located south of the courthouse on the other side of Fourteenth Street from the Coulter Building. They saw a green car turn north on Fifth Avenue off Thirteenth Street, going so fast it seemed to go up on two wheels as it made the turn. Shortly after, they heard sirens approaching the Coulter Building.[45]

Phenix City police logged Mrs. Bentley's call at 9:09 P.M. Officers Dewey Chestnut and William Griffin heard the dispatcher call a squad car to investigate a reported shooting at the Coulter Building. Because they were only three blocks away, the two policemen decided to head in that direction to provide backup. They beat the other car, arriving only three minutes after Mrs. Bentley's call. As soon as they saw Patterson's lifeless body, they radioed for an ambulance. Before the call was completed, officers Tom Scroggins and Glenn Holloway pulled up. Scroggins asked if anyone had called an ambulance yet. Griffin replied, "You don't need an ambulance, you need a hearse." A small crowd had already formed when an ambulance from the Colonial Funeral Home arrived. Attendants James Elkins and John Leslie picked up Patterson and put him on the waiting stretcher. As they did so,

Patterson's keys fell out of his hands. They retrieved these along with his hat, which was lying on the sidewalk, and headed toward Cobb Memorial Hospital.[46]

At the Patterson home at 1302 Pine Circle, Agnes Patterson answered the telephone at about 9:10. It was Abbie Cochran calling from the Elite Café to tell her that someone had been shot at the Coulter Building and that she believed it to be Mr. Patterson. Mrs. Patterson called down to a married couple who rented the basement apartment at the Patterson home and asked them to take her downtown. They met the ambulance a few blocks short of the Coulter Building and turned around, toward the hospital. There, Dr. Clyde Knowles informed her that her husband was dead. She sat there stunned until her second-oldest son, Maurice, appeared, breaking down as he put his arm around her. Only then did her tears come.[47]

4
June 18, 1954,
Part 2

If you catch the son-of-a-bitch, turn him over to me. They didn't even give him a chance.

John Patterson, June 18, 1954

At the Redmont Hotel in Birmingham, Si Garrett finished his telephone conversation with Arch Ferrell and called his wife in Montgomery to tell her to bring the children up for the weekend. He then entered the main room where the party was still in progress. Noticing Mrs. Gold's Phi Beta Kappa key, Garrett kidded about how smart she must be. At about 8:45 CST, the telephone rang again. It was Associated Press night reporter Stanley Atkins, who, hearing of the murder, remembered that Garrett had checked into the Redmont after his grand jury testimony. Atkins was calling to get the attorney general's reaction. The first words out of Garrett's mouth were, "My God, can that be true?" He then inquired as to when the murder took place, and when Atkins told him, Garrett paused for a moment and remarked, "If that time is correct—and I see no reason to doubt your word—then at that very time I was talking to the solicitor of Russell County."[1]

Garrett turned from the telephone and instructed Horne: "Take down these numbers." Horne busily wrote as Garrett ticked off a slew of telephone numbers from memory. When Garrett was finished, Horne began dialing. The first on the list: Governor Persons. Before anyone answered, Garrett said with some emotion, "It's the worst thing that ever happened to Alabama. I'll put the dirty son-of-a-bitch in the electric chair! I don't necessarily believe in capital punishment, but I'll strap the son-of-a-bitch myself!"[2]

After Ferrell had completed his telephone call to Garrett, he culled a few papers from the stacks on his desk and stuck them in his pocket to carry home. He walked downstairs to the basement, exited the rear of the courthouse, and headed home in his car. A few minutes later, he pulled into Huckaby's Store, just a few feet from his own driveway. Once inside, he helped himself to a can of beer and chatted with Mr. Huckaby, the owner. He had barely started on his second when James Money, a young man who lived across the road, came in and asked excitedly if they had heard the news: Albert Patterson had been shot and killed.

Incredulous, Ferrell asked where he had heard that. Money explained that he had just heard it on the radio. Just then, Mrs. Huckaby stepped out from the back of the store and confirmed the news, the flash having just come over the television. Ferrell stepped to the back to see for himself. When he had heard enough, he got back in his car and drove to his house. His wife, Madeline, was in bed reading. Ferrell relayed the news to her as he was dialing the sheriff's office. No one answered. He tried the jailhouse, but that line was busy. He next attempted to call Governor Persons at his home. No one answered. He then tried the residence of Public Safety Director L. B. Sullivan. Busy. Then Tom Carlisle, the head of the state highway patrol. Busy. As soon as he hung up, the telephone rang. It was his father, asking excitedly if the news was true. Ferrell said that it evidently was. He would let him know when he had more information. Ferrell hung up, and again the telephone rang. This time it was Garrett, wanting to know what the hell was going on in Phenix City. Ferrell filled him in with what little information he had; right now, he was calling for all the assistance he could get. Garrett said he was doing the same thing. They agreed that a local coroner would not do in this murder case. There was only one person who could perform Patterson's autopsy in such a volatile situation. Garrett's last instruction to Ferrell before he hung up was to find Dr. C. J. Rehling, the director of the Alabama Department of Toxicology and Criminal Investigation (now the Alabama Department of Forensic Sciences), and get him to Phenix City right away.[3]

As Robert Lee Smith and Johnny Dees passed Fourteenth Street on their way to Smitty's, they could see some commotion down by the Coulter Building. A policeman directing traffic told them what had happened. Dees told Smith, "I bet the sheriff doesn't know about this!" and got out of the car at a trot, headed back toward the jail.[4]

In Ben Clark's private quarters at the Russell County jail, Sheriff Mathews was telling Fuller that he had received a phone call earlier in the day from Vernon Merritt, Governor Persons's executive secretary. Merritt said that the governor's office had received complaints about gambling. Mathews asked him who had been complaining; Merritt had replied that he wasn't at liberty to say. Mathews now wanted Fuller to check around town and see if gambling was so out in the open that a little reminder might be called for, like a few arrests. Mathews and Fuller had been talking for no more than ten minutes when Dees returned. Finally locating Mathews and Fuller, he announced, "Someone's just shot Mr. Patterson." Fuller didn't think that was funny: "Johnny, cut out the damned bullshit!" When Fuller saw that Dees wasn't joking, he jumped up, grabbed his hat, and ran to the door; Mathews and Dees were close behind. The three took off in Fuller's car to the murder scene, parking in the street.[5]

Fuller and Mathews spent five or ten minutes getting details from police. Patterson had already been taken to the hospital. No one knew if he was dead or alive, but the money was on the former. Independently of Ferrell and Garrett, Mathews also concluded that the local coroner would be inadequate. He instructed Fuller to call Dr. Rehling and request his assistance at once in Phenix City. Fuller went to the jail and tried the number, but he couldn't get an outside line. He told highway patrolman Phillips to keep trying. Fuller returned to the scene, but there was still no word on Patterson's condition. Mathews decided to go to the hospital and find out for himself. As he got in the car with the assistant police chief, Buddy Jowers, he told Fuller to take charge of the crime scene. Fuller ordered the area roped off from the growing crowd. He then asked Mrs. Cochran if she had anything he could use to cover the huge puddle of blood on the sidewalk. She gave him an empty cardboard shipping container, which Fuller placed over the stain and secured with a short wooden plank. After about fifteen minutes at the murder scene, Fuller drove to the hospital.[6]

When Sheriff Mathews arrived at the hospital, he went straight to the emergency room. Dr. Knowles told him that Patterson was dead on arrival. Mathews wandered outside just as highway patrolmen Patrick Mihelic and Clint Hall pulled up outside the building. Minutes before, they were headed south on Highway 431 out of Phenix City when they received a call to check out the shooting at the Coulter Building. Mathews now told them who the victim was, and Mihelic and Hall realized immediately that this was no ordinary Friday-night shooting. There was potential for real trouble, and they didn't hesitate when Mathews asked them to radio for state investigators and more patrolmen. A few minutes later Fuller drove up, and he and Mathews conferred for a moment. Fuller went inside, examined the body, offered his condolences to Mrs. Patterson, and headed back to the jail with Mathews.[7]

Meanwhile, patrolman Phillips's call to the home of Dr. Rehling had finally gone through. Mrs. Rehling said that her husband was in Montgomery. Phillips told her of the shooting and requested, on behalf of the Russell County sheriff, that Rehling come to Phenix City to perform the autopsy. If she couldn't contact her husband, he added, someone else from his office should be sent. She said she would do her best to locate Wendell Sowell, her husband's assistant. "Tell him to hurry," said Phillips. In between calls to Montgomery trying to locate her husband, Mrs. Rehling called the Auburn Police Department and asked them to locate Sowell at the city park, where his son, Wendell Jr., played Little League every Friday night.[8]

Red Porter had been in the Jefferson Davis Hotel in Montgomery all evening waiting for Garrett to call. While he was at the Stockyards Café earlier in the day, Garrett was talking a mile a minute and was anxious to get to Birmingham, so Porter decided to wait until later to tell him that he had already made a deal with Folsom and wanted Garrett to drop his idea for an election contest in the attorney general's race. Garrett had told Porter to wait in Montgomery until he got back from Birmingham, which would be about 5:00 CST. By 6:00, Porter and his wife, Martha, were getting anxious, having left their children with the maid at their Gadsden home with the expectation that they would be back by bedtime. Porter tried to call Garrett at the Redmont but was unable to reach him. About an hour later, Martha called. This time Frank Long answered. She heard Garrett say in the background, "I know who's calling. I am very busy now and will call them in a few minutes." At 9:10 CST, Porter called again. This time Garrett answered. Before Porter could ask if Garrett was going to make it back to Montgomery that night, Garrett told him that Patterson had been killed and that Porter must come to Birmingham immediately.[9]

At Felton Little Park in Auburn, Wendell Sowell was watching his son and eight other teammates on the Auburn twelve-and-under Yankees play the Camp Hill White Sox. Toward the end of the game, the crowd's attention was drawn to a couple of policemen scanning the crowd. Signaling Sowell, they pulled him aside and told him that Albert Patterson had been killed and that Sowell should call Mrs. Rehling immediately.[10]

Sowell took his family home and called Mrs. Rehling, who informed him that Russell County officials had requested that a state medical examiner go to Phenix City as quickly as possible. Sowell placed an emergency long-distance call to Sheriff Mathews, only to be told by the operator that an emergency call was already in progress on the sheriff's telephone and that she would not interrupt one emergency call with another. While his wife held the line, Sowell changed his clothes. Finally, a deputy gave Sowell a quick rundown of the situation. Twenty minutes later, after a quick stop at his toxicology laboratory to pick up some of his traveling equipment, Sowell was on his way.[11]

Arch Ferrell arrived back at the courthouse at about 10:00. In contrast to the scene some forty minutes earlier, the building was now full of people, and at least six highway patrolmen stopped Ferrell and quizzed him as he made his way to the sheriff's office. Mathews was talking on the telephone, but he stopped long enough to ask Ferrell if he knew what was going on. Ferrell said he was just finding out and wanted to know what leads had been uncovered so far. The sheriff mentioned two suspicious cars in the area and one suspect fleeing the scene. Ferrell went to the city jail to interview one of the suspects and determined that the man could not have been in the area at the time of the shooting. When Ferrell returned to the county jail, Mathews said that Garrett was trying to reach him. Ferrell replied that he already had, but he called Garrett just to make sure. Garrett wanted to know if Rehling had been located yet. At that moment, Sowell drove up.[12]

It was now 11:05, two hours after Patterson's murder. Mathews and Ferrell gave Sowell a quick rundown on the situation, and then Sowell and Ferrell drove to the crime scene. When Sowell entered the roped-off area, he was perturbed to see the large number of people within reach of the car. In addition to what seemed to be every law enforcement officer within fifty miles of the Chattahoochee River, various reporters, witnesses, and even quite a few spectators who had no reason to be there were milling about Patterson's car. Exasperated, Sowell asked Fuller, "Has anyone touched the car?" Not that he knew of, said Fuller. Sowell immediately gave orders that the car be kept under guard, that no one touch it, and that no one except official investigators be allowed inside the ropes.[13]

The initial investigation of the crime scene was well under way. The car, a two-tone blue 1953 Oldsmobile 88, remained parked as Patterson had left it, with the driver's-side door still open. Most noticeable was the bullet hole in the car's front passenger-door window. Several detectives and policemen were scraping through the surrounding gravel searching for the bullet. Inside the car, the driver's seat and the floorboard were covered with blood. Investigators removed one of the blood-soaked floor mats for evidence. Police found Patterson's cane on the rear floorboard.[14]

Fuller ordered deputies and policemen to round up and question the furniture movers, teenagers, and patrons of the local restaurants. Only Ross Gibson had seen any suspects, and he now gave them his description of the man he saw running from the alley: a white man wearing a light brown suit and a light-colored hat. Based on Gibson's information, lawmen searched along the paths behind the Coulter Building looking for evidence. Before the boundary changes of the 1920s, the alley itself had been an extension of Line Street (it has

since been renamed Fifteenth Street), so named because it marked
the border between Girard and Phenix City and connected Fifth Avenue with Broad Street one block to the west. Now, in 1954, it officially
terminated at Fifth Avenue, with the pavement petering out a few
yards beyond the Coulter Building and the Elite Café. To the right, a
small driveway ran behind Smitty's, and this is where Gibson was when
he saw the killer. To the left was a pair of unfenced footpaths that
wound their way behind the Coulter Building through untended back
lots. One of these ended at the Fifth Avenue service entrance and
loading dock of the post office. The other veered off to the right and
emerged onto Fourteenth Street between the post office and the Raiford Building. Policeman Glenn Holloway found a footprint near the
back corner of the building. Another policeman, Houston Ragsdale,
noticed it was longer than his own shoe, a size ten. They showed the
print to Assistant Police Chief Buddy Jowers. A little later, policeman
Walter Sanders led Fuller to the footprint. The two covered it with a
board to protect it until crime scene investigators could take a plaster-of-paris cast.[15]

Pete Miller had already learned in his fifteen years the value of not
being too observant or nosy, especially around Phenix City, so he almost instinctively let the police believe that he was almost at the bottom of the stairs, right behind Schermann and Elwer, when the shots
rang out and had therefore seen nothing. In reality, Miller was *first*
on the sidewalk, *ahead* of Schermann and Elwer. He had clearly seen
not only Patterson's final, jerky steps on the Fifth Avenue sidewalk but
also a man crossing Fifth Avenue, headed toward the vacant lot to the
north of Fifteenth Street. Once or twice, the man looked over his
shoulder toward Patterson, almost as if he expected to be pursued.[16]

When Fuller returned to the hospital it was with Willie Painter, the
first state investigator to arrive in Phenix City. By this time, the corridor outside the emergency room was swarming with people. The
two lawmen talked for a while with Dr. Knowles, who offered the opinion that the bullets were of a .25 caliber. Knowles based that conclusion on a bullet he said he had removed from Patterson's mouth
and had given to Police Chief Pal Daniel. At about the same time,

three RBA members—Howard Pennington, David Morris, and J. T. Pickard—arrived. Pennington sought out Mrs. Patterson, who was down the hall from the cubicle that held her husband's body. She had told ambulance driver James Elkins that she wanted to see who came in to examine the body. Agnes looked at Pennington: "Well, they got him first, didn't they?" "Yes, they did," Pennington agreed softly.[17] Stepping out in the hallway, Pennington, Morris, and Pickard took a close look at Fuller. Something was different about him, perhaps a new hat or a different haircut. It took a minute, but then they all noticed. Fuller had an empty holster; it was the first time any of them had seen him without a side arm.[18]

Across the river in Columbus, John Patterson was at home reading on the evening of June 18. He had only recently moved into the residence, and his telephone was not yet connected. He was roused by a knock on the door, and his neighbor, Sherman Sylvia, told him he had an emergency phone call. John walked next door and picked up the receiver. On the line was Mr. Estes, the man renting his father's basement apartment, who said that John's father had been shot. Running back home, Patterson told his wife what had happened and asked her to call her sister's husband, Clanton attorney Morgan Reynolds, and ask him to come to Phenix City right away.[19]

When John arrived at the Coulter Building, a huge crowd had gathered on the street and sidewalk in front of his father's car, the door of which was still open. Local police quickly informed him that his father had been shot. Judging by the amount of blood on the sidewalk, John could see that the wound was serious. Deputy Aaron Smith expressed his sympathies and offered the department's help on anything Patterson or his family might wish. John had only one request: "If you catch the son-of-a-bitch, turn him over to me. They didn't even give him a chance."[20]

At the hospital, John learned that his father was dead on arrival. Entering the emergency room cubicle, he took a look at his father's body and muttered, "Fine people we have here." Local mortician James McGehee arrived, and Patterson told him he wanted him to take care of his father's body after the autopsy. Morgan Reynolds arrived about 11:30, and Patterson had a special assignment for his brother-in-law:

stay with the body and let no one around it until a state examiner arrived. He then left to find his mother.[21]

By this time, the news of Patterson's murder was hitting the rest of the state like a tidal wave. In Montgomery, Fred Andersen, the managing editor of the *Montgomery Advertiser,* received a call at his office from a near-hysterical Jabe Brassell at 10:00 CST. Brassell excitedly told Andersen about the murder and claimed that his life was in danger. He had been trying to call the governor for an hour but hadn't been able to reach him. He now told Andersen that armed men were attempting to break into his house and that he and his son were fighting for their lives. Brassell nearly screamed into the telephone, "Call Gordon Persons and tell him if he doesn't call out the National Guard we are going to have to kill every goddamned gambler in Phenix City!"[22]

During the evening, Governor Persons had been watching a movie, and he didn't learn of Patterson's murder until his return to the Governor's Mansion. Like his predecessors, Persons had left Phenix City and Russell County to their own devices in dealing with vice and corruption. Now, in Persons's final year as governor, the news hit him with an element of betrayal. He knew the Phenix City machine wouldn't like what he was about to do, but he had no choice. The first priority was to keep order. If the RBA and other sources were to be believed, the town was on the verge of anarchy, with swarms of armed vigilantes out to avenge Patterson's murder. He first called Sheriff Mathews and told him of Brassell's complaint. Mathews said he hadn't heard of any trouble, but he agreed to send a couple of deputies to check it out. Then, noting that the governor had said nothing specific about Patterson's murder, he asked, "You know about the other trouble?" Persons assured him he had and hung up. The governor next ordered Public Safety Director Sullivan and highway patrol chief Carlisle to put in as many highway patrolmen as could be reached. There were already eight on hand; by midnight there would be at least twenty more. He also called the FBI's local office in Mobile and requested federal assistance on the theory that since Phenix City bordered Georgia, there was a good chance that Patterson's killer had crossed the state line while fleeing, thus falling under federal jurisdiction. Special agent Gordon Shanklin said he would pass the request on to Washington.[23] Lastly, Persons put in a call to "Crack" Hanna, his National Guard adjutant general, and told him to go to Phenix City, assess the situation, and use his judgment as to whether troops were needed to keep the peace.[24]

Major General Walter Hanna, military commander of the Alabama National Guard, was no run-of-the-mill weekend warrior. At fifty-two, Hanna was already a millionaire from his two primary businesses, National Safety Engineers and Hanna Steel Corporation. Born on December 29, 1901, Hanna had an unlikely start at soldiering. There was no military tradition in his family; on the contrary, his father had even objected when Walter wanted to join the Boy Scouts because he thought the organization was too militaristic. At Central High School in Birmingham, though, Walter signed up for ROTC but was kicked out after he pummeled his captain during a disagreement over when cadets were required to salute (Hanna was right).

Hanna attempted five times to join the service during World War I, lying about his age each time. Once, after loading up on bananas and water to make the weight requirements, he achieved a stint of two weeks before army officials discovered his true age and sent him home. In 1919, Hanna enlisted in the legendary 31st (Dixie) Infantry Division, again lying about his age (his true age was not corrected on his military records until 1961, two years before his retirement). In 1921, after being chosen as the best-drilled man in the Alabama Guard, Hanna was promoted to second lieutenant, an impossibility had the National Guard known that he was not yet twenty-one.

In the years following the war, Hanna earned the nickname "Crack" for his ability as a marksman, breaking the world's record and winning a variety of medals and titles in regional and national competition, including state champion for thirteen years. By the time he was called to active duty in 1940, Hanna had worked his way up to major, and as the only noncareer officer to command such a unit in the Pacific, he led the 155th Infantry Combat Team in New Guinea, the Philippines, Morotai, and the Dutch East Indies. When he returned to Alabama after the war he had a chestful of medals, including the Legion of Merit, the Silver Star, the Bronze Star, and the Air Medal.

Hanna had arrived at his current position because of his obstinate character. When the Korean War broke out, the 31st Infantry Division, with General A. G. Paxton as the commanding officer and Hanna as second in command, was called up for duty. Hanna had caused a dispute through his insistence that each and every soldier in the division—including clerks, chaplains, and cooks—undergo full combat training. Paxton disagreed, and when Hanna made the dispute public, Paxton relieved him of command and sent him home. Governor Persons, though, was quick to appoint him adjutant general. Although an honor, the appointment was not Hanna's first choice. The stateside-bound job offered little excitement, especially during peacetime. Even making money in Birmingham offered more action than did the largely administrative and ceremonial duties of adjutant general. That was about to change drastically.[25]

On the night of June 18, Hanna was on his way home to Birmingham after activating a new National Guard unit in Gadsden, sixty-five miles to the northeast. As Hanna and his driver, Lieutenant Colonel Tony Jannett, reached the outskirts of Rainbow City, Hanna's name came over the car radio along with the request that he contact Birmingham headquarters immediately. The general tried to raise Birmingham, but a highway patrol dispatcher was broadcasting an unfamiliar code and would not let Hanna cut in. After a few minutes, the caller asked who was "trying to bust in." Hanna identified himself, and the dispatcher explained what a signal 7 was: an Alabama Highway Patrol precedence signal excluding all other calls. He was in the process of rounding up as many patrolmen as possible to be sent to Phenix City. After completing his lecture, the dispatcher relayed a message for Hanna to telephone his home immediately.[26]

Because of the late hour and isolated location, Hanna and Jannett had trouble finding a public telephone. They finally located an ancient hand-crank model outside Springville in St. Clair County, and from there Hanna heard the news of Patterson's murder and an urgent request to call Governor Persons. Instead of trying to call Montgomery from the antique telephone, Hanna hopped back in the car and told Jannett to step on it. Jannett did, and a few miles later a Trussville police officer pulled the car over for speeding, only to hurry him on when he saw who it was. On the outskirts of Birmingham, Hanna's car was pulled over by another policeman, this time to escort Hanna and Jannett through downtown Birmingham at eighty-five miles an hour.[27]

At the armory, Hanna telephoned the governor and received his instructions. He was to make a personal assessment of the public safety situation in Phenix City. If he believed that troops were called for, he should muster as many as he thought were needed. He was also to shut down gambling and vice operations wherever he found them. Hanna first notified the local Phenix City outfit, Company C of the 167th Infantry, to alert its men and stand by. He then called Lieutenant Colonel Jack Warren, a twenty-two-year veteran of the guard and the 31st Infantry Division's provost marshal. Hanna snapped, "Jack, Albert Patterson's just been killed. The governor's ordered us to Phenix City to take a look. Get your fat ass over here to the armory at 4 A.M., ready to go." Hanna next roused his seventeen-year-old son, Pete, a private in the guard, to drive him and Warren to Phenix City.[28]

Joe Smelley, chief of Alabama's equivalent of the FBI, the Investigative and Identification (I & I) Division of the Department of Public Safety, was visiting relatives in Huntsville when he learned of Patterson's murder. From there he radioed orders for three state investigators to head out for Phenix City at once, then hopped into his own car to make the 220-mile trip. Coming into town at about 12:30, Smelley could see that the local police had not set up any roadblocks—if the killer had decided to flee Phenix City, he was already gone. At the scene, Smelley assessed the situation quickly. Although the alley was now brightly illuminated, he noticed the crime scene was well lit, even without the portable lights the fire department had brought in to assist the police. Up above, an almost full moon shone brightly in the June sky. Numerous street lights dotted the street and back alleys. Both sides of the show windows in the Coulter Building were lit up, as was the Elite Café across the alley. Certainly, it was possible that someone had seen the killer.[29]

Ferrell and Sowell inspected Patterson's car closely, paying close attention to the hole in the front passenger-door window. A few of the city policemen pointed out some aspects of the crime scene, such as the trail of blood that led from the car to the sidewalk. In a few minutes, Police Chief Daniel arrived and told Sowell to call Garrett in Birmingham. He also gave Sowell a small box, saying it contained the bullet that Dr. Knowles had removed from Patterson's mouth. After Sowell and Ferrell arrived at police headquarters, Sowell opened the box and was surprised to see it was not a bullet at all but rather one of Patterson's gold teeth. Sowell told Ferrell and Daniel that it would be a good idea not to mention this fact.[30] When Sowell called Garrett, the attorney general gave him a direct order: he was not to touch the body until Rehling arrived. Although Garrett had confidence in Sowell, the matter was too important for anyone but the top two medical examiners in Alabama. Sowell just as urgently emphasized the importance of performing the autopsy as soon as possible and asked Garrett to consider the possibility that Rehling couldn't be reached. Garrett's answer was authoritative: "I gave you an order not to touch that body and it still stands!" He then went off the subject: "You know I'm up here before the grand jury on this vote fraud and we're going to show that Mr. Patterson did not win the election? You know that I supported Mr. Porter very strongly in this election even though he opposed me four years ago and made me campaign? You know the Governor was also supporting Mr. Porter, but not as openly as I was?" Losing patience, Sowell asked Garrett if he wanted to talk to Ferrell and handed off the receiver. All Sowell heard from Ferrell was a series of "yes, sirs."[31]

When Ferrell finished talking to Garrett, he, Sowell, and Daniel returned to the county jail, where they discussed with Mathews how many shots had been fired and the caliber of the gun. After a few more attempts to contact Rehling, Ferrell told Sowell that it would be OK if he went ahead and performed the autopsy. Sowell agreed to do so, but only if Ferrell got Garrett's approval first.[32]

At that point, Albert Fuller drove up with Dr. Knowles. Ferrell asked Knowles if he would assist Sowell with the autopsy, and he agreed. Ferrell again called Garrett and laid out his case. He had called every single place he and Sowell could think of, and Rehling was nowhere to be found. He repeated Sowell's conviction that the autopsy must be performed soon and told Garrett that he was going to enlist Knowles's assistance. Garrett accepted Ferrell's decision but insisted that Sowell and Knowles perform the autopsy together and that Knowles take an active part.[33]

When they arrived at the hospital, Sowell, Ferrell, Daniel, and Mathews went straight to the emergency room cubicle where Morgan Reynolds sat with the body. By this time, John Patterson had returned from his mother's house, and Mathews introduced Sowell to him. Patterson gave no sign of acknowledgment. Instead, he looked sharply at the three Phenix City and Russell County law officials flanking the assistant chief medical examiner and bluntly asked who would head the investigation. Before Sowell could reply, Ferrell informed him that he and Mathews were in charge. Patterson walked out. Sensing his animosity, Sowell followed him into the corridor and explained that he had the authority, recently granted by Garrett, to conduct the autopsy and that he would brook no interference from local officials. Patterson seemed satisfied with that, and he provided Sowell with information about his father's office and offered to share a large envelope that held the contents of Albert Patterson's pockets. In the meantime, Ferrell introduced himself to Reynolds and pulled back the sheet to view the body. Ferrell was visibly upset at the sight of Patterson's corpse, which Reynolds thought quite unusual for a seasoned circuit solicitor.[34]

After his conversation with John Patterson, Sowell ordered police and deputies to clear the hallway to the autopsy room. The body was wheeled in, and the autopsy finally got under way at 2:35 A.M. Eight people crowded around the corpse: Sowell, Dr. Knowles, Ferrell, Mathews, Daniel, undertaker James McGehee, coroner Roy Thornell, and Richard Aldinger, the administrator of Cobb Memorial Hospital. Sowell removed the sheet. Patterson's body was as the ambulance attendants had delivered it DOA—still dressed in a brown striped suit, white shirt, blue tie, and tan dress shoes. His light-colored straw hat rested nearby, a bullet hole through the brim's left underside. The most obvious sign of violence on Patterson's body was a bullet wound directly to the mouth, which had blasted both upper and lower lips and had been fired from such close range that it left a powder burn more than an inch in diameter.[35]

After Sowell and Knowles lifted the body onto the examination table and removed the clothing, Sowell took out a tape measure and ran it the length of the body. As he measured, he asked Ferrell to explain to the room that any information gained from the postmortem was official and confidential. Then he handed Ferrell a notepad and told him to take notes. Before Ferrell started, however, a policeman entered to announce the arrival of I & I chief Smelley and agents Robert Godwin, John Williams, and Willie Painter. Relieved, Ferrell handed the notepad to Painter.[36]

Ferrell officially announced that the autopsy was being performed on his order and at the request of Sheriff Mathews. The first order of business was to obtain prints from Patterson's palms and fingers, a standard police procedure, so that any prints found at the crime scene could be compared with Patterson's. Investigator Williams assisted Sowell in this task. Next, Sowell and Knowles examined the individual wounds. Beginning with the mouth injury, they saw that the bullet had shattered the right side of Patterson's jawbone before embedding in the back of his neck. Sowell removed the projectile, a damaged .38 caliber lead bullet.

The second wound examined was to Patterson's back, almost centered behind the left lung. After puncturing the lung, the bullet had ranged upward and to the right, severing Patterson's trachea, glottis, and epiglottis—the organs that made speech possible. This explained why the three furniture movers could hear only choking and gasping noises after Patterson rounded the corner. The killer was indeed lucky with this shot. As was later determined, the bullet wound to the mouth was the first shot, and more than one observer believed that this could have been either a conscious or subconscious symbol of silencing Patterson. But had the shot to the back not ricocheted upward through the throat, Patterson, although dying quickly, could have very well identified or described his killer in the remaining ten minutes or so of his life. Sowell also recovered this bullet, another lead .38.

A third bullet wound was observed about one inch above the left elbow. From the location and path of the bullet, Sowell concluded that Patterson saw this one coming and tried to shield himself from its impact. This bullet, also a .38, had broken Patterson's arm and left only two fragments, which Sowell also removed.

After examining the wounds and retrieving the bullets, Sowell began the task of determining the exact cause of death. As he opened the abdominal and thoracic cavities to examine the internal organs, he could see that the victim's whole left side was filled with blood, a result of the lung puncture from the shot to the back. Sowell then called for an electric saw to remove Patterson's skullcap and check for brain hemorrhages or fractures. Ferrell left at this point; he knew what was coming and would just as soon not see it.[37]

After an hour and a half, the autopsy was finished. Sowell and Knowles agreed in their report that "the bullet into the left upper back, which penetrated the lung, caused copious and fatal internal hemorrhage, and this is concluded to be the immediate cause of death." When the group filed out of the autopsy room, Ferrell remarked to the undertaker, McGehee, "I understand now why you are waiting here and watching this postmortem." McGehee replied, "Yes, sir, Mr. Ferrell, I have to do this. I'm going to have to fix it back up."[38]

As daylight approached, Ferrell rode back to the Coulter Building with Sowell and watched as detectives finished processing the crime scene. Photographs were made of Patterson's car, the sidewalk where Patterson had died, and, after first light, the footpaths behind the Coulter Building. With the rising of the sun at about 5:30 also came dusting of the car by state investigators Godwin and Williams. The results were disappointing. Although they lifted a partial palm print from the bottom center of the chrome strip that lined the driver's-side window frame, they found no clear fingerprints. After some thought, they decided to dust underneath the rain guard positioned over the driver's-side window, a metal awning approximately two inches wide designed to keep rain out while allowing a margin of ventilation. There, about two inches from the rear edge of the door, they found and lifted a fully legible thumbprint. When they were finished dusting the car, Phenix City policeman Walter Sanders led Godwin and Williams to the wooden plank he had placed over the footprints the evening before so they could take plaster-of-paris impressions. He was astounded to find that the prints had been practically erased.[39]

5
The Initial Investigation

The murder investigation has run into a blank wall.
                                        Ralph Mathews, June 23, 1954

After concluding the autopsy, Sowell and Ferrell returned to the Coulter Building to take a second look, this time in the light of day. They agreed that the killing was an audacious move considering the amount of traffic around the Elite Café, the post office, the courthouse, Smitty's Grill, and the Palace Theater. Sowell raised the possibility that the killer could have waited unnoticed at the bus stop at Fourteenth Street and Fifth Avenue. Someone waiting there would have had a clear view of the Coulter Building, including the lights in Patterson's office, but probably wouldn't have attracted very much attention. Ferrell was inclined to agree.[1]

Sowell found it hard to believe that only one witness saw the killer flee the scene. Could he have hidden somewhere after the murder until he felt it was safe to come out? They searched for possible hiding places, examining each for footprints or other evidence, but didn't find anything. Next, they walked along the paths behind the Coulter Building looking for possible avenues of escape. They concluded that Patterson's killer took one of two likely routes. The first, the old Line Street extension, ran directly west between a pair of houses and on to

Broad Street. This path would have been longer, but there were fewer buildings and natural obstacles in that direction. The second route, which they believed more likely, turned behind the Coulter Building toward Fourteenth Street, split, and emerged on both sides of the Raiford Building.[2]

By this time, Phenix City was stirring. Sowell and Ferrell returned to the courthouse, where Sowell finally received a call from Dr. Rehling. It turned out that Rehling wasn't in Montgomery at all but at a friend's house in Clanton. After providing a quick status report, Sowell told Rehling that he thought it best if the chief toxicologist came to Phenix City. At the Coulter Building, police removed the crime scene rope and a wrecker towed Patterson's car to the large yard surrounding the Russell County jail. Not long after, three workmen appeared with mops and buckets to clean up Patterson's blood. Across the street, a thoughtful Arch Ferrell watched them, hands folded behind his back.[3]

General Hanna and Lieutenant Colonel Warren, driven by Hanna's son, arrived at the Russell County Courthouse about 6:00 A.M. Pete Hanna had covered the 160 miles in a little more than two hours. Years later, Warren would claim this ride caused his hair to turn prematurely white. Sheriff Mathews gave Hanna a quick briefing on the situation, concluding that while Governor Persons's concern was appreciated, there was really no need for National Guard troops. Hanna could have taken Mathews's word for it and headed back to Birmingham, but he didn't trust local officials. Besides, Persons had made it clear that the decision to post troops was completely his, not the Russell County sheriff's. Getting back in the car, Hanna, Warren, and Pete set off on their own inspection tour.[4]

The governor arrived later that morning to tour the area. After inspecting the crime scene, he went to the Patterson home to pay his respects. As he was leaving, RBA president Howard Pennington handed Persons a resolution. It was a tall order, requesting a suspension of alcohol licenses in Phenix City until the killer was captured, the establishment of a special grand jury to investigate the murder, the appointment of a special prosecutor, and authorization of the maximum reward for the killer's capture. The visit to the Patterson home had been difficult for Persons, and the last thing he wanted just now was a political discussion. He looked at the resolution as if it were a dead rodent and told Pennington to mail it to his office.[5]

Persons didn't need advice from the RBA on what to do next. He stopped by the courthouse for a talk with local officials. At a news conference afterward, reporters asked if he had spoken to Sheriff Mathews and Solicitor Ferrell. Yes, Persons replied, he had: "I told them that the show is over and they might as well pass along to all gamblers, prostitutes and petty criminals to get out of town and stay out of town, because there is not going to be any more vice in Phenix City. . . . No governor likes to encroach on local government," he continued, but "when it is definitely proven that local government and law enforcement is not able to provide protection for its citizens, then it's time for the governor to move in. . . . I make a solemn promise to the people of Alabama that the present pressure on the lawless element in Phenix City will not let up as long as I am governor."[6] To show he meant business, Persons contacted the commander of Fort Benning, Major General Joseph Harper, and asked that he place the whole town off-limits to military personnel. By noon, military police moved into position on the Fourteenth Street Bridge and the Dillingham Street Bridge with orders to turn back any military personnel unless they could prove they were residents of Phenix City.[7]

As the army cut off the demand, the Alabama National Guard cut off the supply. Completing his survey of Phenix City shortly after noon, General Hanna declared, "We're going to stay," and began ordering in guardsmen from neighboring towns. Placing Warren in command, he instructed him to prevent property destruction, disperse crowds, and, most of all, shut down gambling in Phenix City. Troops began arriving sometime after 4:00, and by nightfall thirty-three were on duty, most handpicked because of their civilian experience in law enforcement or government. They were immediately assigned to patrol duty.[8]

People were beginning to worry about Arch Ferrell. Always high-strung, Ferrell seemed to have been turned into a nervous wreck by Patterson's murder. Although he and Sowell covered a lot of investigative ground that morning, the assistant chief toxicologist thought Ferrell reeked of liquor. When Dr. Rehling arrived at Sheriff Mathews's office about 1:20 that afternoon, he could see that Ferrell was "noozle-eyed" from whiskey. The resulting discussion was a chore. In all the cases he had worked with Ferrell, the state's chief toxicologist had never seen the circuit solicitor like this. Although Ferrell appeared to have been drinking, which should have had a calming effect, he seemed extremely emotional, his lower lip trembling throughout the discussion. Mostly, he just chain-smoked and stared out the window. Rehling had to coax the answers out of him.[9]

Later in the afternoon, Ferrell issued a statement to the press in which he expressed outrage at the murder and the hope that "the vicious murderer will be apprehended at the earliest possible moment and dealt with according to the severest limit of justice." He urged Sheriff Mathews and Police Chief Daniel to round up "all known criminals in hope of picking up some thin spread of evidence."[10]

RBA members were not impressed. They suspected that Ferrell might intentionally misdirect the murder investigation, but when they asked the attorney general for a special prosecutor, Garrett angrily responded that he had no intention of replacing Ferrell, whom he called one of Alabama's top solicitors. And, he added, not the governor, the legislature, or the state supreme court could direct him to do otherwise.[11]

The FBI was also taking notice. Less than two hours after the murder, special agent Shanklin telegraphed J. Edgar Hoover to apprise him of the murder and warn him that although there was no evidence of a federal violation, "undoubtedly numerous allegations will be made alleging Patterson [was] killed as result of recent election activity and desire to clean up gambling in Phenix City and State of Alabama."[12]

Following up on his telephone call the night before, Governor Persons contacted Shanklin on Saturday morning to ask whether there was any justification for FBI involvement. Shanklin said that although the FBI could provide limited assistance as a matter of routine police cooperation, it could only enter the case officially if there was sufficient evidence that the suspect fled the state. In that event, the FBI could intervene under the unlawful flight to avoid prosecution (UFAP) statute. Persons agreed that for the time being it was a state case.[13]

The RBA's attitude was a different story. As Shanklin had predicted to Hoover the previous evening, the RBA mistrusted both local and state officials and wanted to enlist the FBI's help. Hugh Bentley had already called to ask for federal intervention, and Shanklin had flatly denied the request, owing to the absence of any evidence suggesting a federal crime. Bentley threatened to pursue the matter with the U.S. attorney general because the people of Alabama, who had elected Patterson, had been deprived of their civil rights. If racial unrest was sufficient reason for federal intervention, Bentley said, then certainly Patterson's murder deserved attention.[14]

After checking out of the Jefferson Davis Hotel on Friday night, Red Porter took his wife home to Gadsden and then drove to Birmingham, arriving at the Redmont at about 3:00 A.M. CST. He spent most of Saturday with Garrett at the Redmont. Most of the time, he just held his head and repeated to no one in particular, "I can't believe it. I just can't believe it." Garrett finally checked out at about 4:30 P.M. CST. On the way back to Montgomery, he spent the time telling his driver, Kenneth Horne, that he was worried about how tough the murder investigation would be on his health. Did Horne know that he had been institutionalized the year before? At that time, he was "out of his head." Luckily, the attorney general's office had gotten along without him, but this situation called for perseverance: "I know I'm a little tired, but I know I've got this to do and I'm going [to go] ahead and do it!"[15]

In addition to the highway patrol and National Guard personnel pouring into Phenix City, a third element was converging on the town, the press. State newspaper headlines on Saturday morning and afternoon screamed the news of the murder, pushing back the otherwise sensational headlines of the CIA-backed invasion of Guatemala. Area motels and hotels were filled with reporters from throughout the country, and even some from overseas. They easily outnumbered investigators, and their fieldwork over the next few days and weeks would prove crucial to the outcome of the murder investigation. In the meantime, expressions of outrage dominated the editorial pages. Alabamians had in the past tolerated the lack of law in Phenix City, but Patterson's murder was the last straw. Patterson himself had predicted that it would take at least ten years to clean up Phenix City, but with his death, public opinion could wait no longer. "If there is anything good to come from such a tragedy . . . [it is that the] death of Mr. Patterson should set public opinion at such a high pitch that gangsterism will be put to an end in Phenix City," judged the *Decatur Daily*. The *Montgomery Advertiser* editorialized that "this crime and its possible ramifications . . . [call] for action going far beyond the realm of regrets and condolences."[16] The *Tuscaloosa News* declared that "[Patterson's] pledge now must be carried out with promptness and smashing finality."[17] *Columbus Ledger* editors pointed out that the murder was "no mere local, Phenix City affair" but rather "a crime against the people of the whole State of Alabama [which] must marshal all of its forces to upturn the evil, slimy mess in Phenix City from which the assassination undoubtedly stemmed."[18] The *Selma Times-Journal* declared, "The cold-blooded assassination of Albert L. Patterson makes it mandatory for the state of Alabama to stop temporizing with entrenched corruption at the border city and stamp it out for once and all."[19] The *Mobile Press-Register* urged that "other men must pick up the charred threads of the things which Albert Patterson believed in, so that his dream may not die with him."[20] "This is one of the times when the State must step in and use all the resources at its command to put an end to the reign of crime and vice," said the *Huntsville Times*.[21]

The idea that state officials were also at fault surfaced in numerous opinion pieces. The *Mobile Press-Register,* for example, noted that the conditions in Phenix City were possible "only in circumstances of official and civic abdication. To attribute it to anything else would necessitate an admission that the combined strength of official and civic structures in Alabama is unequal to the challenge of the lawless."[22] The *Dothan Eagle* was even more blunt: "The blood of Albert L. Patterson is on the hands of Alabama governors and attorneys general who have refused or failed to use the powers of their offices to stamp out organized crime in Russell County although they have had full knowledge of its rampant and arrogant rule."[23] Patterson's assassination, then, was not just a crime committed by Phenix City criminals. The whole state was guilty by association, and elected political officials were especially culpable for their sins of omission. Alabamians comfortable in the belief that they lived in a peaceful society found the reports from Phenix City especially disturbing—and strange. The *Montgomery Advertiser* judged that "assassination of political figures . . . is something we think of as happening in some Balkan principality, or Latin dictatorship, not in a free American commonwealth with a tradition of due process under the law."[24] The *Mobile Press-Register* viewed the killing "as though it were news from another planet."[25]

The story would have been unbelievable if it were not true. Patterson's murder set off a chain of events that heightened the public perception that the government of Alabama had been deeply compromised by corruption and graft. For Governor Persons, who was already genuinely outraged, the course was clear. Any indication that he had been lax on Phenix City during his term as governor must be neutralized immediately. Phenix City would be cleaned up, and Patterson's murderer would be brought to justice.

Governor nominee Jim Folsom, who had preceded Persons as governor and would regain the position seven months later, was in a less pressing but even less enviable position. Although Folsom had swept the Democratic primary without a runoff and had little to fear from the state Republican Party, the Phenix City situation already threatened to cloud his second administration. As the press quickly pointed out, Phenix City vice and corruption had thrived during his first term; in fairness to Folsom, however, the same could be said for almost every Alabama governor during the last fifty years. But no one was complaining about Chauncey Sparks, Frank Dixon, or Bibb Graves; instead, Folsom—partly because he was the incoming governor, partly because he was highly controversial—received all the attention. Folsom, unlike his predecessors, would now have to deal with Patterson's death in a highly volatile environment where one false move could have dire political consequences.

The state Democratic Executive Committee was now faced with choosing Patterson's replacement as the attorney general nominee, and Folsom's supporters on the committee were discussing candidates as early as Friday night.[26] The committee had two options: name a nominee outright or call a special election to let the people decide. Under normal circumstances, the committee would have chosen the first runner-up, Red Porter. Designating Porter would not only avoid a costly statewide election but also allow the Folsom camp its favorite. But these were not normal circumstances. Patterson had been murdered in cold blood, and there was widespread suspicion that he had been gunned down because Porter had not won. Given that fact, Porter was out of the question.

If not Porter, then who? Perhaps third-place MacDonald Gallion could be a compromise candidate. Another name mentioned was former state senator Gordon Madison, an assistant attorney general friendly to the Folsom camp. According to insiders on the committee, Folsom himself favored Circuit Judge George Wallace, who had managed Folsom's campaign in south Alabama. Feasibly, any established politician friendly to the Folsom camp had a shot. The last person anyone expected as Albert Patterson's replacement was another Phenix City lawyer.[27]

Although John Patterson had joined his father's law practice shortly after his return from Germany in late 1953 and had campaigned for him during both the primary and the runoff, the two clearly did not agree on political matters. John had no political aspirations and little understanding of why anyone—at least any lawyer—would want to enter that comparatively nonlucrative profession. Before June 18, 1954, his aspirations had involved fishing and making a comfortable living as a Phenix City attorney.[28]

All that changed at 9:05 Friday night. John's initial reaction to the murder was to get out of Phenix City forever; upon reflection, he decided to stay and fight it out. Years later, he described himself at that time as "one mad fella" with little to lose: "And when you don't have nothing to risk . . . you can play it wide open." By Sunday he had made up his mind. Surrounded by reporters in his father's law office, he announced that he would offer himself as a candidate for attorney general nominee to replace his father, should the state Democratic Executive Committee decide to hold a special election. The public loved it—the avenging son replacing the martyred father. Patterson's declaration took the question of his father's successor from a political question to a moral crusade. The state committee didn't stand a chance against this sentiment.[29]

On Sunday morning, Si Garrett called the *Montgomery Advertiser*'s managing editor, Fred Andersen, and told him that he was going to Phenix City later in the day to take over the murder investigation. For Andersen, who wasn't normally a reporter, this was an important scoop, and he could hardly believe his good luck when Garrett asked him if he would like to ride along. Garrett wasn't in much of a hurry. Andersen met him at the Bonnie Crest Country Club in Montgomery and waited for him while Garrett took a swim with his family and then ate a leisurely lunch. Afterward, Garrett and Andersen climbed into the attorney general's state car with Kenneth Horne. The three engaged in small talk as Horne drove at a normal pace east on Highway 80 toward Tuskegee. Suddenly, without warning or provocation, Garrett reached over and began honking the horn and waving people out of the way. Taking the cue, Horne floored the accelerator and began running red lights and weaving in and out of Tuskegee traffic. It didn't take long for the car to gain attention. An ABC agent recognized the state car, and, guessing Garrett's intent, pulled in front and turned on his siren. Garrett continued to honk the horn, and in this way the trio arrived at the courthouse in Phenix City shortly before 6:00 P.M.[30]

Garrett let Andersen out, telling him that he, Horne, and Sheriff Mathews were going to pick up Arch Ferrell, but he instructed Andersen not to tell anyone. Milling about, Andersen spotted Rex Thomas, a veteran reporter for the Associated Press's Montgomery bureau. Comparing impressions, Andersen discovered that he and Thomas agreed that the recent Birmingham vote fraud investigation and Patterson's murder were connected and that Ferrell was somehow involved. However, according to Thomas, the talk around the courthouse was that Patterson was having an affair with one of his young secretaries and had been killed by the woman's husband. By the time Garrett, Mathews, and Horne returned with Ferrell, other Phenix City and Russell County officials had gathered, including Mayor Reese, Police Chief Daniel, Chief Deputy Fuller, and most of the other deputies and policemen. Garrett's arrival created a stir with the reporters, and a barrage of flashbulbs punctuated shouted questions. The attorney general, dressed in a white suit and ten-gallon cowboy hat, pulled Mathews and Ferrell close and insisted that photographers snap a picture of them together: "I just want it goddamn plain that I have full confidence in these two public officials." To Andersen, this directly contradicted what Garrett had told him on the way from Montgomery—that he was going to Phenix City with the express purpose of taking over the investigation.[31]

Garrett then called a press conference in the grand jury room upstairs, and although he talked incessantly, he really didn't provide anything of substance, only that he was exploring "three theories" of the murder. Sometimes he was contradictory, one moment expressing

confidence in Mathews and Ferrell, calling Ferrell the "best damn solicitor in the state," the next announcing that he would send two assistant attorneys general, who, at his direction, would take charge of
the investigation.[32]

After the reporters left, local officials (which now included Lieutenant Colonel Warren, head of the National Guard detail) entered
the grand jury room. Garrett assured them that he had full confidence in their abilities and would continue to have that confidence
until he had reason not to. As far as this case was concerned, Garrett
was in charge and Ferrell, as solicitor, was his assistant. The two assistant attorneys general he planned to send the next day, Lee Barton
and Maury Smith, would coordinate the disparate law enforcement
agencies. As for the local officials present, each knew his duty and
Garrett was certain they would perform it well. Ferrell mentioned that
there had been some talk about bringing in a special prosecutor and
judge for the case and asked Garrett what he thought about it. Garrett
had heard nothing along that line, and as far as he was concerned,
Ferrell was the solicitor. Replacement of a judge was another matter,
in that Garrett had no responsibility in that field. Garrett acknowledged political differences between Patterson and some of those present, but he believed that no man in the room would have murdered
Patterson or anyone else. As lawmen, they knew that their primary
duty, regardless of political differences, was to catch the murderer and
obtain the evidence necessary to convict him.[33]

With this official conference ended, Garrett stepped into the corridor and invited a few of the reporters to dinner: Clancey Lake and
Ed Strickland of the *Birmingham News*, Andersen and Bob Ingram
from the *Montgomery Advertiser*, and Rex Thomas of the Associated
Press. First, however, the group met in Thomas's hotel room in Columbus. Russell County deputies Albert Fuller and Jeff Dudley accompanied them. Garrett decided to order whiskey for the group and
dispatched Fuller. Although Sunday liquor sales were illegal, it took
Fuller only eight and a half minutes to produce a bottle. After a few
drinks, which Ferrell took straight, the group left for the CoCo Club
in Columbus.[34]

Despite his announced purpose of going to Phenix City to direct
the murder investigation, Garrett—for the rest of the evening, at
least—showed a greater concern for Ferrell's welfare than for finding

Patterson's murderer. At dinner, with the main topic turning to the murder investigation, Strickland asked Garrett if he would replace Ferrell in the case. "Never," Garrett answered. When the meal was over, Ferrell, Garrett, and Andersen returned to Ferrell's office for an off-the-record interview. Garrett wanted to know what the general talk was among the reporters, particularly if they thought there was a connection between the vote fraud and the murder. Andersen said, yes, they did. Garrett then asked if they thought Ferrell was involved. Andersen lied this time and said he didn't know. He glanced at Ferrell to gauge his reaction, but Ferrell wasn't listening. Although he had been drinking heavily since early evening, the circuit solicitor was wild-eyed and his mouth twitched. On the verge of tears and seemingly oblivious to the conversation between Andersen and Garrett, Ferrell stared at the floor, hat in hand, and murmured repeatedly, "Arch Ferrell has never done anything wrong in his life." According to Andersen, Ferrell chanted this mantra forty or fifty times, "like he was trying to sell himself the idea." To Andersen, Ferrell seemed like a man on the brink of suicide.[35]

Then Garrett had an inspiration. They would go to see Ferrell's father and tell him "that his boy was not a killer." Garrett and Ferrell took Ferrell's car while Andersen rode with Horne in Garrett's car. It was long after midnight when they got to Seale. At the intersection of the Montgomery road, the cars pulled over at a closed gas station, where Horne and Andersen were instructed to wait. Garrett and Ferrell drove on past Mr. Ferrell's home, where they could see that no one was awake. They then went to one of Ferrell's sisters-in-law, where Madeline was staying, and Ferrell called out for his wife. There, in the late June night, Garrett tried to reassure her. He and Ferrell brought her to the closed gas station to meet Andersen and Horne. She had obviously been crying. Dressed in a housecoat, she asked Andersen, childlike, if everything was going to be all right. Andersen said he hoped so. Then, Garrett, Andersen, and Horne started back to Montgomery, with Andersen driving. Garrett didn't say a word all the way back.[36]

Governor Persons called J. Edgar Hoover early Monday morning to ask if there was any way the FBI could help in the Patterson murder case. Local and state authorities were simply not equipped to handle an investigation of this magnitude, the governor admitted. Hoover replied that the FBI would be happy to perform laboratory examinations on any evidence acquired, but as to an active investigation, the bureau lacked jurisdiction. That could change if the UFAP statute were invoked, but Persons didn't even have a suspect yet. Persons then asked if he could issue a statement saying he had contacted the FBI and that Hoover had said the agency would help in any way possible. While Persons realized that such a statement meant little, it would help to "take the heat off." Hoover agreed. Persons asked Hoover if he would send him a wire stating, "In response to our telephone conversation in which you requested the assistance of the FBI, permit me to say that this Bureau will assist in any way it possibly can." Hoover told Persons that he would be happy to send the wire and that he hoped the statement would have the desired effect.[37]

Around midmorning, Mr. F. B. Patterson (no relation to Albert), district manager of the Southern Bell Telephone and Telegraph Company in Columbus, received a call from the state attorney general. Garrett was interested in securing information on a telephone call made by Ferrell from Phenix City to the Redmont Hotel in Birmingham on June 18. Patterson explained to Garrett that the toll tickets were in Atlanta but that he would secure the information. After contacting Atlanta, Patterson called Garrett and explained that Ferrell had actually made two telephone calls to the Redmont on the night of June 18. He provided Garrett with the precise times for both calls.[38]

On Monday, June 21, more than a thousand people attended Albert Patterson's funeral service at Trinity Methodist Church, some standing in the street. All of the pallbearers were members of the RBA's executive board: Hugh Britton, Hugh Bentley, Howard Pennington, George Findlater, Leland Jones, Jack Gunter. Honorary pallbearers read like a list of Patterson's campaign coordinators from the recent political race.

Phenix City and Russell County officials were conspicuously absent from the funeral.[39] This was probably a prudent move, considering the tremendous amount of anger over Patterson's murder, much of it directed toward local officials. Rev. T. E. Steely of West Side Baptist Church blamed the murder on "not the man who pulled the trigger in this tragic and shameful thing, but the brains, the director of the people who worked this out and had him do it." Rev. R. K. Jones, pastor of Pepperell Methodist Church, said the assassination was caused by "the agencies of hell, because he stood for honesty, because he stood for the brighter and nobler things of life, and because he wanted a good state for you and for us." After the services in Phenix City, a cortege of more than one hundred cars traveled eighty-five miles to the Bethlehem Church cemetery at New Site. There the American flag was removed from Patterson's coffin and handed to the family.[40]

It was nearly 10:00 A.M. when Garrett's two assistant attorneys general arrived at the Russell County Courthouse. At twenty-seven, Maury Drane Smith was one of the youngest members of the attorney general's staff, taking a job with Garrett immediately after graduating from the University of Alabama School of Law two years earlier. Smith's elder partner, Lee Edward Barton, was a forty-nine-year-old Virginia native and a 1930 graduate of the University of Virginia Law School. He had served six years with the FBI and three years as a special agent for the Home Owners Loan Corporation. During the war years he was principal investigator for the Army Air Force Material Command. Barton had been on the attorney general's staff since 1947.[41]

The first task for Smith and Barton was to interview local law enforcement officials and determine what headway had been made. In the grand jury room that Ferrell had secured as headquarters for the attorney general's staff, Phenix City police and Russell County deputies related the information they had received since the killing and offered their opinions on suspects and motives.[42]

One of the first interviews was with Police Chief Daniel, who outlined the status of the investigation. Asked to give his views concerning motive, Daniel completely ignored Phenix City vice and corruption and instead painted a sordid picture of Patterson's private life. He mentioned one of Patterson's secretaries, who, according to Daniel, had maintained a long-running affair with the former state senator. Although she had quit some time ago, she had returned to work for Patterson during his most recent campaign for attorney general. The situation had been so bad, according to Daniel's sources, that John

Patterson intended to quit the family practice because of his father's outrageous behavior.[43]

Barton and Smith also talked to Sheriff Mathews, who, like Chief Daniel, gave little indication that Phenix City vice and corruption were in any way related to the murder. Mathews listed a number of local men worth investigating, generally well-known undesirables who had the misfortune of being in the vicinity of the crime scene, those having expressed a wish to do Patterson harm, or people whom Patterson had gotten the best of in court. Only one of these men had actually been arrested, and he had an airtight alibi. Mathews listed a number of possible paid assassins, including an ex-racketeer who was presently a paid informant for the Muscogee County (Georgia) Sheriff's Department and a professional gambler from Chicago with underworld connections in Phenix City. Despite these possibilities, however, Mathews emphasized that he did not believe Patterson was killed by a professional. Had that been the case, the murder would have taken place at a different place and at a different time. There were simply too many lights and too many people in the area for it to have been anything but a crime of passion.

Following this logic, Mathews suggested that either John Patterson or his father might have had an affair with another one of Albert Patterson's former secretaries, an attractive eighteen-year-old whose husband had been stationed in Korea. The husband had returned to Alabama on June 18, only to be told by his wife that she wanted a divorce and that Albert Patterson was performing the necessary legal work. Although the husband was a good suspect as far as motive was concerned, sheriff's deputies had already determined that he was out of town when Patterson was murdered.

Mathews also told of another alleged girlfriend. Word had it that the woman's almost-grown son had "raised lots of hell about his mother and Mr. Patterson" and might be worth checking out. Barton and Smith seemed skeptical. Wasn't Albert Patterson, at sixty years of age, a bit too old to be playing the role of paramour? Mathews admitted that "age would stop him some, but they still say he was hot after women." Cautiously, Mathews indicated that John Patterson might be worth investigating as well. He believed that John and his late father had had a rocky relationship and had been told by a local court official that John had joined the army mainly because of animosity toward his father. Their most recent legal partnership was failing, and John planned to open a separate office.[44]

Meanwhile, in Montgomery, Garrett had telephoned Andersen and asked him if he wanted to go to Phenix City again. This time, Horne was escorted by a highway patrol car with sirens and flashers and made the trip in record time. When they arrived at the courthouse, Garrett introduced Andersen to Smith and Barton and indicated that a question-and-answer period was in order. When Andersen started the questioning, Garrett insisted that he quote the tight-lipped Barton, the former FBI man, even though Smith did most of the talking. Andersen believed that Garrett, standing right next to him, sensed that his own word was tainted in the public perception and wanted to provide Andersen with an authoritative statement by someone other than himself. As he talked to Garrett's two assistants, Andersen had no doubt that they were present in Phenix City only to provide window dressing for Garrett. And although he didn't know it at the time, Barton and Smith had already reached the same conclusion.[45]

While Garrett was at the courthouse, Sheriff Mathews informed him that John Patterson had stated that more people in Phenix City were carrying guns than not. Garrett was livid after hearing this and urged Mathews to institute a person-by-person search on the streets and to confiscate any gun for which the owner lacked a permit. This, according to Garrett, would "prove that goddamned John Patterson is as big a liar as his father was." Mathews, however, didn't think it was a good idea. Garrett threatened to order the searches himself.[46]

By midafternoon, Barton and Smith had concluded that the only way to effectively conduct the murder investigation would be to have it completely taken over by state law enforcement authorities. They were apprehensive not only about the poor reputation of Phenix City and Russell County officials and the apparent mismanagement of the Patterson case, but also about the lack of coordination between the disparate law enforcement agencies.[47]

It would be logical for Barton and Smith to share their concerns with their boss, Garrett, who was on the scene, but the two men faced a dilemma. They were convinced that local officials could not perform a credible investigation, yet Garrett had made it clear that he had full confidence in these same officials, specifically Mathews and Ferrell. And they knew that RBA members and many reporters were openly discussing Ferrell as a suspect in the murder. At first, Barton and Smith thought that Garrett might distance himself from his friends at the Russell County Courthouse, but that afternoon they learned that Garrett was supplying Ferrell with an alibi of his whereabouts when Patterson was gunned down. Instead of backing off, their boss was growing closer to the Phenix City elements. Garrett would have to be bypassed, and this was risky business for government workers. Barton and Smith left Phenix City at about 7:00 P.M., arriving in Montgomery about an hour and a half later. There they tracked down Bernard Sykes, a career employee in the Office of the Attorney General, to get his impressions.[48]

Sykes, a thirty-six-year-old Montgomery native, received his law degree from the University of Alabama School of Law in 1942, placing third in his class. He was immediately employed as a legal research aide in the attorney general's office and had risen steadily ever since. When Albert Carmichael died in early 1954, seniority rules bumped Sykes up to first assistant attorney general. Sykes was the second in command in the attorney general's office, serving his fifth attorney general, when Barton and Smith arrived in Montgomery that night.[49]

Sykes listened as Barton and Smith revealed their apprehensions about the Patterson murder investigation and Garrett's support of local officials. When they finished, he suggested that they speak to Governor Persons. In a few minutes, Barton and Smith stood in front of the governor urging a complete state takeover of the investigation. Because of Garrett's situation, they also suggested that Sykes be appointed to direct it.[50]

While Barton and Smith were in Montgomery, Garrett stayed behind in Phenix City with Andersen, Horne, and their escort from Montgomery, highway patrolman John White. Checking into the Ralston Hotel in Columbus, Garrett invited *Montgomery Advertiser* reporter Bob Ingram to join them. The first thing Ingram observed was that Garrett had been drinking heavily, but not alcohol, even though there were numerous bottles of whiskey set up; as was his habit, the attorney general was consuming large amounts of soda water, and there were already numerous empty quart bottles of the carbonated beverage scattered about. Garrett was worried about Ferrell, and he told Horne to summon him to the hotel. While Ferrell was on his way, Garrett outlined to Ingram and Andersen the plan to search everyone in Phenix City for the murder weapon. The following morning, Russell County sheriff's deputies and Phenix City police would methodically detain and search every person on the streets of Phenix City. Strangely, Garrett gave the reporters permission to announce the plan in the following morning's edition of the *Advertiser*. Garrett confided that as soon as Ferrell arrived he would leave the room and make some telephone calls regarding the proposed search but that the reporters and his assistants should not let Ferrell leave, nor should they tell him what Garrett was up to.[51]

At that moment Ferrell arrived, neatly dressed and sporting a new straw hat. He had already been drinking, and Garrett immediately wanted to know how many drinks he'd had. Ferrell insisted that he'd had only a couple but that the warm room "was making him feel them." Seeing the bottles of liquor on the nightstand, Ferrell helped himself. As planned, Garrett sidled along Ingram and asked for the key to his room. Ingram surreptitiously turned it over. Garrett then informed Ferrell, "Arch, I've got some things to take care of, but I'll be back in a few minutes. You wait here with the boys until I get back and then we'll go out and get us a steak." Garrett then left for Ingram's room, presumably to telephone the Russell County and Phenix City authorities and discuss the proposed gun search. After Garrett left, Ferrell passed the time telling everyone what a great guy Garrett was: "Si Garrett is the best friend I've got. He's one of the greatest men in Alabama, and there's nothing I wouldn't do for him to repay him for the many things he's done for me."[52]

Garrett returned shortly, and the topic again turned to Patterson's murder. Ferrell observed that "Patterson had a lot of enemies in town, and maybe some of them hired somebody from outside to do the job. I don't know who did it, but I hope who killed Pat gets what's coming to him." Fred Andersen was not known for his tact. Perhaps that explained why he was on the *Advertiser* staff as the managing editor instead of a full-time reporter. He now looked up good-naturedly from his drink and, without the slightest hesitation, told Ferrell, "I guess you know a lot of people in Phenix City think you killed him." Although it was a hot night, the comment chilled the room. Andersen's observation was common talk among reporters and others, but its frankness in the face of the circuit solicitor shocked Ingram as much as it did Ferrell.[53]

Ferrell stared into his bourbon and water a long time as he collected his thoughts. "I know all about that talk," he finally answered. "I've heard it ever since Pat was killed. I'm tough and mean, nobody knows that better than me. I'm not a religious fellow, never have been, but this thing is making me wish I were. But no matter what anybody says, I didn't kill Patterson. I just couldn't kill a man." To put an emphatic end to his statement, Ferrell polished off his drink in one long gulp.[54]

Garrett had listened to Ferrell's speech as attentively as the reporters had. Then, in the grim silence that followed Ferrell's remarks, Garrett strode to a nightstand and dug out a crumpled sheet of paper from his stuffed briefcase. He now spoke: "I'm getting goddamned tired of all this talk about Arch killing Patterson. I'm going to put an end to it once and for all right now." Reading from the paper, Garrett now said with some authority, "A telephone call was placed from 8-6028—that's Arch's office—at 8:53 P.M. on the night of the murder. The call was made to Room 718 in the Redmont Hotel in Birmingham, which was assigned to Frank Long Jr., where I was staying."[55] "The call was connected at 8:56 P.M. and continued for three minutes and 45 seconds, ending at 8:59 P.M. Two minutes later a second call was placed from Arch's office, this one to Room 720 in the same hotel. This call continued for twelve minutes and seventeen seconds and ended at 9:17 P.M. That's Arch's alibi, and I'd like to see anybody pin the murder rap on him." Ferrell listened to his alibi, spellbound.[56]

In short order, the subject of the Jefferson County Grand Jury came up. Someone suggested that Garrett and Ferrell volunteer to testify and waive immunity. Garrett agreed, saying that the move would be good "psychologically." After some discussion, Ferrell reluctantly went along, saying he would "only if Si wants me to."[57]

As he had the previous evening, Garrett invited the reporters to dine with him and Ferrell at the CoCo Club. The restaurant had already closed when they arrived, but Garrett beat on the door until the manager was summoned. Identifying himself, Garrett persuaded the manager to allow the party in for steaks all around. By this time,

Ferrell was extremely drunk. Had anyone else been in the restaurant, his behavior would have been embarrassing. He alternated between shouting, cursing loudly, and breaking down in tears as he told of his great love for Attorney General Si Garrett.[58]

Garrett grew annoyed at Ferrell's behavior and asked Horne to mix a particularly stiff drink to finish him off. It did, but not before Ferrell spilled another drink and a cup of coffee and, for the grand finale, threw up on the table. Ingram, White, and Horne grabbed their steaks and fled to another table while Ferrell joined Garrett and Andersen in a booth. Within five minutes, Ferrell, like a torpedoed ship, sank slowly down in the booth and passed out with his head in Garrett's lap—what Andersen called "a very touching sight." But before he did, Andersen heard Ferrell say, "I wish I was dead."[59]

Returning to the Ralston at about 3:00 A.M., Horne and White deposited Ferrell in White's bed. In a few minutes, Garrett came in and searched Ferrell's wallet, helping himself to forty-seven dollars, all the cash Ferrell was carrying, for operating expenses. While doing so, Garrett noticed a list of names with numerical notations next to each; this he also pocketed. Garrett, Horne, and White then drove out to Ferrell's home, opening the house with a key lifted from Ferrell's pocket. In one of the bedrooms, Horne pointed out a notebook to Garrett. Inside were the names, telephone numbers, and addresses of several Phenix City gangsters. Entries for Hoyt Shepherd and Jimmy Matthews gave Garrett an idea.[60]

Garrett returned to the courthouse and, with the information supplied by Ferrell's address book, dispatched White and Horne to fetch Hoyt Shepherd. By now it was about 4:30 A.M. After about a twenty-minute talk, Garrett released Shepherd and told White to bring in Jimmy Matthews; Shepherd offered to go with him. After Matthews's interview, White took him back home.[61]

Later that morning, Madeline Ferrell showed up at the Ralston wanting to know where her husband was. Garrett told her he was resting in another room. Then he asked for her keys, which she gave up without question. Taking Horne into the bathroom for a private conference, Garrett handed over the keys with instructions to go to Arch's car and retrieve his gun from the glove compartment. Horne returned shortly with the pistol, a .357 Magnum. After Madeline left, Garrett took the gun, ejected the cartridges, and invited Andersen to examine it to see if it had been fired recently. Andersen said he didn't know a lot about guns, but it appeared that it hadn't. Garrett agreed and urged Andersen to print a story to that effect in the *Advertiser.*[62]

The day after the funeral, John Patterson went to the law office he had shared with his father to clean out Albert Patterson's personal effects. As he was sorting through papers and files in his father's briefcase, Patterson found a newspaper or magazine clipping that his father had deemed worthy of keeping. It was merely a scrap of paper with a single sentence by English statesman Edmund Burke, but it spoke volumes of Albert Patterson's philosophy regarding Phenix City: "The only thing necessary for the triumph of evil is that good men do nothing." While Patterson was pondering these words, I & I chief Joe Smelley and Chief Deputy Albert Fuller arrived unexpectedly and questioned him at length. Given the tone and content of the questions, Patterson became extremely suspicious of the men's motives. He decided he would indeed do something.[63]

On Tuesday, June 22, Governor Persons finally answered the RBA resolution that Howard Pennington had tried to hand him the previous Saturday, and the answer was no. He had authorized a reward of $5,000 for information leading to the arrest and conviction of Patterson's murderer even before the RBA's request. As to their demand that he revoke beer and liquor licenses in Phenix City until the killer was captured, Persons pointed out he did not have the authority but had given General Hanna full leeway to close any establishment that might cause trouble. He scoffed at the idea of calling a special prosecutor or grand jury for Russell County. Constitutionally, Pennington had as much authority as the governor to do that, since it could only be achieved by the attorney general and the state judiciary system.[64]

Bill Miller, the owner of the pickup truck that James Elwer had borrowed on the night of the murder, had had nothing but trouble ever since the Columbus papers had reported that Pete had been at the Coulter Building when Patterson was shot. On Sunday morning, someone called the house but never spoke. Within the next hour, Miller received five more similarly unnerving calls. That night, one of his trailers was broken into and trashed. The following morning the telephone calls came again. On Tuesday, Miller sent his son to live with relatives in Ohio. The phone calls stopped.[65]

Si Garrett again testified before the Jefferson County Grand Jury on Wednesday, June 23, regarding the alleged vote fraud in Birmingham, but this time members were not as accommodating. The Birmingham investigation had taken on a more sinister cast due to press reports that Patterson had planned to testify on the vote fraud allegations. Shortly after the murder, Circuit Judge Alta King made a supplementary charge to the grand jurors: "It has been rumored that these alleged violations of our election laws in our own county have stemmed from, or were tied in with, the so-called lawless elements in our neighboring county of Russell." King urged jurors to keep Patterson's murder in mind during their deliberations.[66]

In addition, Lamar Reid had two days earlier made a sixty-eight-page confession to Jefferson County circuit solicitor Emmett Perry of his involvement in the vote fraud and a full accounting of how Garrett convinced him to help steal 600 votes for Lee Porter. Reid told his story after being confronted with evidence from Fred Bodecker, the detective Reid had suggested hiring to determine how the recapitulation sheets for Jefferson County had been altered. With Reid's testimony in their possession and the Patterson murder casting a new sense of importance on the proceedings, grand jurors quickly reduced Garrett's usual bullying with pointed questions which indicated that they were not just guessing about his activities in Birmingham on June 4 and 5. The interrogation lasted ten and a half hours, and when it was over, Garrett announced that he was leaving the state to rest up from the ordeal of the Patterson murder. He told Horne to take his briefcase to Montgomery and give it to his secretary; the Phenix City material he should give to Barton. Asked by reporters where he was going, Garrett wouldn't specify, saying only that they would "have one hell of a time finding me."[67]

6
Sykes Takes Over

After careful consideration and under the circumstances, it is my
view that the services of Mr. Ferrell will no longer be required in
this investigation.

Bernard Sykes, June 25, 1954

By Thursday morning, the whole state was abuzz with the news of
Garrett's departure. For Governor Persons, who had been wrestling
with what to do with Garrett ever since Barton and Smith raised their
suspicions, the attorney general's sudden departure was a godsend.
The governor knew as well as anyone inside the state government what
had happened to Garrett: he had either cracked up again or was
avoiding answering any more questions in the vote fraud case. Either
way, it didn't look like he'd be back soon. After conferring with Alabama Supreme Court Chief Justice Ed Livingston, Persons felt confident enough to authorize Bernard Sykes not only to take over the
Patterson murder investigation but also to assume the role of acting
attorney general. In a press conference that night, Sykes announced:
"I am taking over this investigation. . . . I want it clearly understood
that I am not acting through instruction of Si Garrett. Mr. Garrett has
gone and I am the designated assistant to act in his absence." Reporters wanted to know where this left Arch Ferrell. After a brief pause,
Sykes answered, "After careful consideration and under the circumstances, it is my view that the services of Mr. Ferrell will no longer be
required in this investigation."[1]

John Patterson didn't know what to make of Bernard Sykes. He trusted the attorney general's office about as much as he did the local officials. Garrett's involvement had made him suspicious because he was sure the attorney general had been covering for his good friend Ferrell. The day after Garrett left, Patterson accused him of "poor judgement . . . and complete indifference as to the outcome of this investigation," and he expressed surprise that authorities let him flee the state. He didn't know a lot about Barton and Smith except that Garrett had sent them to Phenix City and that they had spent a lot of time talking to Sheriff Mathews and Chief Daniel. Sykes he didn't know at all. In any case, Patterson wasn't going to sit by and let himself be steam-rolled, especially after Smelley and Fuller's unnerving interview. On Wednesday, the same day Garrett went before the Jefferson County Grand Jury a second time, Patterson made a scathing indictment against the whole statewide political apparatus: "The murder was a direct result of my father's opposition of the political machine and crime syndicate, which here are synonymous. The same prominent people who are connected with the vote fraud in my father's election run the machine. The administration in office, the incoming administration and the crime syndicate were against my father."[2]

By this time, Patterson had already requested an interview with U.S. Attorney General Herbert Brownell Jr. Reluctant to get directly involved, Brownell asked J. Edgar Hoover to handle the matter. The FBI agreed to hear Patterson out, without comment, and receive the allegedly incriminating documentation Patterson said he would bring with him. After flying to Washington, Patterson on June 25 told FBI agents who he thought the likely suspects were and why he trusted neither local nor state officials. At the end of the interview, the agents told Patterson what they had already told Persons and the RBA: in the absence of any evidence of a federal crime, such as unlawful flight, the murder remained a local problem to be solved by local officials. After the conference, a Justice Department spokesman told reporters, "We're all sorry for young Patterson. He's got a right to be demanding action. His father's murder was a disgrace to the state and to the nation. But unless Patterson can give us something we can base federal jurisdiction on, we can't give him anything but our sympathy." Patterson returned to Columbus empty-handed.[3]

As Patterson was on his flight back from Washington, Sykes arrived in Phenix City to take over the case. Garrett had once bragged to Lamar Reid that if Circuit Solicitor Perry started causing trouble in the Birmingham vote fraud inquiry, Garrett would use his powers as attorney general to take over the case and appoint Perry to "cow-stealing cases" in remote parts of Alabama. Utilizing the same provisions under the Alabama Constitution, Sykes officially superseded local authorities and put the investigation under the authority of the attorney general's office, following up with an official letter to Ferrell formally removing him from the case. In quick succession, Sykes promised protection for anyone with evidence in the Patterson murder, prohibited the issuing of public statements about investigation details, and moved his headquarters from the Russell County Courthouse to the Ralston Hotel in Columbus, a clear indication that he did not trust Russell County or Phenix City officials.[4]

That evening, Sykes called a conference between his staff and Dr. Rehling, Captain Smelley, and Smelley's superior, Public Safety Director L. B. Sullivan, to review the progress of the investigation to date. The conferees first discussed how the case was being handled by local authorities. Everyone agreed that Sheriff Mathews had not shown a great amount of interest. He hadn't made any breakthroughs in the case; indeed, he had hardly done anything on his own initiative. The *Columbus Ledger* had already criticized Mathews for failing to follow the most elementary police procedures after the murder, such as setting up roadblocks, employing bloodhounds, or alerting the Columbus authorities. Ferrell's situation was even more unusual. Like Mathews, Ferrell seemed to show little interest in the investigation. And, they had to agree, Ferrell was a nervous wreck. Rehling and Smelley both remarked how jumpy and distracted he seemed. Despite these acknowledged criticisms, Smelley and Sullivan denied that any additional help was needed. They claimed that the Phenix City Police Department and the Russell County Sheriff's Department, assisted by the state investigators already on hand, were quite able to conduct a proper murder investigation. Sykes overruled them. The attorney general's office was taking over.[5]

Getting down to the particulars of the case, Sykes turned to Dr. Rehling, who now outlined the results of Sowell's investigation. Because of the highly public setting of the crime, Rehling had deduced that the murder was an act of desperation. All indications pointed to the theory that Patterson knew his killer. The fact that a crippled sixty-year-old man walked thirty-seven feet with three bullet wounds was extraordinary; Rehling's guess was that Patterson was trying to reach the street and tell someone who had shot him.[6]

Both the Alabama Department of Toxicology and the FBI had examined the three bullets recovered from the body. The first bullet, the one that smashed into Patterson's mouth, was a .38 caliber copper-coated lead bullet of Western or Winchester manufacture, commonly known in shooters' circles as a "Lulaboy." Because the bullet was so badly damaged, the particular gun model could not be definitely established, although there were some similarities to a .38 Special. The second bullet, also a probable .38, split into two fragments after breaking Patterson's arm. The fatal bullet was definitely a .38 caliber lead bullet. Although the FBI could determine neither the specific model nor the manufacturer, some of the physical characteristics suggested a type of bullet known as a "wad-cutter," used primarily for target practice. Interestingly, none of the three bullets appeared to be of the same manufacture but rather a random selection. It seemed to Rehling that the killer did not do a lot of shooting and had probably just collected a few shells from home. FBI ballistic tests showed that the bullets were fired from a gun, or guns, having six lands and grooves with a left twist. These rifling characteristics pointed to a Colt revolver or possibly an overseas manufacturer.[7]

The group next heard from Captain Smelley. One week after the murder, he didn't have a lot for Sykes to work with. Although investigators reasoned that with the number of people in the area someone must have had a clear view of the killer, the only witness who saw the suspect was Ross Gibson, the elderly cook at Smitty's Grill, and he got only a fleeting glance some distance away. Physical evidence was scant and inconclusive. Investigators had only the one clear thumbprint and some smeared prints, supposedly from fingers of the same hand. Smelley agreed with Rehling's theory that the killing was an act of desperation.[8]

The lawmen went over motive theories. From their perspective, Patterson was murdered for one of two reasons. The fact that he was to be the next attorney general and had pledged to clean up Phenix City was the most promising lead, though the question remained which set of enemies might have pulled the trigger—the Phenix City racketeers or the crooked public officials. Patterson's upcoming tenure as attorney general posed a serious threat to both of these groups, but each had something different to lose: the gangsters would lose their income and probably serve some jail time; the politicians would lose their careers. There was also the possibility, pushed by local law enforcement officials, that Patterson was murdered for personal reasons. The most sensational theories concerned his alleged affairs, but the group also considered the possibility that Patterson, like any other attorney, might have made some enemies in the courtroom.[9]

As far as suspects were concerned, the fact that both John Patterson and the RBA were saying semipublicly that Ferrell was the number one man to be investigated could not be ignored. Ferrell was Patterson's political enemy; no one disputed that. More interesting was Ferrell's proximity to the area where Patterson was killed. True, Garrett had provided telephone records showing that Ferrell was on the telephone at the moment Patterson was gunned down, but that alibi was just a little too tidy for Sykes and his staff, and they now discussed the possibility that the telephone calls which supposedly established Ferrell's alibi were made specifically for that reason or made from another location. In any case, Rehling wanted to determine if Ferrell's gun could have been the murder weapon.[10]

At the end of the day, Sykes and his staff had a lot of suppositions, innuendoes, downright lies, and, somewhere in that heap of information, possibly some hard facts. They couldn't even pick up where the local investigation had left off, since the local officials were themselves suspect. They were on their own.

Another headache facing Sykes in Phenix City was the hornet's nest of political intrigue with the local authorities on one side and the RBA on the other. RBA members, who now looked to John Patterson for guidance, did not trust local officials and for the moment were unsure of Sykes and the state investigators. For his part, Patterson kept Sykes at arm's length, and the RBA began conducting its own investigation. When Smelley found out about this, he demanded that they be brought in and forced to provide whatever information they had.[11]

But Sykes didn't have to ask. On Saturday morning, to his surprise, one of John Patterson's younger brothers, twenty-five-year-old Maurice, showed up at the Ralston. He said he wanted to share some information but didn't want his name mentioned. Emphasizing that his older brother was not to know he was talking to Sykes, Maurice told him, "John knows things you don't know. He's going to talk to you, but he will take his time and when he comes to see you he will have something. Your biggest problem is to convince John and the RBA you mean business."[12]

The following morning, John Luttrell and Howard Pennington of the RBA arrived. To show them he meant business, Sykes put in a call to J. Edgar Hoover, who wasn't available. Impressed, Pennington and Luttrell started talking. One of the RBA's top suspects was Tommy Capps, a local hood who, they believed, was responsible for dynamiting Hugh Bentley's home two years before. According to Pennington and Luttrell, Capps would have been prosecuted had Governor Persons's office not halted the investigation. At any rate, Albert Patterson would have made Capps's prosecution his first case as attorney general.[13]

So, was Capps the killer? Well, actually Sykes should also seriously consider Fuller, Ferrell, and Porter. The RBA had reason to believe that Porter was in Ferrell's office when Patterson was killed, left Phenix City at 9:15 Friday night, and checked into a Montgomery hotel at 10:30 CST. And Fuller was at the hospital Friday night without his gun. So Fuller killed Patterson? No, Ferrell did, but he used Fuller's gun. So what was the motive? Pennington and Luttrell claimed that it had something to do with Patterson's visit to Montgomery on Friday, something they couldn't tell Sykes about. This something had caused Patterson to call Albert Rosenthal from the Exchange Hotel and tell him that he would appear before the Jefferson County Grand Jury on Monday. And it was big—so big that Sykes wouldn't be able to handle it. That's why the FBI had to get involved.[14]

Luttrell and Pennington filled Sykes in on what they knew about the vote fraud. Birmingham was just the tip of the iceberg—the effort to steal the election was statewide and involved scores of high-ranking politicians. Porter was going to contest the election and ask for a recount. His supporters gave Patterson the ultimatum in Montgomery on Friday: either quit or the Democratic Executive Committee would throw him out. There was only one man who could put it all together, and he would only talk to the FBI. They were sworn to secrecy as to the man's identity, and there was no way they would reveal it to Sykes. OK, the man was John Pruitt (Pennington begged Sykes not to let John Patterson know where he got the name). Pruitt knew the exact motive.[15]

Sykes followed up on the RBA's information. Tommy Capps was picked up on June 25 for fingerprinting, but there was no match. Capps, a small-time gangster, had been no trouble to bring in. But John Pruitt, Patterson's campaign coordinator for south Talladega County and the man who would supposedly break the case, was nowhere to be found. Finally, on June 28, the state highway patrol set up a roadblock in Clay County and detained Pruitt between Phenix City and Talladega. Sykes and his staff questioned him for an hour and a half, but Pruitt wasn't able to tell them anything pertinent to the case. Sykes would eventually judge Pruitt "unbalanced" and require him to produce an alibi for the night of the murder.[16]

On Monday, June 28, Lee Barton talked with Hugh Britton, the RBA's intelligence officer for the past three years. Britton emphasized, "You're not going to get anywhere until you get those .45s off of those armed gangsters" (that is, the police and deputies). In other words, there were plenty of witnesses, but no one would talk until the deputies were disarmed. In fact, the more the witnesses knew, the more reluctant they would be to talk. Britton then launched into a litany of Phenix City gossip involving most of Russell County's law officers. As Mathews and Daniel had played up Patterson's love life, Britton now provided details on Ferrell's supposed indiscretions.[17]

Sykes took the RBA's information under advisement. To him, the RBA's observations were useful but skewed. In order to get an accurate view of the entire situation, he wanted to hear the other side of the story. After Britton had been ushered out of the Ralston, two of Phenix City's most recognized gangsters, Godwin Davis Sr. and Jr., arrived for a talk. Both admitted that they didn't particularly care for Patterson's nomination as attorney general, but recent indications were that Patterson would not be the crusader he had promised during the campaign. Their plans had been to keep operating until he took office, then close down and see what happened. If the opportunity presented itself, they would try to make a deal. Neither believed

Patterson's murder was a gang killing; they thought it was more likely the result of a personal grudge over a woman, or maybe even the Russell County Draft Board. What about the draft board? asked Sykes. The elder Godwin alluded to Patterson's ouster three years earlier. Barton was skeptical. So how did that get Patterson killed? Godwin answered, "Because some son or brother was sent to war when somebody else should have gone."[18]

And then there were what Sykes called "the screwballs." Within two days of Sykes's arrival, the first of many unbalanced individuals confessed to the killing of Albert Patterson: a Fayetteville, North Carolina, man who claimed he had been paid $500 to kill Patterson. Sykes was skeptical, but it had to be checked out. After investing considerable man-hours, Sykes determined that the man was miles from Phenix City at the time of the murder.[19]

In addition to hearing the confessions of self-described killers, Sykes and his staff had to deal with those compelled to say that they had seen one aspect or another of the crime. Some wanted the reward, some wanted a little notoriety, and some were mentally unbalanced. On June 28, Barton contacted a woman in Rockford, Alabama, where Patterson had once been the high school principal. She had information on the homicide. Barton listened impassively as she detailed a conspiracy involving a rural mail carrier, his wife, the owner of a local store, and the sheriff of Coosa County. The conspirators had a mysterious method of communication that employed a sound system undetectable by most humans, though the woman could hear it. It was something like radar, but it was definitely voices. While she could not always tell what they said, she distinctly heard one time, "Schuman committed the Patterson murder and was the actual triggerman." Barton deadpanned in his memo to Sykes that the woman "was thanked for this information and requested to furnish us with any information which may be to her choice."[20]

On Saturday, June 26, the Democratic Executive Committee voted to call a special election thirty days hence to decide who would replace Albert Patterson as the attorney general nominee. Although committee members had discussed the possibility of handpicking a candidate to replace Patterson, public reaction soon discouraged it. *Alabama: The News Magazine of the Deep South* spoke for many when it said, "Handpicking of an attorney general by a political committee under existing circumstances would be unthinkable." Given the widespread belief that Patterson had been murdered not for his announced program to clean up Phenix City but for the very real and immediate threat of exposing vote fraud, the Folsom camp was in no position to wield any influence in the race for attorney general.[21]

State politicians also saw the futility in trying to buck John Patterson's candidacy, judging an electoral challenge to the slain martyr's son "political suicide." Yet the committee wasn't ready to hand Patterson the nomination on a silver platter, thinking that cooler heads might prevail by July 27. Although the special election would be costly (upward of $200,000), the committee voted to "let the people speak." But the voters never got the chance. MacDonald Gallion immediately announced that he would not seek the office, offering his unqualified support to John so he could "carry out the program of his martyred father." That same day, Gordon Madison, another potential candidate, announced that he would not run either. Two days later, Porter stopped all talk of reentering the race when he made it clear that he would not seek the nomination.[22]

The only opposition Patterson encountered was from Birmingham attorney C. E. ("Bud") Huey, who announced his candidacy on June 29. Huey claimed that "the office of attorney general is far too important to allow it to go by default to someone obviously lacking the experience necessary to execute its many-fold duties fairly, impartially, and to the betterment of the whole state of Alabama." Within hours of his announcement, however, Huey had backed out after learning that Patterson would "select competent assistants."[23]

By the July 1 qualification deadline, John Patterson was the only candidate and the party declared him the winner. The younger Patterson's succession to attorney general nominee ensured that the murder investigation would not fade away for at least four years. Certainly, most of the men investigating the murder, from both the Office of Attorney General and the I & I, appreciated the fact that the son of the murder victim would be Alabama's top law enforcement officer in six months.[24]

MacDonald Gallion, the odd man out in the May primary, had been in Texas since the middle of June, seeing to the business interests of his late stepfather, a Dallas optician. Friends in Montgomery had called and told him of Patterson's murder shortly after the news broke, dashing Gallion's expectations of being appointed first assistant attorney general, but only temporarily. In a few days, John Patterson made Gallion the same offer his father had, and Gallion accepted second place again.[25]

As Gallion made his way down U.S. Highway 80 toward Fort Worth, a Texas highway patrolman pulled in behind him and lit up the rearview mirror with flashing red lights. At the moment, Gallion could only think how embarrassing it would be for a future assistant attorney general to come home with a Texas speeding ticket. Convinced that he was well within the speed limit, Gallion started to protest. Before he could say a word the patrolman asked, "Are you MacDonald Gallion?" Gallion nodded. The patrolman told him he had an urgent message for him from Montgomery, Alabama: call the governor immediately. Gallion found a telephone and called his old Public Service Commission boss, Gordon Persons. Persons had an assignment for Gallion. He wanted him to go to Phenix City as his legal representative on the Patterson case.[26]

Governor Persons was furious over John Patterson's Wednesday press conference, in which he accused the administration of being beholden to Phenix City interests. He was trying his best to govern responsibly in Phenix City, but the state couldn't gain anyone's confidence if Patterson kept undermining the investigation. On July 2 the governor telegraphed Sykes and urged him to appoint young Patterson as an assistant attorney general. The purpose, according to Persons, was to "assure the people of Phenix City there will be no letup in the determination to forever keep crime and rackets out of Phenix City." But there was another reason, too. Maybe Patterson would be less likely to criticize the investigation if he were directly involved in the process. To sweeten the deal with Sykes, Persons even offered to pay Patterson's salary out of the governor's emergency funds. Eventually, Persons made the offer, but Patterson turned it down.[27]

For the first few days of Sykes's tenure as acting attorney general, one nagging question kept popping up: What would happen if Garrett returned to Alabama and resumed his duties as attorney general? That question was resolved, at least for a while, on June 28. Broox Garrett, Si's younger brother and a Brewton attorney, called a press conference to read a joint statement from his father and Dr. E. J. Kocour, Si's personal physician in Montgomery:

> It became an immediate necessity last week to return Si Garrett, Attorney General of Alabama, to John Sealy Hospital, in Galveston, Texas, for additional treatment. He was ordered confined to this hospital in August and September 1953, where he was a patient of Dr. Hamilton Ford, psychiatrist. About six weeks ago, Dr. Ford and his personal physician recommended that he again enter the hospital for treatment, but hope was maintained by the family that he might improve without hospitalization. Instead he grew steadily worse. Upon his physician's advice of Tuesday, June 22, that Si Garrett was a very sick man mentally and should be returned at once to the hospital for treatment, the family had him carried on Wednesday night, immediately after he had appeared before the Jefferson County Grand Jury, to the John Sealy Hospital in Galveston for psychiatric treatment.[28]

No timetable was provided for Garrett's recovery, but it was clear that it would not be soon.

As Sykes began the Patterson investigation anew, the state judiciary began the process of finally cleaning up Phenix City. Accusations concerning Russell County's peculiar judicial system, aired before the election subcommittee during the first half of June, along with new revelations since the Patterson murder, convinced Governor Persons that Phenix City could not clean its own house. On the same day Sykes arrived to take over the murder investigation, Chief Justice Livingston ordered a special grand jury impaneled in Phenix City and appointed Circuit Judge Walter Jones of Montgomery to take over the duties of Judge Julius Hicks.[29]

Walter Burgwyn Jones, sixty-five, had been on the bench since 1920 and had served as presiding judge of the Fifteenth Circuit since 1935. There were few Alabama families as respected as Jones's. His father, Thomas Goode Jones, was a Confederate officer, a twice-elected governor, and a major force behind the state's 1901 constitution. By 1954, Judge Jones had made his own mark. In 1927 he had founded Jones School of Law, a Montgomery night school that offered a legal education to those who could not forego their day job. Jones was a titan in the state legal community. In addition to his election as presiding judge of the Montgomery circuit, he was acting president of the Alabama Bar Association and editor of its monthly newsletter, *The Alabama Lawyer*. Jones reveled in the law, and through his weekly column, "Off the Bench," in the *Montgomery Advertiser,* he sang the praises of his profession.[30]

In spite of his respectability, or perhaps because of it, Jones was also stubborn and righteous, exhibiting a tendency to classify people as good or evil. Thirty days after his appointment as special judge in Phenix City, Jones wrote of the men who would soon appear as defendants in his courtroom: "The mobsters and gangsters who have for years and years controlled Phenix City might as well realize that their day is over, and that Phenix City is not again going to live under their lawless reign. . . . The gang which has controlled Phenix City in days gone by," he continued, "is now backed to the wall, and the law-abiding people of Alabama . . . don't propose to let the mobsters return to their sordid rule of plunder and terror. . . . Phenix City won't be cleaned up in a day or a week, or a month, but the gangsters are on their way out. Looks like they are headed for Kilby Prison."[31]

Three days after Jones's appointment, Governor Persons demanded and received the resignations of Russell County's three jury commissioners and replaced them with Phenix City reformers. The following day, Judge Jones invalidated Russell County's jury pool (the official list of qualified jurors) and ordered that a new list be drawn. Jones instructed the new commissioners: "You are to have a notable part in the effort being made to bring back to Russell County a government of law and to take from it the rule of the gambler and racketeer."[32]

Less than two weeks after Patterson's murder, only Arch Ferrell remained of the Russell County judicial hierarchy, and he was barred from the murder investigation. On June 30, in Birmingham, the Jefferson County Grand Jury capped its three-week investigation by indicting Ferrell, Garrett, and Reid for vote fraud. Ferrell suffered the indignity of being hauled off to Birmingham in handcuffs, despite

Sheriff Mathews's guarantee of bond. Garrett remained in a Galveston hospital, out of reach.[33]

As the third week of the Patterson murder investigation got under way, Sykes's team began separating fact from fiction. They spent much of their first week on the job becoming acquainted with the setup in Phenix City, determining who were the criminals and who were not. They talked to anyone who could give them information on Patterson's murder, and even though they had little faith in local officials' judgment, they dutifully checked out leads provided by Phenix City police and Russell County sheriff's deputies. One of their first targets was the young secretary whose alleged relationship with Albert Patterson—according to local officials, at least—figured so prominently in the murder. Local gossip produced two scenarios regarding her and the Pattersons. The first involved her husband, a lieutenant who had returned from overseas duty on the morning of the murder. Learning of his wife's liaison with her former employer, he murdered Patterson as soon as he found him. The second scenario was even more titillating. In this version, John Patterson had begun a relationship with the young secretary as soon as he returned from Germany and started working with his father. When Albert fell out of the young woman's favor, he fired her, claiming lack of money. This dismissal, in addition to other troubles between the elder and younger Pattersons, soon led to a jealous rage in which John killed his father.[34]

On July 2, Lee Barton and Maury Smith interviewed the former secretary. She confirmed that she had worked for Albert Patterson from September 24, 1953, to about April 20, 1954, when, against John's wishes, Albert dismissed her for financial reasons. Smith and Barton asked about her marital problems. She said that her husband was generally jealous and abusive and that problems had existed in her marriage long before she met either Patterson. What, exactly, was her relationship with John Patterson? Strictly good friends, she replied. In fact, just the day before, he had helped her secure the divorce. While employed at the law firm, she often traveled around town with him on business and once went out of town when he needed a witness to a mortgage closure. As far as she knew, there were no bad feelings between Albert and John, much less any jealousy over her. One of the investigators asked her point blank if she had had sex with either Patterson. She answered equally shortly: No. In fact, she offered, she didn't think Patterson's murder had anything to do with extramarital affairs, but rather Patterson's planned testimony in Birmingham. She denied the possibility that her estranged husband killed Patterson, and in fact confirmed her husband's whereabouts at the time of the murder.[35]

Following up, Barton and Smith interviewed the husband. He frankly admitted that he was divorcing his wife because he was too jealous: his tours of duty away from his wife drove him crazy. Jealous of whom, the investigators wanted to know? Well, not Albert Patterson, he said, because Patterson was "a much older man." The lead went nowhere. As far as Sykes and his staff were concerned, the interview proved that information from local officials had a lot in common with information provided by the RBA: it was small-town gossip.[36]

The scores of reporters in Phenix City were in a unique position to help Sykes. Not only had they been early on the scene, but they were also inquisitive and observant by nature. Desperate for official information, they would tell everything for the tidbits Sykes occasionally revealed. On July 1, Barton and Smith interviewed Fred Andersen of the *Montgomery Advertiser* to hear about his two nights with Garrett directly after the murder. Andersen related the two trips, the Sunday-night press conference, the late-night dinners at the CoCo Club, Ferrell's bizarre behavior, and the trip out to Seale to see Ferrell's wife on Sunday night. What did he think Garrett was up to? Andersen offered the opinion that the only reason Garrett had asked him to go to Phenix City was to manipulate the press. Smith asked Andersen if he believed Garrett had sent him and Barton on Tuesday as a sham. Andersen had no doubt. It was his opinion that Garrett didn't do anything to solve the case, that he was more concerned with protecting Ferrell. In fact, to Andersen's way of thinking, Garrett's defensive maneuvering, even more than Ferrell's actions, led him to believe that Ferrell was involved in the murder.

Barton asked if Andersen thought the telephone calls were authentic. Yes, Andersen said, but only to establish the alibi: "I believe he connected, laid the phone down, walked across the street, killed Albert Patterson and came back." Barton brought up the possibility that Ferrell made the calls from another telephone. After some thought, Andersen agreed that the call could have been made from somewhere else and charged to Ferrell's office number. The only way an operator could confirm a caller's number was to call back, a common occurrence because it usually took the operator some time to contact the party.

Now that Barton mentioned it, Andersen recalled that the telephone records produced by Garrett showed that the operator had *not* called Ferrell back for the second call, the one that covered the time when Patterson was murdered. Ferrell had instead held the line while waiting for the connection. Barton asked Andersen if he thought Garrett was crazy enough to lie about the phone calls. Andersen replied that he had never been around Garrett when he was supposed to be sane and therefore had no basis for comparison.[37]

By the second week of July, Sykes's operation was spread out over ten rooms in the Ralston Hotel, incurring five hundred dollars a day in hotel bills, food, long-distance calls, and incidental expenses. Bureaucratically speaking, nothing like it had ever been attempted in Alabama. Sykes had taken over not only the functions of the local circuit solicitor in regard to the murder investigation but also the investigative machinery of the Phenix City Police Department and the Russell County Sheriff's Department. While he had at his disposal the services of Barton, Smith, and Gallion, the heart of the investigative team was the Alabama Department of Public Safety's I & I Division.[38]

The I & I unit had been in operation since 1936 when a criminal investigator was added to the highway patrol, itself established only the year before. Since then, the unit had evolved into an official division with the purpose of assisting local police agencies upon request. Composed of highly trained men who had paid their dues in the highway patrol, the I & I over the years had helped crack a number of cases that local police forces had found beyond their capabilities. The I & I was a closed brotherhood; applications were by invitation only. The state investigators—plainclothes detectives all—were better trained and had faster cars, more money, and access to the latest crime technology. They knew all about forensics, ballistics, metallurgy, fingerprinting, crime scene photography, and criminal psychology. When the state men (the official title was criminal investigation officer, or CIO) arrived, people noticed. While superior to their localized counterparts, the I & I men limited their assistance to services requested by the local authorities, who (in theory, at least) retained control of the investigation. But the I & I men brooked no interference in their activities and certainly didn't take orders from anyone outside the division, including sheriffs and police chiefs.[39]

By the time Sykes arrived on June 25, there were already four I & I investigators on duty in Phenix City, and more were on the way. Sheriff Mathews had made the original request within thirty minutes of the murder, asking patrolmen Mihelic and Hall to radio for state help as soon as they arrived at Cobb Memorial Hospital. Receiving the request in Huntsville, I & I chief Joe Smelley radioed for three investigators almost immediately. First on the scene was Willie Painter, who arrived as early as 11:30 from his assigned station in Montgomery. A native of Paint Rock in northeast Alabama, the thirty-six-year-old Painter was tall, lanky, and unassuming. He had joined the highway patrol in 1948 and was accepted by I & I four years later, as soon as he completed training at the FBI Academy. A plodding yet successful investigator, Painter rarely raised his voice except when he believed it would prove valuable in interrogations, never got excited, never leaped to a conclusion, and never revealed his thoughts until it was absolutely necessary. These sphinxlike traits earned him the ironic nickname "Loudmouth" from his coworkers. Although Painter was intelligent and a good investigator, some of his fellow detectives considered him overly ambitious and too eager to please his superiors.[40]

John H. Williams Jr., thirty-three, was a likable Huntsvillian who in his eight years as a highway patrolman had been stationed in Montgomery and Cullman. Although he had been with I & I only since January, he was considered a capable investigator, and Smelley had called him in from his latest station in Dothan on the night Patterson was murdered. Williams was teamed up with Decatur-based Robert W. Godwin, nine years Williams's senior, who had in April 1952 given up a sixteen-year career in the highway patrol and the rank of lieutenant to join I & I.[41]

Captain Smelley himself led the detail. Smelley had joined the highway patrol in 1937, shortly after it was formed, and rose to the ranks of sergeant and lieutenant before transferring to I & I in 1952. Typical of Smelley's character, he mourned the loss of his beloved motorcycle patrol duty more than his temporary loss of rank. In February 1953 he was appointed chief investigator. Bearing some resemblance in both appearance and demeanor to a grizzly bear, the forty-six-year-old Smelley was considered a father figure by many of the younger CIOs who owed their career in I & I to him. Smelley was no diplomat; he either liked you or he didn't. Either way, there was never any doubt where he stood.[42]

These four CIOs would have been plenty for most murder investigations, but this was no ordinary murder. Governor Persons had said that the state would spare no expense in finding the killer, and he meant it. Smelley was given carte blanche on the number of investigators he would need to solve the case. His first choice was Walter L. Allen, who, in seniority at least, outranked everyone else in the division, including Smelley. Proud, stubborn, and highly intelligent, the forty-one-year-old Birmingham native joined I & I in July 1947. While some of his fellow CIOs complained that he carried a chip on his shoulder, no one denied that he was a good investigator, probably the best I & I had to offer. Pulled out of training at the Police Institute in Louisville, Kentucky, Allen arrived in Phenix City on June 24.[43]

Smelley also brought in two other veteran I & I investigators, Oscar Coley and Maurice Chambers. Coley, forty-eight, was a bona fide old-timer. A Montgomery native, he was one of the original highway patrolmen when the department formed in 1935, but he had taken time off to fight in World War II and the Korean War. He had been with I & I a little over a year. Chambers, forty-five, was a native of eastern Madison County, close to Willie Painter's hometown, and had joined the highway patrol in 1939, working out of Decatur. Like many of his coworkers, Chambers took time out to join the army in early 1944 and didn't return to the patrol until 1946. He had been a CIO since September 1952.[44]

In the first week after Patterson's murder, the I & I men were in a familiar position: supplementing local authorities in a murder investigation. After Sykes took over, however, the bureaucratic waters became muddied. Smelley believed that Sykes's role would be strictly prosecutorial. From his point of view, Sykes and the other assistant attorneys general were lawyers, not criminal investigators. The relationship between I & I and the attorney general's staff, Smelley and his investigators believed, would be much the same as that between a local police force, which the I & I had replaced, and the local circuit solicitor, whom Sykes had replaced. In practical terms, this meant that I & I would run the investigation, while Sykes would take what they produced and make a case with it. Sykes had other ideas, however. Given complete power over the investigation, he was not about to share authority with anyone.[45]

After concluding the interview with Patterson's former secretary, Sykes and his staff were much less likely to listen to local officials. And the more they rejected a personal grudge as the reason for Patterson's murder, the more the investigation led them back to Circuit Solicitor Ferrell. The motive was too great to ignore. As the reputed head of the Phenix City machine, Ferrell was Patterson's avowed political enemy. If Patterson took office, he would become Ferrell's constitutional superior, with chances better than even that he would immediately relieve Ferrell of his office and replace him with an aggressive prosecutor who would indict every crooked official in Russell County, with Ferrell as a prime target. Detectives also learned that Ferrell was a heavy drinker subject to violent outbursts. In 1953 his temper had cost him an assault-and-battery conviction after he broke a friend's jaw in a fistfight. The victim, city clerk Jimmy Putnam, said they were having a political discussion. Ferrell paid a fine of $101.50.[46]

Also difficult to ignore was the certainty of the RBA and John Patterson that Ferrell was the killer. Sykes had to coax Pennington and Luttrell to share their suspicions, but John Patterson could hardly conceal his feelings. In a July 7 press interview in his Coulter Building law office, Patterson was asked who he thought murdered his father. In reply, the young lawyer pivoted his chair until he was facing the Russell County Courthouse, visible in the distance. After staring at the structure for some time, he replied, "This man I believe killed my father is a known drunkard with an uncontrollable temper. He is deeply enmeshed with the stinking criminal element of Phenix City. What's more important than all these—this man had the motive and the opportunity. I don't believe his alibi worth a damn."[47]

There was also the matter of Ferrell's bizarre behavior immediately after the murder, as related by Fred Andersen and others. Their impressions of Ferrell were confirmed by Smelley and assistant chief toxicologist Wendell Sowell, who described how the usually cool and collected Ferrell was visibly upset while attending the autopsy, his shaking hands barely able to hold the cigarettes he was chain-smoking.[48]

Although his actions appeared to be those of a man experiencing deep remorse, Ferrell had an impressive alibi, confirmed by the state attorney general and the telephone records which indeed showed that Ferrell's line had been connected to Garrett's Birmingham hotel suite at the time of the murder. Instead of letting Ferrell off the hook, however, this telephone call only made investigators suspect Garrett even more, such was the extent of suspicion against Ferrell. They knew that Garrett was no friend of Patterson's either, politically speaking. Sykes very much wanted to talk to Garrett, but he remained holed up behind the locked doors of a psychiatric ward in Galveston.[49]

The vote fraud investigation in Birmingham particularly held Sykes's attention, for it indicated how far Garrett and Ferrell were willing to go to defeat Patterson. Some of the Jefferson County Grand Jury's activities could be gleaned from the papers, and they indicated that Garrett and Ferrell had pulled out all the stops after the May primary to keep Patterson from being elected. But Sykes needed something more direct. He requested and received from Solicitor Perry transcripts of Garrett's grand jury testimony on June 18 and June 23 to help determine the whereabouts of Garrett and some of his aides on the day of the murder. In a cover letter, Perry cautioned Sykes at length about the impropriety of supplying this information and the probable legal consequences if anyone found out. Sykes also apparently used the Jefferson County Grand Jury to access witnesses he wanted to question. Perry had offered to subpoena anyone Sykes wished to question. When Sykes provided a lengthy list, Perry simply sent him blank subpoenas to fill out himself.[50]

On July 6, Sykes officially stripped Ferrell of his remaining duties as circuit solicitor and replaced him with George Johnson, circuit solicitor of Alabama's Eighth Circuit (comprising Limestone, Morgan, Lawrence, and Cullman Counties). The forty-seven-year-old Johnson, deceptively mild looking but tough as iron, began a practice in Athens after graduating from the University of Alabama School of Law in 1928. He served two terms as county solicitor before he won the circuit solicitor post in 1942. Conrad "Bulley" Fowler, who as solicitor of the Eighteenth Circuit had already made headlines for bringing down gambling kingpins in Shelby County, was hired to assist Johnson. Their job was to clean up Phenix City; the murder investigation remained the domain of Sykes and I & I.[51]

Sykes decided it was time for a little talk with Ferrell. On the night of July 8–9, Sykes, Barton, Smith, and Gallion interrogated Ferrell for ten hours, questioning him in detail about his movements and contacts the day of the murder and the two days immediately following. In most instances, Ferrell's memory was faulty. He couldn't recall seeing or hearing anyone in the courthouse that night and had no recollection of the Boy Scout honor court or the sirens passing by later. In other situations, he could recall seemingly minute details, such as Garrett's room number at the Redmont. He also gave a detailed account of Patterson's autopsy, admitting that he had to leave the room when Sowell and Knowles began sawing into Patterson's cranium, and was able to rehash much of the conversations that took place at the CoCo Club on Sunday and Monday night, despite Andersen's observation that Ferrell was drinking heavily.[52]

Ferrell held up pretty well until Sykes produced a paper toward the end of the marathon session, the one that Garrett and Horne had taken from Ferrell's wallet the Monday night after the murder as Ferrell slept off his drinks. This simple sheet, written in Ferrell's hand, listed the attendees of the Red Porter fund-raiser at the Bama Club following the May primary, along with the names of Sheriff Mathews and Chief Deputy Fuller. To the right of each name was a single digit. Sykes suspected that the list showed how many thousands of dollars each had pledged to Porter's primary runoff campaign. In response to this line of questioning, Ferrell clammed up. Given his indictment for vote fraud, he was not about to give up his rights as a defendant. Besides, he could see no connection between the list and the murder investigation. He told Sykes, "I have my doubts as to whether you would reveal it [the meaning of the list] under the present circumstances." Sykes replied icily, "I believe under the present circumstances, if I was sitting in your place, I believe I would reveal just about everything I could think of, just as quickly as I could think of it."[53]

Ferrell also antagonized Sykes when he asked the acting attorney general whom he, as solicitor, should answer to: the out-of-town Garrett, who had assigned him the position as assistant on the Patterson murder case, or Sykes, who had relieved him of all his official duties. Sykes told him curtly that due to Garrett's absence, he was acting attorney general with full authority over any solicitor in the state. It was 3 A.M. when the interrogators cut Ferrell loose, but not before they fingerprinted him.[54]

Ferrell had been a suspect from the beginning, but by the middle of July another prominent Russell County official fell under suspicion: Albert Fuller, Sheriff Mathews's chief deputy. If only half of what the RBA said about Fuller was true, he would be toward the front of the line of indictees in a Patterson-led cleanup of Phenix City. And there were some strange coincidences involving Fuller on the night of the murder, such as his empty holster at the hospital and the disappearance of the suspect's footprints when only Fuller and another policemen knew about them. Still, Fuller had a very good alibi, better even than Ferrell's. Six witnesses, including a highway patrolman, two deputies, the sheriff, and an ABC agent, said that Fuller was at the county jail when Patterson was shot.[55]

Although Fuller's activities were suspicious, investigators spent more time on Ferrell, partly because Fuller wasn't going anywhere for a while. On July 4 he fractured several vertebrae when, he later told doctors, he took a fall while horseback riding. Word on the street had it that Fuller had run afoul of Buddy Jowers, the six-foot-four, 230-pound assistant police chief who was allegedly Fuller's main rival for Phenix City protection money. Jowers, who detested Fuller and believed he was involved in Patterson's murder, had been fired on July 1 as part of the Phenix City cleanup. As it became apparent that the Patterson murder would result in the cleanup of Phenix City, Jowers beat the chief deputy within an inch of his life and left him for dead. At any rate, investigators took their time developing leads on Fuller.[56]

Although Garrett seemed safely out of the way in a psychiatric hospital, there was still concern over what would happen if he decided to return to Alabama. On July 10, Governor Persons answered that question in a *Montgomery Advertiser* interview. Quite frankly, the governor said, there was little he or anyone else could do if Garrett decided to resume his duties as attorney general. Persons and his legal staff had researched the problem, and the Alabama Constitution and statutes were quite clear on removing an elected official for insanity. Simply being treated for mental illness was not sufficient. The incumbent had to be judged insane in a legal proceeding in court. No such proceeding had taken place, nor was one contemplated.

The fact that Garrett had been indicted didn't mean much either. For one thing, he hadn't been convicted, and even if he had been, vote fraud was a misdemeanor, the same legal status as speeding. To justify removal from office, the crime had to result in a sentence of hard labor in a penitentiary, a doubtful outcome for the current charges against Garrett. It was also highly unlikely that the state senate could impeach Garrett with the available evidence. Accepted charges to remove an incumbent officeholder included willful neglect of duty, corruption in office, incompetency, or intemperance to the extent that it rendered the officeholder unfit. And finally, Persons cleared up the misperception that Garrett had vacated his office. Constitutionally speaking, this could only be done through death, resignation, forfeiture of state residency, or a court decision declaring his appointment or election to office void or his tenure ended.[57]

Almost as if the governor had cued the action, Garrett returned to Alabama the next day, turned himself in to the Jefferson County sheriff on the vote fraud charge, and announced his intention of resuming his duties as attorney general. Garrett's surprise return set off a near panic in Phenix City. To deny Garrett access to the murder investigation records, Sykes rushed through a legal maneuver before Judge Jones in which Jones impounded the documents on behalf of the Russell County Circuit Court and appointed Sykes as custodian. But Garrett wasn't the only one who had considered the options laid out by Governor Persons the day before. In the few minutes it took Garrett to pay the $1,000 bond, Solicitor Perry, in Birmingham, moved with amazing speed to file lunacy proceedings, asking the court to determine Garrett's mental condition as soon as possible. Under Alabama law, a prisoner who shows signs of mental imbalance may be forced to undergo a court-ordered psychiatric evaluation. The purpose of the law—and Perry was quick to point out the humanitarian aspect—was to ensure that mentally ill persons were treated at a hospital, not locked up. Circuit Judge J. Russell McElroy of Jefferson County set a hearing for July 21. Given the earlier public statement by Garrett's father and doctor that Si was a "very sick man, mentally," Perry felt justified in filing the petition to protect Garrett's rights.[58]

But there may have been some ulterior motives, too, as Garrett's lawyers would soon accuse Perry. The worst thing that could happen to the Patterson murder investigation and the Phenix City cleanup was the return of Attorney General Silas Coma Garrett III. As Governor Persons had pointed out, Garrett could not be removed from office for insanity because no commission had officially ruled him insane. With Perry's filing of lunacy proceedings, however, Garrett now faced that distinct possibility.[59]

After posting bond, Garrett departed on a vacation to Laurel, Mississippi, with his two children, Silas Garrett IV, age eight, and Pamela, age four. Just outside Waynesboro, Garrett's 1949 Ford left the highway at a high rate of speed and smashed into a telephone pole four hundred feet from the road. The Garretts were lucky to survive. The impact was so severe it drove the steering wheel halfway into the backseat and the engine block into the front floorboard. All three were thrown from the car. Pamela, asleep in the front seat, was shaken up but not seriously injured. Silas IV, asleep in the backseat, suffered a concussion. Si had the most extensive injuries: a broken neck, a fractured elbow, and an ear that was nearly ripped off the side of his head.

But Garrett's spirits were good. Asked to comment on Perry's request for a lunacy hearing, Garrett quipped, "I believe I am as sane as Mr. Perry, although momentarily not as mobile." The accident most definitely would postpone any legal proceedings against Garrett. It would also keep him away from Montgomery and Phenix City.[60]

7
Three Suspects

You will disregard oral instructions given you on July 16 relating your present assignment. . . . [Instead], you will be expected to report at 8:00 A.M. each day to Sykes for the assignment of the day.

Joe Smelley, July 20, 1954

While Sykes was plodding along in the murder investigation, special prosecutors George Johnson and Bulley Fowler, along with Judge Jones and a sympathetic, reformed Russell County Grand Jury, were unraveling 120 years of Phenix City vice and corruption. Phenix City was already under a journalistic microscope because of Patterson's murder, and as the special prosecutors uncovered new acts of lawlessness each day there was a corresponding rise in media accounts relating how law enforcement officials had ignored it over the years. This was certainly bad news for Ferrell, Daniel, Jowers, Mathews, and Fuller, but there was some statewide blame, too. One of the first casualties was the I & I chief, Joe Smelley, who had won the RBA's animosity when he testified on behalf of Sheriff Mathews at his 1952 impeachment trial. RBA members were also unhappy with Smelley's lack of results while investigating the bombing of Hugh Bentley's home that same year. Lastly, the RBA said, Smelley was far too intimate with the gang at the Russell County Courthouse. On July 16, Public Safety Director L. B. Sullivan ordered Smelley back to Montgomery to resume his normal duties. Although Sullivan hotly denied that the recall was anything but routine, Smelley himself claimed publicly that he was the victim of RBA intrigue and was being, in his words, "made the goat" for the failure to find a suspect in the Patterson murder case. He also strongly indicated that the RBA was wielding undue influence in the Patterson murder investigation. In Sykes's office there were mail baskets for each of the state investigators, Smelley pointed out, and alongside these was one for Hugh Britton, the RBA's "intelligence officer."[1]

It is a matter of conjecture how the investigation would have unfolded had Smelley remained in charge, but one direct result of his reassignment was the loss of I & I's independence in the Patterson murder investigation. But on July 16, Smelley didn't know that yet. Before he left, he told senior investigator W. L. Allen that Allen was now in charge of the investigative detail. Allen's tenure turned out to be short lived. Four days later, he and every other CIO in Phenix City received an official memorandum in which Smelley reversed himself and specified that the attorney general's office—specifically Bernard Sykes—was running the investigation. Smelley ordered Allen to "disregard oral instructions given you on July 16 relating your present assignment. There will not be an investigator in charge of the detail in Phenix City." Instead, "you will be expected to report at 8:00 A.M. each day to Sykes for the assignment of the day."[2]

Sykes, then, found himself heading the biggest murder investigation Alabama had even seen. He may not have wanted to direct the day-to-day work—publicly he denied any responsibility for Smelley's removal—but he was unwilling to delegate the actual detective work to anyone else after Smelley left. Totally untrained in police work, Sykes had never done anything remotely resembling a murder investigation in his twelve years as an assistant attorney general. His specialty up to this point had been researching and preparing appeals.[3]

But there was a more fundamental problem than Sykes's inexperience in police matters. The Patterson murder investigation was now in the hands of lawyers instead of detectives. In a criminal investigation, the questions the police must answer are what happened and who was responsible. The job of the prosecutor, on the other hand, is to take the results of the investigation and make a case against those to whom the evidence points. In the Patterson murder case, it appeared that prosecutors were making a case *before* those fundamental questions were answered.[4]

Another victim of the intense publicity from the Patterson investigation was Lee Barton. In early July, Governor Persons and a number of newspapers throughout the state received some very unflattering wanted posters from Rhode Island featuring the assistant attorney general. It appeared that Barton was wanted by police in Pawtuxet, Rhode Island, for an illegal wiretapping charge dating from 1939. An embarrassed Barton explained to reporters that when he was younger he had been on the staff of a detective agency hired by Rhode Island's Republican governor to check up on his Democratic opponent during an election. The Democrats found out about the wiretaps after they won the election, and a warrant had been issued for Barton's arrest. Barton found it an opportune time to find another job some distance from Rhode Island . . . like Montgomery, Alabama. Governor Persons, a Democrat, laughed off the incident and joked how Barton had chosen the wrong side to spy for, but he was concerned enough to check with the Rhode Island state police, who said that as far as they were concerned, Barton was not a fugitive.[5]

In the meantime, Sykes had acquired four more investigators. Ben Allen was brought on board in early August. Allen, thirty-eight, was raised in Sheffield in northwest Alabama but had moved to Birmingham when he joined the highway patrol. He had been working only a few months when he joined the Marine Corps during World War II. Although he was no relation to W. L. Allen, the two had much in common and were good friends. Both had joined the patrol in 1941 and, six years later, the I & I, with W. L. only two weeks senior to Ben.[6]

Sykes also went recruiting from outside I & I. Concerned over what they viewed as the provincialism of the state investigators, the attorney general's staff searched for an outside, yet experienced, point of view. Birmingham detectives Robert A. MacMurdo and Maurice H. House filled the bill. MacMurdo, forty-eight, was a Pittsburgh native who had come south as a young man following steel industry jobs. At six foot two and two hundred pounds, MacMurdo was intimidating, but not physically; rather, he had an uncanny ability to read people. MacMurdo's partner was forty-one-year-old Maurice House, who had grown up in the Pratt City section of northwest Jefferson County. As a sergeant he outranked his partner, although MacMurdo had almost three years' seniority.[7]

Another recruit was Claude Prier, a forty-two-year-old Birmingham native stationed in Dothan. He had been with the Alabama Highway

Patrol since 1939, not counting his four-year stint in the navy during World War II. Known for his daredevil stunts as well as solid police work, Prier cut a striking figure in his green uniform atop a maroon motorcycle. He gave it up in 1947 for I & I but was sent back to patrol duty four years later because of budget cuts. He was rather plainspoken—an unusual trait in an occupation where cunning and intrigue were used against suspects, as well as in the Byzantine world of I & I politics. Blunt with coworkers and superiors alike, Prier was a no-nonsense investigator who said exactly what he thought, usually loudly.[8]

Despite the additional manpower, Sykes was getting nowhere. By the end of the first month of the murder investigation, he and his staff had interviewed more than two hundred people and amassed a pile of information that filled their offices and kept growing. From what they could determine, about a dozen people had seen Patterson emerge from the alley and die on the sidewalk. Possibly twice that many had been close enough to hear the gunshots. The various locations of these people suggested that the killer had been virtually surrounded. Had he disappeared into thin air? A more plausible solution was that people weren't talking. Already a number of witnesses had appeared who, although not close enough to see any suspects, had nevertheless identified others who were.[9]

Take, for example, Raymond Ennis, who was standing at the Palace Theater ticket window when he heard the shots. Ennis looked up Fifth Avenue toward the Coulter Building. There, in the middle of the street, he saw a man looking directly into the alley. If the killer had run in the opposite direction after shooting Patterson, as witness Ross Gibson said he had, then the man Ennis described was practically looking right at him. So where was he?[10]

There was also Mrs. Bentley and her hired hand, Hubert Tharp. Bentley's Grocery was right across Fifth Avenue from the alley, and if either had looked up when the shots were fired, he or she would have seen the killer. It may have been that neither one saw anything, as they claimed, but as MacDonald Gallion found out from local police records, it would have been the first time. Over the years there hadn't been so much as a broken beer bottle without a detailed complaint from Bentley's. And now, four gunshots directly in front of the store didn't raise an eyebrow?[11]

One thing Bentley and Tharp did admit to seeing, though, was Jimmy Kirkland, the seventeen-year-old who passed in front of the alley moments before the shots were fired. They claimed not only that Kirkland was in a good position to look into the alley but that he *did* look in the alley as he passed. State investigator Robert Godwin was sure that Kirkland had something to tell him and brought him in for questioning. Kirkland was extremely nervous and claimed he couldn't remember looking into the alley or seeing anyone there. Although he changed his story three times in one aspect or another, the one thing he did insist on was that he couldn't remember anything. No number of guarantees for his safety could shake his story; he simply couldn't remember. Detectives didn't buy it, but given the circumstances, they really couldn't blame him.[12]

Ben Allen and W. L. Allen, however, came to a different conclusion. Both had years of experience questioning witnesses and believed they could tell when someone was lying. In their opinion, Kirkland was telling the truth when he said he didn't remember. Familiar with the emerging use of psychology in law enforcement, the Allens believed that if Kirkland had seen anything, his cognitive processes simply could not recall it. They therefore decided to try and help him out, proposing that the teenager be hypnotized and regressed back to the night of the murder. Because of the medical aspect of the activity and because Kirkland was a minor, they first had to obtain his parents' permission. This was flatly refused.[13]

The investigators were not as easy on Jimmy Sanders, who, like Kirkland, had been only a few feet away from Patterson when he was gunned down. Sanders was so close that he was the first to arrive at the body. But this didn't intrigue I & I half as much as what Sanders said happened afterward. As Sanders was still leaning over Patterson, he saw a man quickly walking up Fifth Avenue toward Fourteenth Street. The man was about five foot eight or so, his curly hair cut short around the edges, and he was wearing a white shirt and brown pants. Perspiring so heavily that he had to take out a handkerchief and wipe his face, the man seemed to not even notice Patterson's body lying on the sidewalk or the hubbub around it. For a moment Sanders thought the man might actually trip over the body, but at the last minute he stepped around it without even looking. Sanders had never seen him before and hadn't seen him since.[14]

Investigators questioned Sanders twice, but apparently they didn't like what he had to say. The third time, they picked him up at Smitty's and placed him under arrest. While Sanders was in jail, investigator Willie Painter had him go through about forty mug shots. When Sanders identified one of the photographs as a likeness of the man he had seen on the sidewalk, Painter wouldn't tell him who it was. Maury Smith told Sanders that two other witnesses had already identified the man walking through the crowd as Arch Ferrell and that Sanders might as well identify him, too. But when Sanders was shown photographs of Ferrell and Fuller, he swore it was neither of them. He remained jailed two days before being released.[15]

Although investigators weren't having much luck finding witnesses they knew were at the scene, they were beginning to get information from people they didn't know were there. On July 15, James R. Taylor, a Columbus cab driver, contacted investigators with the most substantial story in the investigation so far. On the night of the murder, Taylor was taking a young lieutenant from downtown Columbus to Chad's Rose Room, a nightclub on Fourteenth Street in Phenix City. Soon after they crossed the Fourteenth Street Bridge into Alabama, Taylor stopped at the red light at the Fifth Avenue intersection. While they waited for the light to change, Taylor answered his passenger's questions about Phenix City nightlife. Just then, they heard gunshots coming from the direction of the Coulter Building off to their right. Taylor could see two or three people near Smitty's. The lieutenant, sipping on a fifth of whiskey, joked, "I know I'm in Phenix City now." A few seconds later, as Taylor pulled adjacent with the post office, a man suddenly appeared a few feet in front of him, running toward the street. He was of medium height, five foot nine or so, around two hundred pounds, chunky but not fat. He was wearing light brown pants, a light-colored shirt, and a tan hat that was pushed back on his head. Taylor couldn't say a lot about the man's facial features because he only saw him from the side while he was moving quickly.

The runner was headed toward a large, dark, late-model car that was parked at the curb with its taillights on, the engine running, and the front passenger-side door open. Another man was sitting behind the steering wheel. Taylor couldn't tell much about him, either, except that he was white and was not wearing a hat. It was a good thing the door was open, because the runner hardly slowed down as he jumped in the car. As soon as he was in, the car took off directly ahead of Taylor's cab. The first traffic light it came to was red, but the car didn't even slow down. Taylor soon lost sight of it.

Gallion realized the implications immediately. One of the possible escape routes from the murder scene was along the footpaths behind the Coulter Building, one of which emerged right at the point Taylor described. And the man Taylor described as running from the direction of the murder sounded a lot like Chief Deputy Fuller, already mentioned more than once as a possible suspect. Didn't Taylor agree that the physical description he had just provided perfectly fit Albert Fuller? Well, yes, Taylor guessed it did. Could Taylor positively identify the man as Albert Fuller, then? No, he couldn't. He just didn't see him that well.[16]

Sykes was stymied. Despite setting up headquarters in Columbus and promising protection for anyone who came forward, he could do little to erase a century and a half of state indifference. No amount of assurances or promises could convince residents that this time Phenix City would be cleaned up. They would have to see it to believe it.

"Crack" Hanna didn't trust Phenix City's local officials on the early morning of June 19, and he trusted them even less by the middle of July. Theoretically, the guardsmen were there only to help local officials keep order, but in reality General Hanna had his own ideas about law enforcement, particularly when it came to the gambling and prostitution that local authorities had traditionally neglected. Immediately after he established a guard presence on June 19, Hanna publicly ordered all gambling ceased. The order openly discredited local authorities, who had for years maintained the charade that organized gambling did not exist in Phenix City. Two nights later, Hanna led a combined force of guardsmen and highway patrolmen and confiscated almost one hundred gambling devices. Impressed, townspeople deluged the National Guard and highway patrol with tips on gambling violations. The resulting series of raids netted a record number of gambling machines, but the National Guard and highway patrol were hamstrung by the lack of authority to act on their own; they had to bring along a deputy to actually make an arrest. They were also prohibited from entering anywhere but public establishments and had no access to private clubs or even the back rooms of public bars. And the guardsmen began noticing what most Phenix City residents had known for years: the gambling equipment they were confiscating was totally worn out.[17]

To find out just how bad vice conditions in Phenix City actually were, Hanna appointed First Lieutenant Richard Peacock to organize a counterintelligence unit. Peacock's men, both covertly and in uniform, toured around Phenix City for the next few days and nights. The resulting report concluded that the situation was actually much worse than the guard had imagined, even worse than the RBA suspected, and that local law enforcement agencies were heavily involved. Not only that, the intelligence unit reported, but there were clear indications that both city police and Russell County deputies regularly monitored the guard's movements and tipped off gangsters about impending raids. For Sykes and his staff, the implications were disturbing. How could they guarantee confidentiality to witnesses in the murder investigation when the National Guard couldn't even raid a juke joint without the gangsters' knowledge?[18]

Hanna told Governor Persons that the only way to clean up Phenix City would be to entirely replace local law enforcement agencies. Persons had been hearing the same thing for weeks from the RBA, newspaper editors, state investigators, and the Jefferson County Grand Jury. Though hesitant to take such a drastic and costly action, Persons really had no choice. He directed his legal advisers to search the state constitution, statutes, and court decisions and find out under what conditions martial law could be declared. By July 18 he had his answer. If any situation qualified for martial action, the one in Phenix City did. There was still the question of the extent to which martial law would be imposed. Full martial law meant the complete takeover of civic duties by the military—in this case, the Alabama National Guard. No one saw the need to go that far. Nothing could be gained by having the guard fighting fires and picking up garbage, for example. The problems in Russell County were law enforcement and the courts, and the state had already taken over the local judiciary. Persons decided, therefore, to declare "limited martial rule": the guard would take over the Phenix City Police Department and the Russell County Sheriff's Department and leave everything else alone.[19]

July 22 was a wet, dreary day in east Alabama. In Montgomery, Governor Persons called Hanna into his office during the afternoon and told him what he wanted to hear. Phenix City would be placed under martial rule at precisely 4:30 P.M. CST. With less than two hours before Persons would announce the proclamation, Hanna raced to Phenix City to ready his men. At the appointed time, fully armed guardsmen surrounded the Russell County Courthouse. Hanna and his aides marched into the sheriff's office to read the governor's proclamation to a stunned Ralph Mathews and a handful of deputies. With no introduction save the rustle of military slickers against carbines, Hanna read from the single sheet of paper Persons had handed him earlier that afternoon. The governor, quoted Hanna, was invoking martial rule to "suppress the state of lawlessness, intimidation, tumult and fear which reigns" in Russell County. In a frank indictment of Phenix City and Russell County, the governor accused local authorities of being "unwilling or unable" to enforce the law there. Troops then relieved Mathews and his deputies of their duties and firearms. Minutes later, Hanna repeated the ceremony at city hall, disarming Chief Pal Daniel and city policemen.[20]

The takeover came off without a hitch. The closest things came to violence was when one of the National Guardsmen, Sergeant Edward Ratigan, a Birmingham policeman in civilian life, stormed into the jail office to take it over. A startled jailer began to reach into a desk drawer until Ratigan raised his carbine and demanded he back off. With one eye on the jailer, Ratigan removed a .38 Colt from the drawer. Within days, the gun was delivered to Sowell, tested, and cleared.[21]

Wasting no time, Hanna began another round of raids on local clubs, this time without the cooperation of local officials. Beginning on July 24 and lasting three days, the raids wiped out the Phenix City gambling establishment, netting almost five hundred indictments. As one indication of gangsters' expectations, a large number of gambling machines were found in a warehouse in the heart of Phenix City, having been placed there shortly after Patterson's murder and awaiting a return to normal operations.[22]

Normal operations, however, would never return. While the National Guard and the reformed grand jury decimated gambling operations, the state Democratic Executive Committee dismantled the local political machine. On July 15 the elections subcommittee ruled that there had been widespread fraud in Russell County and Phenix City during the May 4 primary—so widespread, in fact, that it could not determine who the legal winners were, Brassell and Cole or Curtis and Belcher. Because the voting lists would have to be purged, the subcommittee doubted if there would be enough time for a special election and recommended that the full committee choose a nominee. But it didn't stop there. Russell County's vote fraud was so widespread and so entrenched that the subcommittee recommended that *all* nominations in Russell County be set aside.[23]

Two weeks later, the full committee adopted the subcommittee report and voided all nominations in Russell County from the May 4 primary. Curtis and Belcher saw their nominations handed over to Brassell and—instead of Cole, whose reputation was already becoming tarnished in the cleanup—yet another Phenix City attorney, Homer Cornett. Sheriff Mathews, who had won his race by a four-to-one margin, was relieved of his nomination and replaced with RBA supporter Lamar Murphy, a former prizefighter who now ran a service station. Arch Ferrell was completely devastated. Although he had run unopposed (his name had not even appeared on the ballot) and it was therefore impossible for vote fraud to have occurred on his behalf, the committee was not swayed. Its final report concluded that Ferrell had accepted the backing of a "corrupt political machine" with full knowledge that it was responsible for Phenix City lawlessness. Ferrell's friends on the committee didn't give him much help either. While many of them privately expressed the belief that the committee's action was unlawful and that the courts would eventually overturn the ouster, no one wanted to go against the political tide sweeping state politics. By a vote of forty-four to six, the committee replaced Ferrell with local attorney James Caldwell. The committee also took away Ferrell's chairmanship of the Russell County Democratic Committee when it threw out all but one of the members.[24]

Although the declaration of martial rule was instrumental in cleaning up the vice dens of Phenix City, it was also important to the murder investigation. First, it tended to run a large number of hoods out of town, and second, it showed that the state was serious about finding a permanent solution to Phenix City's problems. But that's not how it was first perceived, at least by the press corps, which was impatient for an arrest in Patterson's murder. To them, martial rule meant that Sykes had nothing, since otherwise there would be no need to impose it. In a press conference the day after Governor Persons made the declaration, Sykes pleaded for patience in the murder investigation. In general, however, the city's residents were impressed, and that's who the potential witnesses were. Fascinated, townspeople watched as Phenix City's political and business leaders were publicly unhorsed, their businesses entered without warrant, their belongings piled up and burned. After that, witnesses were much more inclined to talk. And now that the National Guard had replaced sheriff's deputies and policemen, Sykes felt confident enough to move his headquarters back to Phenix City. Instead of using the courthouse or city hall, however, he set up his offices in the Coulter Building, down the hall from the rooms previously occupied by Albert Patterson. Each morning, investigators parked in the same parking lot in which Patterson had been shot and walked directly over the spot where he had died.[25]

The removal of the old guard produced some immediate, though not quite ironclad, results for the murder investigation. On July 26, Gallion interviewed James Taylor again, this time in the company of investigators MacMurdo and House. Since the last interview, Taylor had been thinking over what he had seen and wanted to add some details. He remembered that the lieutenant—Taylor's fare on the night of the murder—was wearing a ring, a large gold-looking piece with a diamond setting. When Taylor had remarked on it, the lieutenant said he had bought it while stationed in Germany. Also, Taylor had given more thought to the car he saw pulling away from the curb. While driving around Columbus and Phenix City recently, he had studied the taillights of various cars and concluded that the car was a late-model Cadillac.[26]

Finally, although he again confirmed that he saw the runner's face only from the side, Taylor had believed at the time that it was Albert Fuller. Then why did he previously say he couldn't identify him? Because he was too afraid. Why should they believe him now? Because, Taylor said, he had told someone else he thought it was Fuller right after the murder. When he first saw Fuller running toward the waiting car, he didn't make the connection with the gunshots he had heard seconds before. But after he had dropped off the lieutenant at Chad's Rose Room and was headed back into Columbus, he heard the dispatcher commenting on what had happened. The radios in the cabs allowed the drivers to communicate with the dispatcher but not with each other. So he heard the dispatcher, C. E. Phillips, obviously in response to another cabbie, say, "They say Albert Patterson's been shot at the Coulter Building." Then Phillips asked, "Do they know who did it?" At that point, Taylor said, he picked up his own mike and blurted out, "Albert Fuller did it." For Barton, the statement was significant because it could be used as evidence that Taylor named Fuller long before he was prejudiced by newspaper accounts of the reward, now up to $10,000. A quick interview with Phillips confirmed Taylor's version of the conversation.[27]

But where was the lieutenant who, according to Taylor, also heard the gunshots and had remarked, "That man is in one hell of a hurry," when he saw the suspect running toward the waiting car? Barton contacted the army's Criminal Intelligence Division (CID) at Fort Benning for assistance. Agents there estimated that there were about one thousand first lieutenants at Benning, but they said they would try to find him.[28] Investigators also asked the hostess at Chad's Rose Room about the missing lieutenant, but she could recall no such person. This was a little disturbing to Barton. Taylor had quoted the lieutenant as saying he was on his way to a party at Chad's, but the hostess was quite certain that she would have remembered a large group that night. Nevertheless, Taylor's statement was enough for Sykes to order a search. Investigators, with the help of National Guard troops, raided Fuller's home on July 27 and confiscated three shotguns, two rifles, and twelve pistols.[29]

Sykes was optimistic about Taylor's statement, but on July 30 another witness muddied the water. Fred Ryals, a truck driver from Eufaula, told investigators that on the night of June 18 he saw a man running between a pair of buildings on Fourteenth Street shortly after Patterson was killed. When the man reached the street, he started walking toward the courthouse at a fast pace. A few days later, Ryals saw a newspaper photograph of the man he saw that night. The caption identified him as Albert Fuller.[30]

So Ryals had seen Fuller, too. Ironically, investigators didn't want to hear Ryals's story, for it contradicted Taylor's account. Ryals said that Fuller continued walking down Fourteenth Street, whereas Taylor swore that the chief deputy jumped into a waiting car and sped off.

Actually, Ryals's account, in one important respect, resembled Taylor's story *too* closely. Ryals, like Taylor, said he heard the shots while stopped at the traffic light at Fourteenth Street and Fifth Avenue. And, just like Taylor, Ryals was headed west. But if that were true, then Ryals and Taylor were sitting in the same place at the same time. Investigator Painter asked Ryals if there were any other cars or vehicles at the intersection, particularly any taxis. Ryals said that he didn't see a cab but that there was a car behind him.[31]

It was clear to investigators that at least one of the men was lying. Ben and W. L. Allen, however, believed that both were. They based their opinion partly on the statement of Charles Eller, the owner of a two-tone green Ford who had parked his car in front of the Raiford Building a little after 6:00 on the night of the murder and didn't retrieve it until after 9:30. Other witnesses who passed by that night confirmed Eller's story. Yet both Ryals and Taylor denied that there was any such car on that side of the street. Given Taylor's detailed account of the large black car parked in almost the same spot, it would have been especially hard to miss the green Ford, which would have either obscured the getaway car or made it necessary for the larger car to swing out around Eller's Ford.[32]

Other witnesses appeared and confused the matter even more. One cab driver said he saw Fuller in a sheriff's car at the cab stand at Fourteenth Street and Third Avenue around 9:00. The dispatcher on duty, however, told investigators that he couldn't remember seeing Fuller—or for that matter any other law enforcement officer—in the vicinity that evening. Another witness claimed that he saw Fuller's car at about the same time in front of the office of attorney V. Cecil Curtis. Curtis proved he was in Columbus at the time.[33]

And now Sykes was hearing doubts from some of the investigators. Ben and W. L. Allen especially distrusted both Ryals and Taylor and specifically warned Barton in early August to be careful if the case went to trial. Ryals, they believed, was a pathological liar out to gain a little notoriety. Their doubts about Taylor were more substantial. As part of a general assignment to check witnesses' statements, the Allens devised an experiment to test the reliability of Taylor's story. In this reenactment, W. L. Allen positioned himself at the approximate position of the killer, just inside the alley next to the Coulter Building. At the same time, Ben Allen drove west on Fourteenth Street until he reached the Fifth Avenue intersection, where Taylor said he heard the shots that killed Patterson. As soon as the light turned yellow, W. L. ran at top speed through the alley and behind the Coulter Building, familiar ground by now, to reach a waiting car on Fourteenth Street. In the meantime, Ben waited until the light turned green again, exactly twenty-two seconds, and unhurriedly proceeded west down Fourteenth Street. When W. L. reached the Fourteenth Street sidewalk, he looked left toward Fifth Avenue for Ben, but Ben was already well to W. L.'s right. According to Ben's stopwatch, he had actually taken a little longer than Taylor's estimated time. The two investigators repeated the experiment twice more. Even though Ben slowed practically to a crawl, and W. L. probably moved faster than the assailant did, Ben beat W. L. every time.[34]

The Allens concluded in a memo to Sykes: "It can be seen that there can be no faith given to the story given by James Ray Taylor and for approximately the same reason, there can be no truth given to the story of Fred Ryals. It will further be noted that both of these men claim to be in the same spot at the same time, yet they had seen different things. It is the writers' conclusion that no attention can be paid the story of either man." Painter agreed, given the wide discrepancy between the witnesses' statements, and judged Fuller's jailhouse alibi witnesses as more believable. Until there was corroboration for the story of either Taylor or Ryals, Fuller's alibi stood.[35]

Lee Barton talked to Margaret Sanks on July 28. The Elite Café cook particularly held Barton's interest because she was an outsider to Phenix City (she had been in town for only five days when Patterson was killed) and not affected by local politics. In her original statement, Sanks had mentioned that she saw two men in front of the Coulter Building minutes before Patterson was killed. Barton had Sanks walk the same path at the same speed in order to establish how soon before the murder she saw these two men. As Sanks reached the spot where she heard the shots, Barton clicked his stopwatch: two and a half minutes. In his report to Sykes, Barton urged, "We should make every effort to identify and locate the two men seen by Margaret Sanks on the sidewalk." But Sykes didn't share Barton's interest. He believed the two were Schermann and Elwer, two of the furniture movers. Barton continued to differ because Sanks was certain that there was no

car or truck parked in front of the Coulter Building, indicating that
the movers had not yet arrived. More interesting to Sykes was Sanks's
observation of a black car in front of the Raiford Building, facing west.
That fit Taylor's statement.[36]

On July 11, the FBI told Sykes that the prints taken during Ferrell's
interrogation two nights before did not match those lifted from Patterson's car. It was a welcome reprieve for Ferrell, but his troubles,
like Fuller's, were just beginning. Sykes's staff had come to the conclusion that Ferrell's motive for killing Patterson was too great to ignore. Investigators determined early on that the local theory that Patterson had been killed in a crime of passion, perhaps by a jealous
husband, was unlikely to be correct. The evidence indicated that even
if Patterson did have affairs, it had nothing to do with his murder. In
fact, Sykes and the other assistant attorneys general believed that local
officials simply wanted some embarrassing facts about Patterson to
emerge and thereby undermine the sympathy factor for the old man,
thus taking some of the heat off the courthouse and city hall.[37]

For Sykes, this left only two reasonable theories: Patterson was
killed because of his pledge to clean up Phenix City or because he
planned to testify before the grand jury in Birmingham. The first theory, while certainly plausible, did not hold up under close examination, for several reasons. First, despite Patterson's private and public
pledge to clean up Phenix City, it was by no means certain that he
would make good on his promise. Although he had made a lot of
noise about his intentions, he would not be the first politician to break
a campaign pledge if he changed his mind before he took office, especially if he could be convinced that the interests of Alabama would
be better served if he hedged on indicting a good portion of Phenix
City's business and political community. Second, Phenix City gangsters, despite their reputations, were businessmen above everything
else and certainly would have hesitated before assassinating a public
official, since the likely result would be precisely the sort of public
backlash they were now experiencing. Third, Patterson wouldn't take
office for seven months. What was the hurry? And fourth, investigators reasoned, if the Phenix City gangsters were intent on killing Patterson, why did they do it on a busy street on a Friday night in the
middle of town? Even Patterson himself, in explaining to Hugh Bent-

ley why he had little need to carry a gun, predicted that he would be ambushed in the dark, probably as he drove into his own driveway.[38]

The second theory—that Patterson was killed to silence his testimony on the vote fraud during the recent primary runoff—made better sense. What, then, was Patterson going to tell the grand jury? If investigators found the answer to this, they would probably discover the specific motive. Sykes began a determined effort to learn what Patterson had planned to tell the grand jury, and he instructed I & I to piece together what had happened in the June primary runoff, who knew about it, and what they were afraid of should Patterson find out.[39]

By June 18, the Jefferson County Grand Jury had already heard about the changes to the recapitulation sheets in Birmingham that sought to transfer 600 votes from Patterson to Red Porter, the probable involvement of Ferrell and Garrett, and the significant Phenix City contributions to Porter's campaign. But the Birmingham vote fraud, investigators learned, was just the tip of the iceberg. By August, Sykes was certain that Garrett and Ferrell were the prime movers behind raising Phenix City funds to defeat Patterson in the June 1 runoff, and he strongly suspected that they were heavily involved in raising the money used to buy or change votes after the election. When Garrett picked up the morning paper on June 18, he could see how far the investigation had progressed. And Ferrell probably had a good idea, too, either from Wortsman's questions early in the evening, from the Columbus paper he read later, or possibly from one of Garrett's calls.

In their attempt to learn what Patterson knew about the statewide effort to steal the election from him, investigators determined that he definitely planned to tell all. Patterson knew all about the Birmingham vote fraud—that much was certain—but he also knew about at least three other incidents where Porter's backers had stolen or bought votes. A Barbour County official had told Patterson all about Stewart McCollister's midnight ride through south Alabama shortly after the runoff. Patterson had also heard from friends about $15,000 in Phenix City funds that had been delivered to a Birmingham beer distributor as a down payment to buy votes in the Jefferson County town of Bessemer. Within minutes of Patterson's murder, in fact, the distributor showed up at Garrett's hotel room, where he and the attorney general retired to the bathroom for a private conference. Finally, Patterson had heard that one hundred votes had been purchased for Porter in Walker County. Whatever threat Patterson posed to the Phenix City hierarchy seven months down the road in Montgomery, his direct and immediate threat to Ferrell and Garrett had clearly reached its zenith the day he was murdered.[40]

But in addition to the matter of vote fraud, investigators discovered that Ferrell had threatened Patterson. As the stack of witnesses' statements piled up, numerous indications emerged showing that the long-standing political feud between Ferrell and Patterson had become increasingly personal in the days and hours before Patterson's murder. Patterson's campaign pledge to clean up Phenix City may or may not have been sincere, but it was consistent. Even in private, Patterson promised he would shut down Phenix City, even if it meant moving in every law enforcement officer in Alabama and letting the rest of the state run wild. After Patterson's impressive showing in the May 4 primary, his talk turned harsher—and more specific. He made dire predictions of the fate of local officials after he took office, pointedly telling Ferrell's acquaintances that Ferrell would find himself transferred to a remote backwoods circuit after January 1955.[41]

Ferrell took this kind of talk very seriously. One witness, waiting for an appointment in Ferrell's outer office on May 30, claimed that she overheard an animated Ferrell tell a group behind closed doors: "If you fuddle, sit on your lazy ass and let Patterson get to Montgomery, you are all through. If you don't get him, I will." Patterson was never one to mince words, and his threats became bolder, even brash, after the committee certified him as the attorney general nominee on June 10. Another witness told investigators that Patterson remarked to her on June 14 that Mathews and Ferrell had recently offered him $35,000 to switch sides. Patterson responded by warning Mathews that if he had not cleaned up Russell County before Patterson took office, he "was going to get it." Before Mathews could say anything, Ferrell snapped, "If you don't keep your mouth shut, I will shut it for you permanently."[42]

Investigators wanted to talk to Garrett, but Garrett didn't want to talk to anyone, and it was going to be difficult to make him do so. On

August 2, Maury Smith, Maurice House, Robert MacMurdo, and W. L. Allen made a roundabout trip to interview Garrett, still recuperating in a Waynesboro hospital. Their first stop was Birmingham, where they talked to Lamar Reid, under indictment for vote fraud. Reid took the precaution of calling in his attorney before answering any questions, but he incriminated himself anyway when he readily admitted his participation in the vote fraud. Although he had no doubt that Garrett and Ferrell received money for their services in Birmingham, he never did. His intimated compensation was future political rewards. In Gadsden, the four investigators talked to Porter about his contacts with Garrett on June 17, 18, and 19. Porter was candid, so candid that he wound up incriminating himself when he told them of the sums he had received from Phenix City.[43]

When the investigators arrived in Waynesboro, Smith went directly to the hospital administrator, who said that Garrett was coming along just fine. In fact, many of his family members had visited him over the weekend. He didn't see any reason why Smith and the investigators couldn't ask Garrett a few questions, but they should check with Garrett's doctor first. Garrett's doctor, a physician by the name of Frederick Shell, flatly refused to grant such permission until Garrett's lawyer was consulted. Smith pointed out that determining whether Garrett could be questioned was a legal judgment, not a medical one. Nevertheless, Shell stood his ground and the investigators went home empty-handed.[44]

Despite Garrett's refusal to talk, the case against Ferrell was compelling. Still, there was that telephone call and the records to go with it. Until Sykes could figure a way around that, it was doubtful that Ferrell could ever be indicted, much less convicted, for the murder of Albert Patterson. On August 9, Barton and Gallion interviewed the two Southern Bell operators who handled Ferrell's long-distance calls on the night of the murder. The first was eighteen-year-old Mary Barden, toll operator number 69, who worked the four-to-midnight shift on June 18. Looking over the toll tickets she had filled out that night, she explained that the call, from Phenix City 8-6028 (Ferrell's courthouse office), was initiated at 8:37 and placed to 2-3177, the Montgomery residence of Mrs. A. A. Carmichael, the widow of Garrett's predecessor in the attorney general's office and now a good friend of Garrett's.

The line was busy on the first attempt. She tried again five minutes later, but it was still busy. When she tried a third time, at 8:48, there was no answer. She called Ferrell's office number to report that the Montgomery number didn't answer. The party at 8-6028 then asked her to try 3-8996, Garrett's Montgomery residence. When that number answered, Barden called Ferrell back and connected him. That call lasted two minutes, thirty-seven seconds. Barden explained that when a long-distance call was terminated, the operator would stamp the toll ticket with a timing clock and then drop it into a pneumatic tube that sent it to the billing department.

Barton and Gallion then interviewed operator number 301, nineteen-year-old Retha Harris, also on duty June 18. She identified the second successful long-distance call made from Ferrell's office number. That call was placed at 8:53 P.M. to Frank Long Jr. in Room 718 in the Redmont Hotel in Birmingham. The caller told her that Mr. Long would probably be registered at one of the leading hotels in Birmingham. Harris then called Birmingham information to secure the numbers of the Redmont, Tutwiler, Thomas Jefferson, and Bankhead. By chance, her first choice was the Redmont, where she got Long on the line. She had thought to herself, "Gee, wasn't I lucky to get him at the first hotel!" That conversation started at 8:57 P.M. and lasted three minutes, forty-four seconds. Harris definitely recalled that it was a man's voice and that his voice and manners indicated that he knew how to place a long-distance call.

The detectives wanted to know if she overheard any of the conversation, but as soon as she looked over at F. B. Patterson, her supervisor, Barton and Gallion realized that they shouldn't have asked that question. Sure enough, Harris explained that operators were prohibited from listening to the call after the conversation started. Because the phone lines were particularly busy on this night, Harris considered it likely that she immediately cut out to take other long-distance calls.

After the four-minute call was terminated, the caller "flashed back"—that is, clicked the receiver a few times to attract the operator's attention. Harris picked up, and the caller said, "Operator, I want to place another call to Birmingham." He wanted to call the Redmont again, but this time he wanted it placed, not to any particular person, but to Room 720. That call was filed at 9:01, with the conversation beginning at 9:03 and terminating twelve minutes, eighteen seconds later. Harris said that she didn't hear any of this conversation, either. Her supervisor told Harris to forget about company rules and regulations; if she heard anything, either intentionally or accidentally, she should tell the investigators. Harris just shook her head.

Barton wanted to know if Ferrell could have placed a call to Birmingham, put the receiver down, and left it off all night, or for Garrett to disconnect the call in Birmingham by hanging up. Both operators said that this was impossible. The only way to disconnect the call at the time it was disconnected would be for Ferrell to hang up the receiver in Phenix City at approximately 9:15.[45]

But if the Columbus operators didn't hear the call, could it have been that Birmingham operators did? On August 12, Barton talked to Birmingham Southern Bell officials to find out. They told Barton that about twenty-five operators were on duty June 18 on the inbound board. Like their counterparts in Columbus, they would be too busy to listen to incoming calls and would have no occasion to monitor them unless there was a problem. As the Columbus telephone office had told Barton already, it was not possible to determine which operators handled the receiving end of a long-distance call because the records only indicate the operator who places the call. Then was it possible for Ferrell to have called from another telephone in the vicinity, one closer to the Coulter Building? There were not many public telephones around. In Smitty's Grill, however, there were three, located near the door. Barton had F. B. Patterson check his records on these telephones. Only three long-distance calls were made from them between 7:00 and midnight on June 18. Of these, only one was to Birmingham, at 7:28, and detectives quickly confirmed the caller's identity.[46]

There was no way to get around Ferrell's telephone call. Barton wrote to Sykes saying he was totally convinced that Ferrell was on the phone almost continuously from 8:35 to 9:15 and that it was impossible for him to have pulled the trigger. Maybe he was standing at his window in the darkness watching the killer escape in the black car parked on Fourteenth Street, or maybe he was reporting the escape move by move to Garrett in Birmingham, but he was on the telephone. And there was no way the motive factor by itself could overcome that.[47]

But while Barton was buying into Ferrell's alibi, a witness appeared and placed Ferrell at the scene. Sergeant Robert R. Moore, a mess hall cook at Fort Benning, contacted investigators and said he had seen a man in the alley by Patterson's car shortly before the murder. Detectives told Moore that they would like to talk to him immediately, and he agreed to drive over. After some time had elapsed, they called his house, and Moore's wife told them that her husband was too drunk to get to the Coulter Building. The next day, Claude Prier and MacDonald Gallion drove to Moore's home in Columbus. He was not there, but his wife tried to convince them that her husband was an alcoholic and unreliable. She said that her husband did not go anywhere on the night of June 18 and that he merely "imagined" he had passed the murder scene that night. Soon after, Moore himself arrived. For a while he had trouble getting through his story because his wife constantly interrupted to insist that he knew nothing about the murder. Finally, Gallion ordered her to leave the room. Thus unencumbered, Moore gave a detailed account of how he and his wife had gone cruising in Phenix City on the night of the murder, passing the Coulter Building sometime between 8:45 and 9:15. Moore saw two men standing in the alley, one of whom he recognized. Prier and Gallion had considerable difficulty getting Moore to identify the man. Since he had called investigators the night before, Moore said, one of his superiors at Fort Benning had "told him to keep his damn mouth shut." After repeated questioning, Moore identified the man as Arch Ferrell, whom he had met through a Phenix City attorney.[48]

Here at last was someone who could place Ferrell at the scene of the crime. Unfortunately, Moore was, as his wife claimed, an alcoholic. Gallion and Prier were unsure how much he had actually seen and how much, as his wife claimed, he had imagined. After the interview, Sykes contacted the army's Criminal Intelligence Division at Benning and requested that Moore be picked up. They kept him several days until he dried out. He was then brought to Phenix City under military guard, where he repeated his story stone-cold sober.[49]

Shortly after Moore gave his statement, Sykes made a crucial decision in the Patterson murder investigation. With impatience growing in the press and the RBA, Sykes concluded that too much of the investigators' time was being spent chasing dead ends and decided to focus the investigation on the three most promising suspects: Fuller, Ferrell, and Garrett. In individual memorandums to the attorney general's staff and I & I agents on August 14, Sykes spelled out the duties of each for the remainder of the investigation. Willie Painter was to sift through the massive number of reports and write a detailed chronology of Albert Patterson's activities June 18. Ben and W. L. Allen would handle crime scene facts, particularly who was in the area and what they saw, and determine the veracity of each witness. MacMurdo and House would review all the material and compile a case against Fuller. Godwin and Prier would do the same for Ferrell. Smith would limit his work to Garrett's activities. Gallion would handle all information on ballistics, including attempts to locate the murder weapon. Barton would act as an executive secretary, sitting in on all interrogations and taking notes.[50]

The directive marked a watershed in the investigation. From now on, so far as Sykes was concerned, there were only three suspects. Although this decision would facilitate the case against Fuller, Ferrell, and Garrett, it would also tend to exclude any information that did not contribute to their indictments.

Albert Patterson. (Alabama Department of
Archives and History, Montgomery)

Albert Patterson as he appeared in a
campaign poster for the 1954 state
attorney general's race. (Alabama
Department of Archives and History,
Montgomery)

Fifth Avenue, downtown Phenix City, showing, clockwise from bottom, (1) vacant lot, (2) Bentley's Grocery, (3) Russell County Courthouse, (4) post office, (5) Coulter Building, and (6) Elite Café. (Alabama Department of Archives and History, Montgomery)

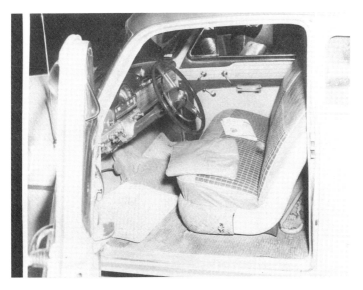

Crime scene photograph of Albert Patterson's car. (Alabama Department of Archives and History, Montgomery)

Chief Deputy Albert Fuller (*left*) and Deputy Aaron Smith (*right*) examine Albert Patterson's blood on the Fifth Avenue sidewalk. (Alabama Department of Archives and History, Montgomery)

Governor Gordon Persons (*left*) visits the murder scene the morning after Patterson's murder. (Steve Franklin Collection)

Fort Benning military police place "Off Limits" notice on the
Fourteenth Street Bridge the day after Patterson's murder.
(Steve Franklin Collection)

Silas Garrett III takes the oath of office as state attorney general, 1951, as his family
looks on. (Alabama Department of Archives and History, Montgomery)

Flanked by Albert Fuller (*standing at window*) and Phenix City mayor Elmer Reese (*seated in corner*), Alabama attorney general Silas Garrett talks to reporters two nights after Patterson's murder. (Alabama Department of Archives and History, Montgomery)

Phenix City "godfather" Hoyt Shepherd. (*Columbus Ledger-Enquirer*)

Major General "Crack" Hanna reads the proclamation of martial rule, July 22, 1954. (Steve Franklin Collection)

Judge Walter Burgwyn Jones. (Steve Franklin Collection)

Circuit Solicitor Emmett Perry. (Alabama Department of Archives and History, Montgomery)

Left to right: Bernard Sykes, John Patterson, and MacDonald Gallion. (Birmingham Public Library Archives)

Left to right: First Assistant Attorney General MacDonald Gallion, Assistant Attorney General Joe Robertson, and Special Prosecutor Cecil Deason. (Alabama Department of Archives and History, Montgomery)

Rod Beddow Sr. (*left*) and Albert Fuller. (Steve Franklin Collection)

Left to right: George Rogers, Arch Ferrell, Drew Redden. (Alabama Department of Archives and History, Montgomery)

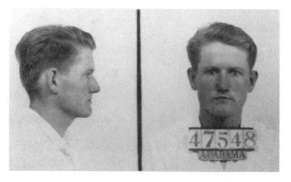

Johnny Frank Griffin in 1941. (Alabama Department of Archives and History, Montgomery)

Former Phenix City cab driver Bill Littleton. (Alabama Department of Archives and History, Montgomery)

RBA cofounder Howard Pennington (*left*) and cab driver James Radius Taylor (*right*). (Steve Franklin Collection)

Assistant Attorney General Joe Robertson (*left*) arrives at the Jefferson County Court-house with Cecil Padgett, the state's star witness in the murder trials. (Alabama Department of Archives and History, Montgomery)

8
Putting the Pieces Together

Everyone is anxious to find a quick solution to this case, but we
must all be patient. We've got to sit down here, calmly sift
through the evidence and calmly build it up so that we will be
able to follow through with it when the proper time comes.

Bernard Sykes, August 20, 1954

Attorney general nominee John Patterson, while vitally interested in
the murder investigation, continued to remain apart from it. That was
just fine with Sykes, who no doubt would have been intimidated by
having his future boss on the staff. The arrangement worked well as
long as Patterson remained quiet, but it became very troublesome
when he didn't. By the middle of September, Sykes still had little to
show for his efforts, and Patterson could hardly contain his impatience. Special prosecutors George Johnson and Bulley Fowler seemed
to have no problem getting indictments; already the whole Russell
County political and judicial infrastructure had been indicted or
kicked out of office. It wasn't as if Sykes had to discover who the killer
was, either. Patterson and the RBA had told him repeatedly: Arch
Ferrell. All Sykes had to do was accumulate enough evidence and present it to the grand jury, which was also beginning to show signs of
impatience. Governor Persons, always sensitive to the charge that the
state wasn't doing all it could to solve the murder, wrote to Patterson
on September 21 and bluntly asked two questions: "Are you satisfied
with the progress of the investigation being conducted by the Attorney General's Office in connection with the death of your father?"

and "Are you satisfied with the National Guard cleanup?" He again offered to put Patterson on the case—in other words, to put up or shut up. In reply, Patterson admitted to the governor that while he had always cooperated fully with Sykes and his staff, "at times, I have been impatient and critical." However, there was no need to shake things up. Sykes, according to Patterson, had recently given him new information indicating that the case was on the verge of a break-through. And no, Patterson did not recommend any changes in Sykes's staff or policy, at least for now: "For the moment, I think Mr. Sykes should continue with a free hand and without change. If what we are now working on bogs down, I will consult with you personally about it." The truth was, Sykes was trying his best to accumulate enough evidence against Fuller, Ferrell, and Garrett to gain not only an indict-ment but also an airtight case. So far, he was unwilling to go before the grand jury with what was on hand.[1]

It turns out that John Patterson wasn't the only one impatient with Sykes's plodding. In early September, Hoyt Shepherd, the Phenix City "godfather," contacted MacDonald Gallion for a private conference with other Phenix City gangsters. Gallion complied, albeit a little un-easily, and met the group at a small shack in the Russell County coun-tryside.[2]

Surrounded by his cronies, Shepherd got right to the point. He told Gallion that he wanted the murder investigation completed so that business could return to normal. To hurry that day, Shepherd told Gallion: "You can cut my heart out and lay it on this table if Albert Fuller wasn't involved." Shepherd had given a lot of thought to the murder and had concluded that Fuller was the one man certain to know the identity of the murderer. Fuller was capable of doing it him-self, but if he didn't, he most certainly knew who did and may have even arranged to hire a killer. There were three men Fuller might have confided in: Head Revel, who wouldn't talk to investigators even if hell froze over; Buck Billingsley, who might provide information if pressured enough; and Red Cook, who was unpredictable. If Fuller had to hire a killer in a short period of time, Shepherd would name as the number one suspect Johnny Benefield, whom Shepherd char-acterized as "a natural-born killer." Benefield's relationship with Fuller was close; despite Benefield's notoriety, he had never even been ques-tioned in any crime, because of Fuller's protection. It was a startling statement to come from the head of the mob, and it carried the weight of gospel with Gallion and, after he was briefed, Sykes.[3]

But it was not feelings of civic duty that motivated the Phenix City hierarchy to finger Fuller. Nor was it even greed. It was politics, and Albert Frederick Fuller had run out of friends just when he needed them most. Despite its monolithic appearance to the outside world, the Phenix City gang was in constant turmoil, and no wonder. Because of the illegality of the operations, wronged individuals within the organization had little recourse in the mild-mannered arenas of law and diplomacy. No gangster could take another to civil court if he encroached on his territory. The only justice was through raw power, and this was exercised in an ugly, straightforward fashion.

Fuller was not only a crooked cop but also an ambitious player in this mobster world. As a protector, he had proved his value by helping to ensure that grand juries and police didn't take the gangsters by surprise. But his assistance came at a high price. He hadn't been content to ease into the existing rackets in Phenix City; he had, over the past few years, carved out a totally new empire protecting an illicit business that had heretofore been left to its own devices by local law enforcement: prostitution. For many old-timers established in the more traditional and benign gambling enterprise, the move seemed extremely risky. Punchboards and slot machines were one thing, but Fuller had extended the law enforcement umbrella over pimps and whores. The move so worried city officials, particularly Mayor Reese, that he appointed his nephew, Buddy Jowers, as assistant police chief in order to counter what he considered an unacceptable imbalance between the city and the county. The appointment was somewhat successful. Fuller eventually split prostitution protection with Jowers, probably the only Phenix City resident not totally afraid of the chief deputy. But lately Fuller had been losing friends at city hall. Later, after the cleanup took him down, Reese publicly accused Fuller and the Russell County Sheriff's Department of trying to take over Phenix City, relating one occasion when Police Chief Daniel ordered gambling operators to shut down, only to have Fuller follow in the officers' footsteps and tell them to keep operating. Patterson's death had, in fact, interrupted a turf war between Fuller and Jowers, who had launched an effort to wrest control of Phenix City from the county deputies.[4]

At the time Patterson was killed, the relationship between Fuller and the mob was at the breaking point. Occasionally, Fuller would selectively harass one operator so as to give his competitor a business edge, and the gangsters found this uncomfortably outside their control. He had once even pursued a business proposition with one of Jimmy Matthews's competitors, but the would-be partner was murdered after he took confidential information from a group of like-minded individuals and beat them to a planned burglary of a hardware store safe in Fitzgerald, Georgia.[5]

But it was not only Fuller's blatant grabs for power and money that worried Shepherd and the rest of the Phenix City order—after all, competition, even of the rough-and-tumble type, was a fact of life in Phenix City. It was also Fuller's recklessness. Ignoring warnings from the older, more established Phenix City gang, Fuller constantly raised his protection rates. Such greed alarmed the mobsters, not so much for the wealth Fuller was amassing but because of the apparent disregard for the consequences. It was this recklessness, perhaps, which led Shepherd to believe that Fuller could have killed Patterson. He was just cocky enough to gamble the electric chair by gunning down Patterson fifteen feet from a main street on a busy Friday night. Years later, when a reporter asked him if he were involved in the murder, an indignant Shepherd said that any self-respecting Phenix City racketeer would have made sure there were no witnesses about.[6]

In the meantime, there had been no headway on identifying the owner of the fingerprints found on Patterson's car. After Fuller became a viable suspect, however, state investigator Willie Painter in mid-September asked the FBI to compare the prints with those of Fuller, who had originally been fingerprinted in August for election law violations. The FBI replied that Fuller's prints were so smudged that they couldn't make a determination. Consequently, Painter and W. L. Allen went to Fuller's residence on September 21 to obtain another set. Fuller didn't know why they were going to the trouble, and again he insisted that he had not touched the car during the crime scene investigation. Two days later, Governor Persons received a call from J. Edgar Hoover. The FBI had the results of the fingerprint comparison, and Hoover wanted Persons to be the first to know: the thumbprint from the rain guard of Patterson's car matched Fuller's left thumbprint. Thrilled, Persons wanted to release the news right away. Hoover declined to give permission, saying it was up to Painter, who hadn't been informed yet. Persons never got permission, and the match remained a secret until Fuller's trial. Sykes and his staff were extremely happy about the identification, yet they were disappointed that the FBI could not identify the partial palm print or the two smeared fingerprints located near the thumbprint.[7]

Not everyone was as happy as Sykes about the fingerprint. W. L. Allen and Ben Allen didn't think it was very incriminating. There was no way to tell the age of the fingerprints, and the sight of Fuller leaning on Patterson's car, left arm and hand over the driver's-side door, was not a rare one.[8]

The FBI's identification of Fuller's prints was a major break in the case, but it didn't provide half as much excitement as the appearance of what was to become the state's star witness against Fuller, thirty-six-year-old Johnny Frank Griffin. Griffin was discovered in large part because of the Phenix City cleanup. On August 23, Sheriff Mathews announced his resignation, effective September 1. His career had effectively ended when the Democratic Committee voided his nomination, and the imposition of martial rule had relieved him of his current duties. A few weeks later, when General Hanna threatened to charge him with willful neglect of office if he didn't resign, Mathews didn't hesitate. He rode to Montgomery with Hanna and Lamar Murphy, his successor, to personally deliver his resignation to Governor Persons. Mathews's resignation represented more than just another sledgehammer blow to the old Phenix City foundation. It allowed Murphy to jump into the cleanup and murder investigation four and a half months before he was to take office.[9]

Murphy, forty-one, was a former boxing instructor from Troy who had settled into running his own gas station in Phenix City over the last eighteen years. Tall, intense, and "nervous as a cat," according to one contemporary, Murphy replaced the cowboy-type outfit worn by his predecessors with a more sedate business suit. Well liked by much of the surrounding community, he had a tendency to call everyone "Doc" after the Bugs Bunny cartoons.[10]

Shortly after Murphy took office, a local mechanic told him that Johnny Frank Griffin was going around town claiming to have seen

Fuller at the murder scene shortly before Patterson was killed. Murphy brought Griffin in for questioning, and in a September 25 statement he related how he was out collecting accounts for his employer, the Southern Furniture Company, on the night of the murder. Shortly after 9:00, he parked in front of Bentley's Grocery. As he was getting out of his truck, he saw Patterson and Fuller standing at the door of the Coulter Building. Griffin correctly described the clothes they were wearing and made an important observation: Fuller had a gun in his holster while he was talking to Patterson, probably a .38. Patterson seemed to be leaving the building, and Fuller was facing him: "They were talking in a low voice and I did not understand anything they were saying. As I started across the street, going to Smitty's Grill to get a cup of coffee, they began walking around into the alley. Mr. Fuller was shaking his head. I could not understand anything they said but every once in awhile he would shake his head. I got up on the sidewalk, in front of the Elite Café, and went on up and got to the paper racks in front of Smitty's Grill." Griffin then heard shots coming from the direction of the Coulter Building. Cautiously retracing his steps, he was within three feet of the alley when Patterson stepped out onto the sidewalk, made a right turn, took a few steps, and fell to the ground. Without waiting around, Griffin re-crossed the street, got into his truck, and went home.[11]

Sykes had some questions for Griffin as well. Griffin reluctantly agreed to another interview, and two weeks later Sykes and Prier accompanied Murphy to pick up Griffin in Columbus. Careful not to be seen by the wrong people, the group pulled into a school parking lot while Griffin told his story again. Sykes wanted to hear more about what Griffin saw after he heard the shots. Griffin said he was almost at the alley when Patterson emerged. He had blood on his face but didn't have his cane, which Griffin was sure had been in Patterson's hand as he walked with Fuller down the street seconds earlier. After Patterson reached the front of Seymour's Dress Shop, his knees buckled and he sank to the pavement. For a few seconds, Patterson kept moving on his stomach, trying to get up, Griffin thought. While on the sidewalk, he kept making sounds. Asked what Patterson was saying, or trying to say, Griffin thought it sounded like "Lord, have mercy on me"—at least that was the tone of it. Griffin repeated that he saw no one in front of the Coulter Building and no one in the alley.[12]

Griffin made an impressive statement, all the way down to his detailed description of Patterson's cane. But Fuller had seven witnesses who supported his claim that he arrived at the jail at about 8:05, a full hour before Patterson was killed, and stayed there until at least 9:10, when he rushed out at the news of Patterson's murder. Sheriff Mathews, jailer Ben Clark, assistant jailer Johnny Dees, Deputy Aaron Smith and his brother, Robert Lee Smith, highway patrolman George Phillips, and ABC agent Curtis Deason all swore that Fuller was at the jail at the time Patterson was killed. Perhaps one or two of these statements could be ignored or explained away as part of the Phenix City crowd, but not all of them. Both Phillips, a visiting driver's license examiner, and Deason, an ABC agent who had recently been assigned to east Alabama, had little reason to commit perjury on Fuller's behalf. Phillips, in fact, had been quite insulted by any suggestion that he might cover up for Fuller. He disliked the man intensely, offering the opinion that he should be in the penitentiary.[13]

In August, Painter had considered Fuller's alibi so airtight that he urged Sykes to disregard Taylor and Ryals. But after Griffin's appearance, Painter took another look at the statements of Fuller's alibi witnesses and discovered a common thread: in describing events and their sequence, none of them had been paying much attention to the clock and could only guess that they saw Fuller at the jail from 8:05 until Patterson was killed about an hour later. When prodded by investigators, however, each offered an opinion of the time in relation to either sunset and darkness or other events. A thought occurred to Painter. Fuller's alibi witnesses weren't lying, but given their lack of precision in relation to the clock, perhaps they were mistaken.[14]

To prove his point, Painter obtained an official U.S. Weather Bureau meteorology report for east Alabama on June 18. According to the report, sunset occurred at precisely 7:50 P.M., with good visibility remaining for twenty minutes and darkness settling in twenty minutes later, at about 8:30. With this report and a little arithmetic, Painter concluded that Fuller did not arrive at the jail until after 9:00.[15]

Take Sheriff Mathews's statement, for example. At about 8:00 P.M., Joe Mathews (no relation), the owner of a filling station in Seale, called the sheriff to report that he had received a bad check. The sheriff drove to Seale, a trip that would have taken twenty-two minutes at his normal speed of sixty miles an hour. Mathews calculated that he spent about fifteen minutes at the station talking to employees and the suspect, whom he then brought back to Phenix City. Allowing another twenty-two minutes to return to Phenix City (and Mathews said he was in no hurry), he would not have arrived back at the jail until approximately 9:00, not 8:30–8:40 as he had estimated in his first statement. Even then, Mathews said he arrived before Fuller did.[16]

Ben Clark, the Russell County jailer, estimated that he had arrived at the jail around 8:55 and recalled that Fuller remained there until he and Mathews rushed out about thirty-five minutes later on their way to the murder scene. But Clark had calculated his arrival time as twenty-five to forty minutes after dark, which, according to Painter's calculations, could have been as late as 9:10. Highway patrolman George Phillips's statement as to Fuller's whereabouts was also based on his recollection of when darkness fell. Phillips said it was "about dark" when he went to a local café, where he spent about twenty-five minutes eating before he walked back to the jail. At that time, Mathews and Fuller had not yet arrived. But if Phillips's perception of "about dark" was correct, Painter figured it would have been about 9:00 when he arrived at the jail, not 8:15 as Phillips believed. Indeed, Phillips didn't see Fuller and Mathews until Phillips had returned from the rear of the jail, where he had brushed his teeth.

ABC agent Curtis Deason, Deputy Aaron Smith, Robert Lee Smith, and assistant jailer Johnny Dees could only guess at the time when they first saw Fuller by relating their activities to other events. Even their vague statements, when closely examined, did not support Fuller's assertion that he was at the jail at 9:05. These four witnesses all agreed that Fuller and Mathews went to the rear of the jail at the same time they left—Aaron Smith accompanying Deason on a liquor raid, Dees and Robert Lee Smith heading to Smitty's for ice cream. Dees recalled hearing a siren as they left the jail. On the way to Smitty's, they saw the gathering crowd and learned what had happened. By that time, the ambulance had already taken away the body. Dees then ran back to the jail to tell Mathews and Fuller about Patterson's murder. According to Clark, Dees was gone about eight minutes. Thus, Painter concluded, Patterson was already shot by the time Fuller and Mathews went to the rear of the jail for their private conversation.[17]

But even if Painter had found a defect in Fuller's alibi, there were some huge problems emerging with the three witnesses who contradicted Fuller's alibi. The first concerned Johnny Frank Griffin. Ben Allen and W. L. Allen, the two investigators assigned the task of tracking all potential witnesses in the area of the murder, were especially skeptical. Over the past two months or so they had spent hundreds of hours interviewing people who had been in the area at the time of the killing, determining their exact locations and movements. None of the three witnesses standing at the door of Smitty's—Leonard David Powell, the man who was on his way into Smitty's for hamburgers, and teenagers Jimmy Sanders and Hugh Buchanan—ever mentioned seeing a man who fit Griffin's description within the small triangle between the Coulter Building, Bentley's Grocery, and Smitty's Grill. Nor did Powell's wife, her sister, or her sister's husband, who were waiting in the car in front of Smitty's. Nor did Mrs. Bentley and her hired hand, Hubert Tharp, who had no recollection of Griffin or his truck parked in front of the store. And Griffin's claim that he saw Fuller walking with Patterson from the front door of the Coulter Building to the alley was directly contradicted by Jimmy Sanders and Jimmy Kirkland, who, as they were headed south on Fifth Avenue from the Palace Theater, were close enough to see Patterson retrieve his dropped keys from the sidewalk in front of the Coulter Building. Neither one mentioned Fuller or any other person in Patterson's immediate vicinity.[18]

When investigators began their routine check on Griffin's history to establish his veracity, they were appalled. Griffin had been charged on several occasions with nonsupport and disorderly conduct. He had been married four times. In 1941 his third wife filed bigamy charges against him, and Griffin pleaded guilty in exchange for probation. He probably wouldn't have gotten that if he hadn't talked a local minister into testifying that he was a changed man. As soon as the judge released him on probation, Griffin went straight to Phenix City and severely beat his ex-wife. In no time at all, Griffin was behind bars again in Dothan, this time with the probation revoked.[19]

It got worse. While Griffin was awaiting trial in Dothan, county jailers found him one morning covered with an unexplainable rash all along his left side. A medical examination revealed that Griffin had actually pricked himself hundreds of times from head to toe with a straight pin. The local sheriff sent Griffin directly to Bryce State

Hospital, the state mental institution, where he remained for three weeks. According to his admission form, Griffin arrived with self-inflicted cuts and burns; the doctors said that in addition to the pinpricks, he had set his clothes on fire. It was apparently not an act. While Griffin was at Bryce, doctors diagnosed him as psychoneurotic. After his hospitalization he stood trial in Dothan, was convicted on the bigamy charge, and served his full term at Atmore State Prison. Investigator Prier contacted Griffin's lawyer in that case, J. Norton Mullins Jr., who recalled, "Griffin was a pitiful case, he was certainly crazy in 1941 and I would not believe him on his oath in a court of law."[20]

There were also the conflicting statements of cabbie James Taylor and Eufaula truck driver Fred Ryals. The issue was resolved with the discovery that Ryals had a criminal record and a reputation for lying. Probate Judge Marshall Williams of Barbour County wrote to Painter that Ryals was "not of good character and would lie if he thought it would help him." A background check on Taylor, however, produced only some insignificant traffic fines and, slightly more disturbing given the by now $10,000 reward, a bad credit report. True, Taylor's story had some weaknesses, as the Allens' experiments showed, but only Sykes and his staff knew that, and there was no reason to let anyone else know. If Fuller came to trial, he could hire a lawyer and perform his own experiments. By the process of elimination, then, Ryals was out, Taylor was in.[21]

Although investigators had little physical evidence to work with, they did have the three bullets from Patterson's body, and these represented potentially the most significant leads in the case. The science of ballistic evidence by 1954 was reliable enough, legally speaking, that such evidence was admissible in court. Spent bullets, provided they remained intact, could be matched to the gun from which they were fired because microscopic manufacturing differences leave distinctive rifling marks on each projectile as it travels the length of the barrel. In effect, the gun leaves a unique fingerprint on each bullet it fires. More than that, rifling characteristics provide a good clue to the make and model of the gun a bullet was fired from, showing investigators what kind of gun to look for.

Based on the two bullets taken intact from Patterson's body, investigators in the Patterson case had a good idea what they were looking for: a Colt .38 caliber. Dr. Rehling and Wendell Sowell tested at least fourteen guns during the investigation, but none matched. Most were confiscated from various suspects, including Hoyt Shepherd, Godwin Davis, Albert Fuller, and two alleged hit men in the area. Some no one claimed, like the one retrieved by Sergeant Ratigan from a jailhouse desk during the National Guard takeover in July. Once, when investigators learned that a Phenix City individual had sent a revolver to the Colt factory in Hartford, Connecticut, for repairs, Sykes asked the Connecticut State Police to quietly obtain the gun, test-fire it, and send the bullets to Alabama.[22]

A determined effort to link Fuller to the bullets that caused Patterson's death continued throughout the summer and fall. In an October 12 raid on Fuller's apartment, the National Guard confiscated seventeen rounds of ammunition consisting of seven different makes and models of .38-caliber bullets. Having failed to tie any of Fuller's guns to the bullets taken from Patterson's body through ballistics tests, Rehling and Sowell performed spectrographic analyses on the confiscated bullets to see if there were any manufacturing similarities. One, a Super-X .38 Special, was similar in chemical composition to the bullet taken from Patterson's mouth, but Rehling sounded a note of caution in this "match." In a cover letter to Sykes, he pointed out that "the identical metal content identified in this particular instance would also exist as between any other specimens of ammunition from that particular lot of manufacture." It was a match, but not a totally convincing one.[23]

Investigators plodded on. By this time both the National Guard and I & I had combed through Fuller's house at least three times. If Fuller had ever possessed the gun that killed Patterson, it was long gone. But maybe it wasn't necessary to produce the gun. In late October, Maury Smith had an idea: if it could be proved that the bullets from Patterson's body matched bullets known to have been fired from one of Fuller's guns in the past, it would be the legal equivalent of matching the murder bullets to a gun still in Fuller's possession.[24]

It was well known around Phenix City that Fuller had killed two men in the line of duty during his tenure as a Russell County deputy. In March 1949, a second-rate bootlegger by the name of Guy Hargett allegedly pulled a gun on Fuller during a liquor raid at Hargett's home. Standing just a few feet away, Fuller shot Hargett five times. The second man killed was Franklin Johns, another small-time hood, who robbed the Manhattan Café in September 1950. Johns and an accomplice escaped with $3,000 and two bullets the bartender had pumped into Johns on the way out. Wounded and seeking to throw off police, Johns had his partner let him off, with the money, at an isolated cemetery. Minutes later, the partner hit another car head-on, killing both drivers, but not before the dying accomplice confessed where Johns was hiding. Fuller and ABC agent Ben Scroggins tracked Johns to the cemetery, where, Fuller claimed, Johns popped up from behind a headstone and leveled his gun at Scroggins. Fuller let loose, emptying both pistols. The $3,000 was never found, although local fortune hunters practically dug up the graveyard over the next few weeks.[25]

No one disputed that Fuller had killed these men, using his gun and his bullets, and even Fuller admitted it with some pride. Smith now conjectured that one of the guns used in these shootings could have been the one used to murder Patterson. There was only one way to find out. On November 4, Sykes ordered that the bodies of Hargett and Johns be exhumed. Later that afternoon, Smith, Rehling, and Sowell watched as workers dug up Hargett's remains from a Columbus cemetery. After the coffin was hauled to the surface, Sowell and Rehling recovered one of the five bullets Fuller had unloaded on the suspect five years before. This bullet, a lead .38, had five lands and grooves with a right-hand twist. Sowell concluded that it had been fired from a Smith and Wesson, not the Colt type used in Patterson's murder.[26]

The process was repeated the next day at Johns's grave in Waycross, Georgia. Like the round retrieved from Hargett, this bullet was a lead .38 fired from a Smith and Wesson. So nothing was proved—except, as Maury Smith said later, that "I didn't like worth a dang being with Dr. Rehling when he pulled those caskets out of that cemetery."[27]

Despite the lack of an exact ballistics match, significant physical evidence—particularly the fingerprint—tied Fuller to the crime. Arch Ferrell was a different matter. So far, there was only motive—everything else was circumstantial, and it didn't amount to much. Any competent lawyer would blow it out of the water. Something concrete was needed to tie Ferrell to the scene.

That revelation came from Quinnie Kelley, the forty-six-year-old janitor of the Russell County Courthouse. Less than a week after Patterson was gunned down, Kelley contacted I & I chief Joe Smelley and investigator John Williams to tell them that on the night of the murder he had run some rowdy kids off the courthouse lawn for disturbing the Boy Scout honor hearing when he happened to look up and see Ferrell in his office, examining books in his bookcase. After the hearing let out, Kelley made a routine walk around the building to make sure that lights were off and windows closed. He was sure that Ferrell's lights were off at that time. While he was on the east-side steps, the side facing Fifth Avenue, he heard gunshots just as he looked at his watch. It was precisely 9:05. Seconds later, as he approached the north side of the courthouse, he saw a man run from the direction of the Coulter Building, turn right on Fourteenth Street, and stop by the flagpole in front of the post office, at which point Kelley lost sight of him. Did Kelley know the man? No, said Kelly, he didn't recognize him. Looking at Kelley's thick glasses, Williams believed him.[28]

Kelley had stuck by the story throughout the summer, but on October 26 he finally identified the man he saw as Arch Ferrell. The reason he was finally coming forward with the whole story, Kelley told investigators, was because he had heard that they were about to arrest Albert Fuller for the murder. He couldn't let them arrest the wrong man.[29]

Initially, detectives assumed that the murder was the work of one gunman and alternately investigated Ferrell and Fuller. This was because Ross Gibson, the elderly dishwasher at Smitty's, said he saw one man fleeing through the lot behind the Coulter Building moments after he heard the shots. As a result, it was never clear who the prime suspect should be; the question was constantly Fuller *or* Ferrell. But as the summer ended, something clicked in the collective mind of the men investigating Patterson's murder, and the new proposition became Fuller *and* Ferrell. The impetus came from two Phenix City neighbors, Emmitt Fulgham and James Young, two family men who went to the crime scene with scores of other Phenix City residents to watch the investigation in progress.[30]

Not long after Fulgham and Young arrived, they saw Ferrell pull up. His appearance caused an appreciable stir among the crowd, and several people pointed out the circuit solicitor. After conferring with police, Ferrell walked up to the passenger side of the car, and, to Fulgham's and Young's astonishment, rubbed his hands over the car door and window. The two men knew the action was reckless, but they had no way of knowing what investigators discovered in September: that the one identifiable print found on the car belonged to Fuller, not Ferrell.[31]

So why was Ferrell rubbing down the car? Assuming that he knew what he was doing, Ferrell obviously was at the scene with Fuller, or for some reason knew that Fuller killed Patterson and was taking a tremendous risk to protect him. With this information, investigators reviewed their notes to look for further signs of collusion between Fuller and Ferrell. Both Abbie Cochran, the proprietor of the Elite Café, and Margaret Sanks, the Elite's night cook, had seen two men standing in front of the Coulter Building moments before Patterson was shot. At the time Sanks was interviewed, Sykes believed they were two of the furniture movers, but in light of Fulgham's and Young's statements, investigators considered the possibility that it was Fuller and Ferrell.[32]

As the pieces of the puzzle fell into place, investigators offered various murder scenarios. Most agreed that Fuller, possibly in a final but unsuccessful attempt to negotiate an understanding with the incoming attorney general, met Patterson at the Coulter Building and walked with him into the alley. Ferrell was either already there or arrived shortly after. It was almost certainly Fuller who shot Patterson. It was his fingerprint on the driver's side of Patterson's car (in fact, it appeared from the smudged palm print and fingerprints that Fuller had actually pinned Patterson with the door first). It was Fuller who was walking around with an empty holster after the murder. And it was Fuller who knew guns and had twice used them to kill. Ferrell, on the other hand, wasn't much of a shooter, and in any case he didn't own a .38. And if Ferrell was wiping down the passenger side of the car, didn't it follow that he was standing on that side of the car when Patterson was shot? After Fuller fired four shots, the two then ran down the alley, westward, away from Fifth Avenue, and turned south behind the Coulter Building. There, investigators reasoned, they separated; Ferrell took a left and headed eastward through the post office loading dock driveway and reemerged on Fifth Avenue, where Kelley saw him trotting toward the courthouse. If he had been a few seconds faster, he would have come face to face with Jimmy Kirkland. As it happened, Kirkland left his spot on Fifth Avenue to see about Patterson. Fuller turned to the right, heading southwest, and appeared on Fourteenth Street, where cabbie James Taylor saw him jump into a waiting car. It would have taken only a couple of minutes to circle back around to the jailhouse.[33]

That was the basic theory, though there were points of disagreement. Barton expressed the opinion that Ferrell watched the whole thing from his courthouse window, reporting Fuller's escape to Garrett. W. L. Allen and Ben Allen refused to believe that Fuller was involved at all. There were some kinks in the story, to be sure. For example, if Ferrell was standing on the passenger side when Fuller shot Patterson, then Ferrell was lucky to be alive, as the bullet hole in the window indicated. And who was driving the car Fuller hopped into? Although Sykes never put any credence in the story, many in the RBA believed it was actually Red Porter, who owned a large, dark late-model car. Investigators looked into the allegation; Porter checked out of the Jefferson Davis Hotel in Montgomery, eighty miles away, a little more than an hour after the murder, making it highly unlikely that he was in Phenix City at 9:05. But for the attorney general's staff, those questions were all academic. They weren't interested in details—they were making a case. Legally, it made no difference who fired the shots. Both assailants were guilty provided the state could place them at the scene.[34]

One detail Sykes could not ignore was Ferrell's long-distance call to Garrett at the moment Patterson was murdered. Except for Barton, the consensus was that somehow Garrett and Ferrell were lying, that in reality Garrett had held an empty telephone line while Ferrell walked across Fourteenth Street and killed Patterson, that the call had been placed specifically to establish Ferrell's alibi. In September, Prier and Godwin believed they had solved the riddle of Ferrell's alibi—with *Fuller's* alibi. They had thought it unusual that it was Johnny Dees who had finally informed Fuller and Mathews of the murder, some ten minutes after it occurred. The reason why no one called the jail, conjectured Prier, was that the line was busy. Not counting prisoners, there were four persons in the jail that night after Deason, Dees, and the Smith brothers left: Ben Clark, patrolman Phillips, and, in a back room that served as the jailer's sleeping quarters, Sheriff Mathews and Albert Fuller. Neither Clark nor Phillips was on the main telephone line, but the back room had an extension. Prier and Godwin concluded, "This would suggest the possibility that the phone calls to the Redmont Hotel . . . were made from the jail phone by Ralph Mathews or Albert Fuller for Arch Ferrell, that being the reason the calls were charged to Ferrell's office phone, possibly the reason too the sheriff was not notified of the killing by telephone, because the jail phone was busy." It was as good an explanation as any, and it might convince a jury. There was only one major problem. Prier and Godwin's explanation conceded Fuller's alibi. Prosecutors could not argue that Fuller was at the crime scene committing the murder *and*, at the same time, in Clark's private quarters when the alibi telephone call was being made. By now Sykes was going after both Ferrell and Fuller, so the matter was dropped. The other problem with the explanation was that Southern Bell officials had said it was practically impossible for Ferrell to have been anywhere but his office between 8:35 and 9:15. Luckily for Sykes, Ferrell and Garrett didn't know that, and in 1954 there was no legal requirement to tell them.[35]

So where did that leave Garrett? The problem was how to charge a suspect with murder when he was 160 miles from the scene of the crime. Conspiracy was difficult to prove without direct evidence of prior collusion among the principals. Sykes ordered investigators to trace Garrett's movements for that day and identify telephones he might have made calls from, but nothing substantial came of these efforts. Detectives found no evidence that Garrett talked to Ferrell at either the Stockyards Café or the downtown Birmingham barbershop, where he had stopped for a trim between grand jury sessions.[36]

There was, however, another avenue of prosecution that might be applied to Garrett, and Sykes's staff went to work on it. If the supposition was accepted that Ferrell and Garrett were lying, then Garrett was, legally speaking, as culpable as Ferrell. Although the charge of aiding and abetting a murderer traditionally involved persons at the scene (as when one perpetrator holds a victim while the other beats him), legal researchers in the attorney general's office found an 1894 case in which the Alabama Supreme Court had upheld an aid-and-abet charge even though the accused had been miles away. If Ferrell could be placed at the scene of the murder, investigators reasoned, Garrett had by definition provided him with a false alibi and had thus aided and abetted Ferrell in the murder of Garrett's duly elected successor. If that could be proved in court, Garrett was as guilty of murder as the triggerman.[37]

9
Against the Peace
and Dignity of Alabama

[An unnamed county official] said unless the attorney general's
office starts presenting whatever evidence it has to the grand
jury within twelve days, the jury will be asked to undertake its
own investigation.

Columbus Ledger, November 1, 1954

Chief Deputy Albert Fuller remained bedridden throughout the summer and fall while recovering from his July 4 mishap. It was an ideal
perspective from which to watch his world crumble. In late July, special prosecutor George Johnson summoned Hilda Coulter, an RBA
Auxiliary leader and now the clerk for the reformed Russell County
Grand Jury, to ask a special favor. Shortly before Patterson's murder,
Mrs. Coulter had testified before the Democratic Party subcommittee
investigating the Brassell/Cole election contest. At that time, she had
told the subcommittee that she saw Albert Fuller marking numerous
ballots at the courthouse polling station during the most recent party
primary. Now, Johnson told her in strict secrecy, the investigators had
located an eyewitness who had incriminated Fuller in the murder of
Albert Patterson. Si Garrett had already fled to Texas, and they were
afraid that Fuller would attempt to do the same despite his supposed
back injuries. Mrs. Coulter was in a position to keep Fuller from dis-
appearing: Would she be willing to swear out a formal complaint
based on her observations during the May 4 primary? Coulter immediately went to a local judge to file charges, and on August 2, National
Guardsmen arrested Fuller on six counts of election law violations.

On September 1, Fuller in effect lost his job for good when Sheriff Mathews's resignation became effective. Chances were slim that Mathews's replacement, RBA supporter Lamar Murphy, would ever allow Fuller to return to Russell County law enforcement. Fuller was arrested again the next day, this time on a bribery indictment. He was specifically accused of taking a payoff from H. C. Harden Jr., operator of the Skyline Club, a hangout on the south side of town known for gambling and prostitution. Fuller was starting to get worried. He had shrugged off the vote fraud charge, a misdemeanor, but bribery was a felony with a potential ten-year prison sentence. Then, on October 8, the bottom fell out. The Russell County Grand Jury indicted Fuller on ten more counts of bribery with bonds totaling $10,000. This time the alleged payoffs came from Cliff Entrekin, operator of Cliff's Fish Camp, an establishment outside the city limits where patrons could just as easily order a prostitute as a plate of fried catfish. Almost as an afterthought, the grand jury indicted Fuller again on November 3 with one count each of vagrancy (the legal term for abetting prostitution) and vote fraud.[1]

The vice and corruption charges were bad enough, but it became clear very early that Sykes considered Fuller a suspect in the Patterson murder. After the July 27 raid in which the National Guard confiscated Fuller's firearms, the former chief deputy was interrogated or searched four more times. On September 2, Fuller, still in his pajamas, was taken to Sykes for questioning. Four days later, following up on Hoyt Shepherd's revelations, MacDonald Gallion grilled Fuller in his hospital room. On October 1 the National Guard again raided Fuller's apartment and conducted a two-hour search, confiscating records that further incriminated Fuller in vote fraud. Ten days later the guard yet again raided Fuller's home, this time taking seventeen bullets of various makes. On October 16, the guard questioned him after he publicly invited a lie detector test. Fuller cut the interrogation short, complaining of chest pains, and was taken to the hospital for observation.[2]

Fuller was not alone in his troubles. What was happening in Phenix City in the fall of 1954 was nothing less than a revolution. By the first of December, the Russell County Grand Jury had indicted 141 persons on 734 counts, a new record for any Alabama grand jury. The list of indicted or convicted persons read like a who's who of Phenix City and Russell County's most prominent officials. Just as in 1916, the proceedings were swift, merciless, and judicially questionable. Under General Hanna, the Alabama National Guardsmen got the job done, but they had little training in search and seizure, and Hanna wasn't inclined to make sure that they did. Their approach to cleaning up Phenix City was to act as if war had been declared. In many ways, it had. Some members of the attorney general's staff were concerned how the courts would look at the guard's disregard for search warrants, but no one was willing to complain about Hanna's tactics. He was getting the job done.[3]

Albert Fuller was one of the more visible indictees. On November 15, the first of his bribery cases involving Cliff's Fish Camp came to trial. Fuller had retained local attorneys Joe Smith and Pelham Ferrell (Arch Ferrell's brother) to represent him. Hoping to delay the trial, Smith and Ferrell claimed that because of Fuller's spinal injuries, suffered more than four months previously, appearing in court could be detrimental to his health. Although the two doctors who had been treating Fuller backed that claim, Judge Jones rejected their testimony and ordered Fuller's lawyers to produce him immediately. Shortly thereafter, Fuller, clad in pajamas and a bathrobe, arrived in the courtroom strapped to a hospital gurney. For those who had not seen him since early July, the change in the former chief deputy's appearance was shocking. No longer the frightening bully, Fuller appeared emaciated and helpless, his voice weak and wavering the few times he spoke. As special prosecutor George Johnson characterized him as a "traitor and would-be dictator," a man who "put a badge on over a black heart and betrayed the people of his county and his state" for a "mess of paltry, stinking dollars," Fuller trembled like a little boy called before the school principal. It took the jury a little over an hour to convict Fuller and sentence him to seven years in prison. Smith and Ferrell served notice that they would appeal the conviction. In the meantime, Fuller was sent home under armed guard to continue his convalescence.[4]

Arch Ferrell's home was never raided, but he had a good idea where he stood, especially after his ten-hour interrogation on July 9. In some ways, the whispers around Phenix City were worse than a straightforward accusation. As an attorney, Ferrell was accustomed to a formal organization of prosecution and defense, but he had little idea how to address rumor and innuendo. By July 24 he was worried enough to invite Fred Andersen to his home for the first press interview since Patterson's murder. Ferrell stated for the record that he did not kill Albert Patterson and did not know who did, but that if the talk around town was to be believed, he was the primary suspect and the grand jury would soon be asked to return an indictment against him. They would be wasting their time, he said, because he could prove, with the records of the Southern Bell Telephone Company, that he was speaking to Si Garrett at the time of Patterson's murder.[5]

Actually, Ferrell (along with everyone else) overestimated Sykes's readiness. It would be some time before the grand jury heard the first witness in the murder investigation. But Ferrell had plenty of other problems to deal with just the same. He, like Fuller, was on a downward slide. His July 31 ouster by the state Democratic Executive Committee, voiding his nomination as circuit solicitor, was just the beginning. On August 4 a National Guard patrol pulled Ferrell over and arrested him for drunk driving. Hugh Sparrow, a *Birmingham News* reporter who witnessed Ferrell's arrest and incarceration, said Ferrell was mostly incoherent when he arrived at the jail, but occasionally the words could be made out. Ferrell kept insisting that while he hated Albert Patterson, he didn't "gun him to death." He offered "three cheers for Albert Fuller" and "three cheers for Carrol E. Bagby." Sykes's investigators took nothing Ferrell said lightly, and they started tracking down Bagby, a small-time Phenix City gambler, as soon as they heard of the incident, but nothing indicated Bagby's involvement in the murder.[6]

One day after Ferrell's arrest for drunk driving, Judge Jones, in his capacity as acting president of the Alabama Bar Association, demanded that the bar's grievance committee begin disbarment proceedings against Ferrell, Garrett, and Reid because of their vote fraud indictments (although none had been brought to trial yet). Jones said, "A criminally-minded person . . . with a license to practice law is a deadly menace."[7] On August 16, the Phenix City cleanup began taking civilians. Three years earlier, Colonel J. T. Johnson, director of the state's Selective Service System, had engineered Patterson's ouster from the Russell County Draft Board by appointing Ferrell's father, Henry A., and Jimmy Putnam, a good friend of Ferrell's. Now Colonel Johnson demanded their resignations, threatening to have President Eisenhower kick them off the board if they didn't resign voluntarily. Putnam eventually gave in, but H. A. Ferrell in effect said that the president could fire him if he wanted, but he wasn't quitting.[8]

On August 28, against all predictions, a three-judge panel in Birmingham ruled that the state Democratic Executive Committee was within its authority when it stripped Ferrell of his nomination. Ferrell said he would appeal to the state supreme court, but he never did. And on November 3, the Russell County Grand Jury indicted him and other former Phenix City and Russell County officials (including Fuller) for vote fraud stemming from the May 4 primary. Ferrell, along with Phenix City attorney V. Cecil Curtis, was specifically charged with distributing a sample ballot that did not have the required "Paid Political Advertisement" logo on it. In a December 6 hearing, Ferrell pleaded guilty and paid a $200 fine; Fuller's guilty plea cost him $250. Ferrell's admission of vote fraud and Fuller's conviction for bribery seemed to prove a point in relation to the Patterson murder. The two men were, whether by their own admission or by conviction through a trial jury, crooked officials. Certainly no one believed they were angels, but their convictions in a court of law made it more believable that they could have killed Albert Patterson.[9]

Attorney General Si Garrett was far removed from the vice and corruption trials in Phenix City, yet his legal problems continued to make headlines. After his July car wreck, Garrett continued to recuperate in a Waynesboro, Mississippi, hospital while his lawyers, Roderick Beddow and G. Ernest Jones, tried first to stave off Emmett Perry's lunacy hearing and next to quash the vote fraud indictment altogether. On September 10 they laid out their case before Judge Robert Wheeler in Birmingham, maintaining that under Alabama law, lunacy proceedings could be instituted only against a confined suspect. Although Garrett had been locked up briefly while awaiting bond, he had already been released by the time Perry actually filed the petition in court. Therefore, forcing their client to submit to a lunacy hearing, which could conceivably result in involuntary commitment, would in effect cause him to surrender his freedom without due process of law.[10]

As for the vote fraud indictment, Beddow and Jones argued that because Garrett had testified before the Jefferson County Grand Jury, he could not be prosecuted. Under Alabama law, providing grand jury testimony on the matter of vote fraud automatically gave him immunity from prosecution. Perry countered that Garrett had waived his right to immunity when he appeared, and produced the transcript to prove it. Beddow and Jones strenuously protested the introduction of grand jury records and said that Garrett could not waive what amounted to a constitutional guarantee. Wheeler agreed with Perry, refused to throw out the vote fraud indictment, and ordered the lunacy hearing to proceed. Garrett's lawyers then served notice of appeal to the state supreme court to address the legality of both the vote fraud indictment and the sanity hearing.[11]

On September 27 the state supreme court rejected Garrett's vote fraud appeal but agreed to hear arguments on his lunacy motion. Solicitor Perry maintained that the only reason he wanted Garrett to submit to a lunacy hearing was for humanitarian purposes. Under common law, an insane person was not to be brought to trial or imprisoned but rather sent to a facility for treatment. Perry was certainly justified in requesting the hearing, because "everyone had heard of [Garrett's] peculiar actions." Beddow took strong exception to that contention. He accused Perry and Wheeler of conspiring beforehand to slap the lunacy motion on Garrett: "They want you to believe it was all done after Si gave himself up, but that's a lot of tommyrot. This is the first time I have ever heard of a solicitor preparing a defendant's case, but I am sure you know as I do what the real reason was behind this lunacy motion and it wasn't to protect Si." The court took the arguments under advisement.[12]

In 1954, Roderick Beddow was widely considered the best criminal defense lawyer in Alabama. A Birmingham resident since the age of three, Beddow had followed his father's footsteps in the legal profession, studying pre-law at Washington and Lee University before going on to law school at the University of Alabama. Upon graduation, he joined the family practice. Beddow was no stranger to Phenix City. In 1946 he had been appointed as a special prosecutor to try Hoyt Shepherd for the murder of Fayette Leebern. Beddow had lost that case to Shepherd's winning defense team, which included Albert Patterson and Arch Ferrell. Now, at the age of fifty-five, Beddow was at the height of his career. Silver-haired and barrel-chested, he resembled a well-tailored lion. Naturally outgoing and quick with a joke, he dominated any gathering; in the courtroom there was no way to ignore him.[13]

Beddow's law partner in the Phenix City cases was forty-two-year-old Bessemer native Robert Gwin, who had gone to Washington in 1932 as Senator Hugo Black's page boy and worked his way through George Washington School of Law. He returned to Alabama in 1940 to open his first law office. Three years later he was appointed assistant U.S. attorney; three years after that he joined Beddow's firm. From his days in Washington, Gwin retained a keen interest in politics. He was active in the state Democratic Committee, an elected delegate to the 1952 national convention, and a co-manager of Folsom's 1954 campaign.[14]

It surprised no one when several well-to-do Phenix City gamblers sought out Beddow soon after the blue-ribbon grand jury handed down the first indictments. The local attorneys were fine for drawing up wills and dealing with the sham raids of the local police, but the Phenix City cleanup was a serious matter. Five of Phenix City's better-known kingpins—Godwin Davis Sr., Godwin Davis Jr., H. C. Harden, Doug Abney, and Shorty Myrick—knew that when it came to lawyers, you got what you paid for. When the grand jury indicted them on various racketeering charges, they didn't hesitate to hire the best they could find.

Beddow approached his new clients' problem in typical sledgehammer fashion. In a preemptive strike, he accused the RBA of controlling the current jury list, pointing out that while there were between six thousand and seven thousand qualified jurors in Russell County, only about seven hundred names had been placed in the jury box, therefore making the indictments fraudulent. Beddow bypassed Special Judge Jones and filed the complaint with Judge Julius Hicks, who still retained noncleanup judicial duties. Hicks promptly ordered the Russell County Jury Commission to show cause why the jury box should not be emptied and refilled with the names of all eligible male voters over twenty-one years old. The maneuver caused Sykes, who normally concerned himself only with the murder investigation, to step in. He first requested that Judge Hicks turn the matter over to

Judge Jones; when Hicks refused, Sykes filed a writ of prohibition with the state supreme court to keep Hicks from hearing Beddow's motion.[15]

Just as quickly, the court ordered Hicks to remove himself from the matter, agreeing with Sykes that only Judge Jones could hear cleanup cases and related matters. Beddow subsequently refiled the petition with Jones, but in a preemptive move, special prosecutor George Johnson filed a motion to dismiss it. During the hearing on Johnson's motion, it became clear why Beddow had wanted to avoid Jones in the first place: the petition was highly critical of the judge himself. In addition to charging that his clients had been indicted by an illegally constituted grand jury, Beddow had requested a change of venue based on widespread newspaper publicity, public statements by General Hanna, and "widespread fear" resulting from the heavy-handed tactics of the National Guard occupation. And, the petition went on, Judge Jones was "acceptable" to the RBA and "hostile" to the defense. Making such an accusation was risky, given Jones's easily offended sense of honor. Solicitor Bulley Fowler watched the judge flush crimson as Johnson read excerpts from what he termed "this damnable petition." Having done his homework, Johnson pointed out that Beddow had in fact violated the Alabama Code of Legal Ethics, which prohibited counsel from attacking a judge in his own court. Then he brought up the fact that the code had been written by none other than Jones's father, former governor Thomas Goode Jones. Too angry to continue, the judge made no offer for Beddow to respond but simply banged his gavel, signaling a recess. On the way out of the courtroom, Beddow complained to Johnson, "Damn, George, you done gone and brought Walter's daddy into it. Ain't no telling what the hell he will do now." When court reconvened, Jones told Beddow that he expected an apology before the week was out. On Friday, Beddow ate crow.[16]

Nevertheless, Judge Jones granted Beddow's request for a hearing, possibly to allow Johnson to dig Beddow's grave a little deeper. While there was plenty to argue, Johnson focused on Beddow's assertion that Jones was unfair. In countering that argument, the ever-dramatic Johnson proclaimed that Judge Jones was a man who had "never lowered his lance of honor." For the likes of Beddow to attack Jones was like "a gnat assaulting an elephant, or the rays from one lone candle trying to annihilate the rays of the blazing sun." Beddow had barely begun his plea when Jones announced that he had heard enough. The fact that only seven hundred names were in the jury box was not reason enough to refill the box, nor had the defense proved the need for a change of venue. There was no doubt that the cleanup had been a major topic in the press, but that didn't mean that the coverage had prejudiced anyone, and Beddow hadn't proved that it did. And, Jones added, he would compare his record any day with that of any of Beddow's clients.[17]

Pressure on Sykes to present an indictment continued to grow. General Hanna, Solicitors Johnson and Fowler, and Judge Jones made it look easy. But Sykes and his staff, by now almost as large as the National Guard detail, had nothing new, or so it seemed. In truth, Sykes had had his suspects since August. He probably had enough evidence for indictments from any grand jury, but certainly enough for the reformed Russell County Grand Jury. Sykes, however, insisted on an ironclad case for a trial jury, and he was still a long way from that. It is unclear at what point he would have felt comfortable going before the grand jury, but that decision was taken out of his hands.

On October 20, nine days after Johnny Frank Griffin's interview with Sykes, one of the state investigators told a reporter that they knew who the killer was: "We feel sure we have a good sound case against the man who did it, but there are a few loose ends to be tied up." And, as an explanation of why no one had been arrested, he said, "There may be others involved and we want to get them." When confronted with the information, other investigators corroborated the story but provided no details.[18]

If this admission had been made to dispel rumors of inactivity, it had the opposite effect. Republican gubernatorial candidate Tom Abernethy of Sylacauga, who had been fighting an uphill battle against Jim Folsom all summer and fall, used the Phenix City situation every chance he could. In a highly publicized campaign speech at Talladega, Abernethy declared that there was no good reason why the murderer wasn't behind bars. Hinting that it was because of the killer's friendship with the Folsom camp that he had not been arrested, Abernethy claimed, "This is the first time in my experience to hear of a primary murder suspect whose identity is known to officers being left to go and come as he pleases." Ever since the murder, "minnows have been raked in by the bucketful, but the big fish have not been caught. The murderer still goes his way. The people of Alabama know almost nothing of the details of one of history's biggest and foulest gang operations." If he were elected governor, Abernethy promised, the people would get the "full story," and all suspects, big or small, would be arrested.[19]

The public discovery that the attorney general's staff had a suspect had immediate ramifications. Overnight, it seemed that no one had faith in Bernard Sykes anymore. Everyone had simply run out of patience. Various newspapers reported that the Russell County Grand Jury had given Sykes an ultimatum: start presenting evidence, or the grand jury would begin its own murder investigation. Sykes himself publicly denied the story, saying that he knew nothing of the ultimatum and doubted its authenticity. Within days, Ed Strickland would claim that although the initial story was untrue, there had been an ultimatum put to Sykes on November 1 at a meeting in Montgomery with John Patterson, Governor Persons, and Chief Justice Livingston. At that meeting, according to Strickland, Sykes was given two weeks to wrap up his case.[20]

It is not clear exactly what happened next in the Patterson murder investigation. Years later, Sykes would tell friends that he was in effect superseded in the case. Who called the shots after November 1 is anyone's guess, but there were a number of people who believed that Sykes should act on what he had. First, they firmly believed that Fuller, Ferrell, and Garrett had committed the crime and that it was useless to look elsewhere. Second, they believed that Sykes had sufficient evidence to indict and convict. There was no need to wait until there was an ironclad case—if Sykes didn't have a case against the three by now, he never would. Sykes, as an appeals lawyer, was selling himself short. He didn't have to have *all* the evidence, just *enough* evidence. And third, there was a time factor. Governor Persons, who had given carte blanche to the cleanup and the murder investigation, would be out of office in seventy-five days. Incoming governor Jim Folsom had expressed support for the cleanup efforts, but he was known to have been friendly with some of the accused. Who knew what would happen after he took office?[21]

So indictments would be handed down whether Sykes was ready or not. In the meantime, all efforts would be made solely to ensure the indictments and convictions of Fuller, Ferrell, and Garrett. Witnesses who contributed to that goal were reinterviewed; anyone who didn't was ignored.

Because grand juries require only enough testimony to send a suspect to trial, prosecutors generally provide the bare minimum for an indictment. Sykes, however, wasn't taking any chances. He produced 118 witnesses, practically the entire retinue in the Patterson murder case. As reporters quickly surmised, it was a circumstantial case. What Sykes lacked in hard evidence he would make up for in sheer volume. Beginning November 29 and lasting two weeks, Sykes, Gallion, Barton, and Smith had witnesses repeat their earlier statements before the sixteen grand jurors. There were few surprises. One exception was Sergeant Robert Moore, the army mess cook who, despite his wife's protests, had earlier told Gallion and Prier that he had seen Ferrell in the alley minutes before Patterson was gunned down. Although Moore admitted that this was the story he had told investigators earlier, he now said that his wife had convinced him that it was a different night when he was traveling down Fifth Avenue. Whatever night it was, he now told the grand jury that he had been drinking and his memory was hazy. Sykes quickly excused him.[22]

There were a few other instances in which testimony did not unfold as prosecutors wanted it to. As part of setting up the crime scene, Raymond Ennis testified about the man in khaki work clothes he saw standing in the middle of Fifth Avenue. Earlier, Sykes had deduced that this man must have been Hubert Tharp, an employee at Bentley's Grocery, who stepped out onto the sidewalk with Mrs. Bentley soon after the shots were fired. But when Assistant Attorney General Maury Smith tried to establish that contention through Tharp's testimony, Tharp contradicted him at almost every turn. True, Tharp said, he was wearing khaki pants on the night of the murder, but he had just changed into a white shirt, not the khaki one Ennis had just described, nor was he wearing a cap that Ennis was positive the man standing in the street had on. Lastly, Tharp testified that he went nowhere near the vacant lot on the other side of Fifteenth Avenue, the place where Ennis said the mystery man disappeared.[23]

Despite these occasional gaffes, the presentation went fairly well.

The most sensational testimony came on Wednesday, December 1, when the grand jury heard Johnny Frank Griffin's story. The next day, Griffin slipped out of the Russell County jail, where he was being held in protective custody. I & I agents had allowed him to come and go as he pleased because, as they told National Guard jailer Sergeant Ed Ratigan, Griffin needed to get food, cigarettes, and other items. He was, after all, a free man. But Ratigan noticed that when Griffin returned, what he had needed more than anything else were a few drinks.[24]

Much has been said about Griffin's frantic efforts on December 2 to contact John Patterson and Sheriff Murphy. Later, Patterson would tell the grand jury that Griffin had come by his home about 11:00 A.M., telling his wife, Mary Jo, that he needed to talk to him. Griffin also called Murphy and left messages, the last being that he needed a ride. It's not clear what he wanted exactly, but eventually he showed up at a diner in Phenix City's Five Points neighborhood, a few blocks west of the courthouse on Fourteenth Street. According to the proprietor, Griffin had been drinking and was already belligerent. Between sips from a near-empty pint of whiskey, Griffin said he was waiting for a ride from Sheriff Murphy. Almost casually, he mentioned that he was going to kill his wife.[25]

Growing restless, Griffin went outside, where he propositioned passerby Barbara Parker. She ignored him and kept walking. At about the same time, James D. Williams, a twenty-five-year-old scoutmaster, showed up with his assistant and fifteen members of Boy Scout Troop 206. They were waiting for a city bus to take them to the Mother Mary Mission, where they were slated to take part in a Christmas program. Griffin, who by now had given up on Murphy, walked up to the group and bellowed, "Where in the hell do you think you're going? You must think this is a holiday or something." Trying to avoid a confrontation, Williams herded his troop down the street. Griffin let them go without further comment. Then he noticed another man standing a few feet away, sixteen-year-old Jerry Washington, who had silently watched the whole incident. Griffin strolled over to Washington: "You don't look like you like what I said." Washington looked away and said nothing. That wasn't good enough for Griffin. With his toe he drew an imaginary line across the sidewalk and challenged Washington: "If you don't like what I said, cross that line." Washington ignored him and turned to leave. This infuriated Griffin, who yelled, "If you don't, I will!" and slapped Washington. Washington stumbled backward, but when he regained his footing he was headed toward Griffin. As Griffin reached into his right front pocket, Washington pulled a knife and stabbed him in the neck. Stunned, Griffin stepped back and then began spitting blood. To the shocked bystanders, Washington breathed, "It wasn't my fault." Apparently, Washington and his fellow bus riders believed the wound was not serious and boarded the bus when it arrived shortly after, leaving Griffin bleeding on the sidewalk. A National Guard patrol arrived to take Griffin to the hospital, where they found a grand jury voucher in Griffin's pocket and contacted Sykes immediately.[26]

Griffin died on the operating table during emergency surgery. Later that evening, when the National Guard went to arrest Washington for Griffin's murder, the teenager burst into tears when he found out that the victim was the star witness in the Patterson murder case. Rumors flew that somehow Griffin had been silenced by the mob. John Patterson told reporters that Griffin's murder was "one of those weird coincidences that could only happen in Phenix City."[27]

The death of the only eyewitness who could positively place Fuller in the alleyway where Patterson was murdered seemed to destroy the state's case. State investigator Willie Painter told *Birmingham Post-Herald* reporter Clarke Stallworth that the case against Fuller "just drained away" when Griffin was killed. Looking back on Griffin's history, however, it is doubtful whether he could have contributed much during a trial. Undoubtedly, defense attorneys would have damaged his credibility by introducing evidence of his mental illness and criminal background. But there were no defense attorneys in the grand jury room. Sykes and his staff had made a convincing presentation.[28]

On December 9 it was all but certain that arrests were imminent. Reporters, along with Sheriff Murphy, I & I agents, and National Guardsmen, waited around the courthouse all day for something to happen. Ferrell also seemed anxious, pacing in and out of his office to chat with reporters, then finally leaving in the afternoon. At 3:26, just a few minutes after Ferrell drove out of sight, grand jurors filed into the courtroom and announced to Judge Jones that they wished to return indictments. Foreman Cloyd Tilley handed what looked like at least three to Clerk I. C. Wheelis. The first one read: "The Grand Jury of said County charge that before the finding of this Indictment that Albert Fuller, alias Albert Frederick Fuller, alias Albert F. Fuller, unlawfully and with malice aforethought, killed Albert L. Patterson with a gun or pistol against the peace and dignity of Alabama." The second indictment was identical except that Fuller's name was replaced with "Archer Bradford Ferrell."[29]

The papers were immediately whisked downstairs to the circuit clerk's office, where the door was locked as the arrest warrants were typed up. Once completed, they were delivered to Sheriff Murphy, who signaled CIOs Claude Prier and Willie Painter. The three then got into Murphy's car and headed directly toward Fuller's apartment. Even before Murphy left the courthouse, a small crowd had gathered in front of Fuller's home. They watched as the three lawmen knocked on Fuller's door, which was opened by his wife, Avon. Murphy confirmed that Fuller was at home and then announced, "I have a warrant for his arrest," as he reached into his coat pocket and found . . . nothing. Two or three minutes of embarrassment passed as he excused himself and went back to retrieve the warrant, which he had left on the front seat of his car. Murphy and the investigators went inside to serve the warrant and place Fuller under house arrest as two National Guardsmen took up positions outside the door. Characteristically, Fuller appeared undisturbed. He told the three that he had been expecting them.[30]

By now, three cars of photographers and newsmen had fallen in behind the sheriff as he headed back to the courthouse to arrest Ferrell, but Ferrell hadn't returned. The caravan then headed for Ferrell's house. Ferrell's car wasn't there when they arrived, so Murphy knocked on the door and asked Madeline where he might be. She didn't know but agreed to let the investigators wait for him in the driveway. At 4:15 Ferrell drove up. Murphy met him in the driveway and told him he was under arrest. Ferrell asked what for, and Murphy handed him the indictment, which Ferrell read ashen-faced. Ready for anything from the sometimes-explosive circuit solicitor, investigators Prier and Painter never took their eyes off Ferrell's hands. Ferrell asked if he could tell Madeline about the arrest himself. Murphy assented, and the three officers accompanied Ferrell inside, where he spoke briefly to Madeline and kissed her and his newborn daughter, Lucille Archer, good-bye.[31]

There was, of course, a third indictee. Everyone knew it was Si Garrett, but as a formality, investigators wouldn't name him until he was arrested, and they couldn't arrest him because they didn't know where he was. The only thing the attorney general's office knew for sure was that Garrett had been released from the Waynesboro hospital where he had been recovering ever since his car accident in July. No one knew where he went after that, but the logical guess was a psychiatric hospital. After a discreet search by the FBI, Garrett was located in the same Galveston hospital where his family had sent him five days after Patterson's murder.[32]

On December 11, Sheriff Murphy, Colonel Warren, and a National Guard staff attorney arrived in Galveston to serve a fugitive warrant on Garrett. The actual arrest was delayed because Murphy had failed to bring along a certified copy of the indictment, as required by Texas law. Finally, with the proper forms in hand, the Alabama lawmen and the local sheriff placed Garrett under "technical arrest." Garrett made no comment, but his doctors quickly issued a statement: "The mental and physical condition of Mr. Garrett is such that it is required that he remain in the hospital for an indefinite period of time. . . . It is affirmed that at the time of his discharge, he will return to Alabama of his own volition." In other words, Garrett would give himself up when he was ready. Sykes was stalemated again. Extradition was highly unlikely given the statement from Garrett's doctor and, back in Alabama, Rod Beddow's public notice that he would fight any attempt to extradite his client until he was well enough to stand trial.[33]

As sometimes happens when a lawyer defends a client charged with two separate crimes, Beddow had placed himself in a difficult position. In his pending state supreme court challenge to Solicitor Perry and Judge Wheeler he had insisted that the state had no right to force Garrett to undergo a psychiatric examination to determine his fitness to stand trial for the vote fraud indictment, yet he was now claiming that Garrett was unfit to stand trial for murder. On December 15 the supreme court acted on Beddow's petition, ruling that the courts had no constitutional authority to order a lunacy hearing because Garrett was not in confinement when Judge Wheeler scheduled it. Writing for the court, Justice Simpson concluded that the purpose of a lunacy hearing was to ensure that a mentally ill person was sent to a hospital rather than to prison. Consequently, "whenever a person ceases to be in jail, the purpose of the statute ceases to exist." On the other hand, the court disagreed with Beddow's corollary argument that Garrett had gained immunity from the vote fraud charge when he testified before the Jefferson County Grand Jury. The way was clear, then, for Perry to try Garrett on the vote fraud charge, but if Perry wanted to settle the question of Garrett's sanity, he would have to bring him to trial first. The question of whether Garrett could be prosecuted for anything remained academic as long as he stayed behind the walls of Galveston's John Sealy Hospital.[34]

Fuller remained in his apartment under armed guard until December 13, when General Hanna ordered him moved to Kilby Prison. The move, according to Hanna, was for Fuller's own protection. At about this time, Fuller decided to drop his local attorneys, Joe Smith and Pelham Ferrell, and hire new ones. He had little to lose; Smith and Ferrell had been unable even to slow down special prosecutors George Johnson and Bulley Fowler during the bribery trial, and this time the stakes were literally life and death. Rod Beddow and Bob Gwin were retained the same day that General Hanna hauled Fuller off to prison. Getting to work immediately, they instituted habeas corpus proceedings to have Fuller released on bond, then had their client issue a public statement from his security cell in the prison hospital: "I did not kill Albert Patterson nor do I have any knowledge as to the slaying of Albert Patterson. . . . I considered myself a friend of Mr. Patterson and at no time did Mr. Patterson and I have any difficulty or misunderstanding. Mr. Patterson did many favors for me, and I trust and hope that the person who killed him will be apprehended and tried for his tragic murder."[35]

Of the three indictees, Ferrell was the only one taken directly to jail upon his arrest. He didn't fare well there. By the next morning he was complaining of stomach pains and asking for a prescription nerve medicine he had left at home. He, too, wrote out a statement for reporters: "I did not kill Albert Patterson and I had nothing to do with the killing of him. I do not know who killed him and do not know who does know. I am not a murderer, and I shall be ready to stand trial before a jury of my fellowmen."[36]

The press assumed that Beddow and Gwin would represent Ferrell as well as Fuller. Because the two men were accused of the same crime, a fully coordinated defense was a logical strategy. Ferrell, though, had compelling reasons to locate another set of lawyers. First, Beddow was already representing Garrett, and now he was taking on Fuller. Could he really devote full attention to Ferrell's case? Second, it might not be a good idea for Ferrell to throw himself in the same boat with his old friend Albert Fuller. Although they had both been brought down in the Phenix City cleanup, Fuller had been convicted of bribery, a felony. And not just bribery, but specifically taking bribes to protect prostitution. Ferrell, up to now, faced only a misdemeanor vote fraud charge. He couldn't afford guilt by association simply because he had the same attorneys. Finally, there was Beddow himself. Ferrell knew as well as anyone that Beddow was the best criminal defense lawyer in Alabama; that's why the top Phenix City gangsters hired him. But Beddow hadn't made much headway against Judge Jones and the re-formed Russell County juries. In fact, about the only outcome of Beddow's work in Phenix City was a much-publicized reputation of defending Phenix City criminals. The last thing Ferrell needed was to be placed in that lineup, especially before Judge Walter B. Jones.

What Ferrell needed, then, was a good lawyer who had never been associated with Phenix City. He settled on George Rogers, another Birmingham attorney, who, with the possible exception of Beddow, had the best criminal defense reputation in the state. Every bit as sharp and urbane as the more flamboyant Beddow, the forty-nine-year-old Rogers possessed a quick intelligence and command of the law that were masked by a low-key and folksy manner in the courtroom. Born and raised in the small town of Morris in northern Jefferson County, Rogers, like Albert Patterson, had taught in the public schools before gaining his law degree. In 1952 he opened his own law firm and hired Drew Redden, a thirty-two-year-old Tallassee native just completing an appointment as assistant U.S. district attorney for north Alabama.[37]

Rogers's first task was to have his client released on bond. Derived from English common law, the habeas corpus hearing requires prosecutors to show cause before a judge why an arrested suspect should remain in jail when he or she has not yet been convicted of a crime. If prosecutors are unable or unwilling to provide such evidence, the arrested individual is released on bond, a monetary guarantee that he or she will appear for trial. Sykes had little to lose by allowing bond because it was doubtful that Fuller or Ferrell was going anywhere. Providing evidence of their guilt, however, could be detrimental to his cases later on. He wasn't about to give any information to Ferrell's and Fuller's lawyers to help them prepare their defense. After posting $12,500 each, the two men were released.[38]

The defendants received some potentially good news just a few days later. Judge Jones, citing a mounting caseload in his regular circuit, decided to remove himself from the Phenix City murder cases and return to Montgomery. It was an opportune time to quit. Handing down the murder indictments had been the last act of the reformed Russell County Grand Jury, making a grand total of 734 indictments. Only hours before, Jones had disposed of the last cleanup cases (not counting nineteen individuals who remained at large) with guilty pleas from Godwin Davis Sr. and Jr. With that accomplished, Jones declared, "Without burning any witches and without vengeance, the state of Alabama has through its court, its jury, its solicitors, and all law enforcement agencies, restored law and order to Russell County and brought about a healthy condition which, I think, will endure."[39]

It also may have been that Beddow's earlier accusations of heavy-handedness were beginning to have an effect. Jones had been merciless in the cleanup trials, but he couldn't risk taking that approach in a murder trial. In fairness to Jones, had it not been for his hard-hitting inquisition during the cleanup to reassure witnesses in the murder investigation, there may have been no indictments in the Patterson case. Now, however, the witnesses had appeared, the indictments had been handed down, and there was no need to risk overturning any guilty verdicts. What was needed was a jurist not associated with the Phenix City cleanup.[40]

On December 22, Chief Justice Ed Livingston announced Jones's replacement, J. Russell McElroy of Alabama's Tenth Judicial Circuit in Birmingham. The fifty-three-year-old McElroy, now in his twenty-eighth year on the bench, had worked his way up from a rural Sumter County crossroads, attending night school to earn his law degree. Following a brief stint as an assistant attorney for the city of Birmingham, he opened his first law office. After practicing for just three and a half years, he was appointed circuit judge, the youngest ever in Alabama. Scholarly, conservative, and soft-spoken, McElroy, in addition to being a well-respected judge, was a popular law professor and author of *The Law of Evidence in Alabama*, a massive compilation and cross-reference of Alabama court precedents on rules of evidence, still used today.[41]

McElroy called prosecution and defense teams for a pretrial meeting on December 27 to agree on a trial date before Ferrell's and Fuller's arraignments, scheduled for January 31. Appearing for the state were attorney general–elect John Patterson and two of his recently appointed assistants, Joe Robertson and Albert Rosenthal, along with Phenix City veterans MacDonald Gallion, Lee Barton, Maury Smith, and Bulley Fowler. George Rogers represented Ferrell; Beddow and Gwin appeared for Fuller. Setting the trial date turned out to be very intricate and contentious. State attorneys, particularly Patterson, wanted the trials held as quickly as possible. Beddow, of course, wanted to delay the trial but could offer no reason to do so. Rogers, however, claimed that Garrett's testimony was absolutely necessary to Ferrell's defense. When McElroy suggested a trial date of February 14, Rogers agreed on the condition that Garrett was available to testify.[42]

Complicating the matter even further was Circuit Solicitor Perry's insistence on first trying Ferrell on the vote fraud charge. It was only a misdemeanor, but the publicity that would certainly accompany the vote fraud trial, now scheduled January 10 before Judge Alta King, could possibly help the state gain a conviction in Ferrell's murder trial. Perry had, in fact, contended that it was "necessary to air the vote fraud charges to lay a background for the murder cases," even though misdemeanor cases ordinarily deferred to felonies. Consequently, Rogers wanted the vote fraud trial held after the murder trial, and again he pointed out the need for Garrett's testimony.[43]

In a December 30 hearing before Judge Wheeler, Rogers asked for a delay in Ferrell's vote fraud trial, which had already been rescheduled twice because of Garrett's unavailability. He produced a letter from Garrett's doctor in Galveston which stated that Garrett would be unable to testify for at least thirty days. Previously, there had been little objection because Garrett had been recovering from physical injuries, but he was now in a psychiatric ward and Perry doubted his inaccessibility. Perry argued heatedly that Rogers was simply trying to keep the vote fraud testimony quiet before the murder trial. Wheeler nevertheless rescheduled the trial for February 7 and transferred the case from Judge King to himself.[44]

John Patterson was sworn in as attorney general on January 17, 1955, and formally took charge of the prosecution. As promised, he named Gallion as first assistant attorney general and, because of Gallion's position and experience in the investigation, placed him on the prosecution team, as well as Barton. Sykes remained on hand because of his encyclopedic knowledge of the investigation. James Caldwell, Russell County's new circuit solicitor, also appeared in court papers as part of the prosecution staff. Caldwell, thirty-five, was a Birmingham native who had gained fame during the war as a crackerjack navy pilot, credited with downing nine Japanese planes in raids off the aircraft carriers *Saratoga, Lexington, Yorktown,* and *Princeton.* His appointment proved to be a formality. He attended Fuller's trial only part-time, never sat at the prosecution's table, and skipped Ferrell's trial altogether.[45]

The scheduling issue carried over to the second pretrial meeting, on January 7. Patterson insisted that the February 14 murder trial date be kept, even though the recently decided February 7 vote fraud trial date threatened to interfere. Circuit Solicitor Perry, included in the group because of the increasing role of the vote fraud trial in setting the date of the murder trial, not only refused to back off the February 7 date but continued to insist that Ferrell be tried before either Reid or Garrett. Then, in an unexpected move, Patterson agreed to delay the murder trial one week to give Perry more time to complete the vote fraud cases.[46]

Rogers would not accept that date. He vowed to continue delaying Ferrell's vote fraud trial until he could obtain Garrett's testimony, which would probably not occur until well after February 7. Beddow, who believed that what was bad for Ferrell was bad for Fuller, protested that Patterson's offer was made with an ulterior motive: "The reason they will agree to delay the murder trial is to get a lot of window dressing and fanfare for the public to mull over just before the murder trials."[47]

Then, a bombshell from Beddow and Gwin. During the cleanup trials, the two attorneys had repeatedly complained that the reformed Russell County Grand Jury and trial juries were purposely stacked with RBA members and sympathizers. Just as repeatedly, Judge Jones had dismissed the complaints. Resurrecting the issue, they now announced that they would file a mandamus petition and force the Russell County jury commissioners to explain why they had recently refilled the jury box with the same names used during the cleanup trials. Beddow said he would insist on a halt of all further proceedings until the matter was resolved. The implications were clear. If the courts granted his petition, the murder trial would be significantly delayed as the matter was hashed out.[48]

On January 10, Judge King granted Beddow a delay in Garrett's vote fraud trial after Beddow presented a signed affidavit from Garrett's doctor affirming that Garrett would be unable to leave the hospital for at least six weeks. Solicitor Perry showed some exasperation, saying that the court shouldn't let "the defendants play leapfrog with these cases." He suggested that the best course would be for Judges King, Wheeler, and McElroy to meet and agree on trial dates for both the vote fraud and murder cases.[49]

On January 14, Rogers, as promised, again asked that Ferrell's vote fraud trial be put off until the end of February, since he was unable to obtain a deposition from Garrett. Solicitor Perry protested, saying that unless Rogers was willing to express what he thought Garrett would testify to, then he was "trying to sell us a pig in a poke." Rogers couldn't say for sure, only that he had tried repeatedly to contact Garrett but had been unsuccessful. Perry pointed out that the affidavit said nothing of Garrett's mental condition, only that he was "physically unable" to testify. When asked of Garrett's mental condition, Rogers said, "I don't say Mr. Garrett is sane or insane." Perry responded that the affidavit was "evidently written by a lawyer and signed by a doctor," leaving Garrett the freedom to plead insanity later. Wheeler granted Rogers's request and set Ferrell's vote fraud trial for March 7, well after his scheduled murder trial.[50]

On January 20, Beddow and Rogers appeared before Judge McElroy and filed separate but identical writs of mandamus to force the Russell County Jury Commission to refill the jury box. The attorneys charged that the commissioners had not only refused to place the names of all qualified Russell County citizens in the jury box but had also purposely excluded anyone who did not share their political philosophy. Therefore, they concluded, it was impossible for their clients to obtain a fair and impartial trial.[51]

For the prosecution, the petitions represented a potential obstacle to the murder trials. Judge McElroy would now have to set a hearing to decide whether the court should issue a rule nisi, or summons, requiring the jury commission to show cause why the box should not be emptied and refilled. If McElroy refused to issue the order, Beddow and Rogers could appeal directly to the state supreme court and delay the murder trials until the issue was settled. If McElroy did issue the rule nisi but subsequently ruled in favor of the jury commission, the defendants could still appeal to the state supreme court. A final scenario presented itself, also potentially favorable to Ferrell, Fuller, and Garrett. McElroy could grant the writ of mandamus and the jury commission would be forced to refill the box, this time with commissioners appointed by Governor Folsom, who had declared only the day before that he was not in favor of "blue-ribbon" juries or grand juries. In any event, the petitions threatened to delay the murder trials indefinitely.[52]

Behind the scenes, the state worked feverishly to neutralize Beddow's and Rogers's petitions. There was much more at stake than just the murder trials. If the courts ruled that Russell County's reformed jury system was unfair—which is precisely what Beddow had been arguing since October—the whole outcome of the cleanup trials would be placed in jeopardy. And, for the murder trials, delay tended to favor the defense. Personal feelings and publicity are not supposed to influence juries, but they do. The longer the passage of time, the less outrage people would feel. There was, however, a solution that would allay Beddow's fears of a one-sided jury box while at the same time keep the trials on schedule: a change of venue to another county.[53]

Prosecutors were not as committed to having Fuller and Ferrell tried in Phenix City as they were to having them tried without a significant delay. Changes of venue were rare in Alabama; an agreement between prosecution and defense beforehand was totally unprecedented. By the time Fuller and Ferrell were arraigned, Patterson had agreed to move the trials to Birmingham. For the state, it would be a huge logistical problem transporting large numbers of witnesses from Phenix City to Birmingham, but there were some advantages, too. Moving the trial to Birmingham ensured that a large number of support personnel—bailiffs, deputies, and so forth—would be available. Another potential advantage was the availability of experienced prosecutors. By rights, Russell County's new circuit solicitor, James Caldwell, would have handled the case, but it had belonged to the attorney general's office from the beginning. Patterson could have named anyone, including Caldwell, to prosecute the case, but what was needed was an experienced prosecutor familiar with Birmingham juries, Beddow and Rogers, and, most of all, Judge J. Russell McElroy. Patterson's first choice was Emmett Perry, but Perry declined, partially because he believed that the trials had the potential of hurting his political career. Instead, Perry suggested that Patterson select Jefferson County assistant circuit solicitor Cecil Deason.

Deason, fifty-one, a former naval commander, had made a name for himself in the Jefferson County circuit solicitor's office by prosecuting some particularly brutal Klansmen. Mild-mannered yet dramatic when the situation called for it, he was hesitant to take the cases because the state had lost its star witness. Then Patterson told Deason that another witness had been discovered, one who would be even more incriminating than Johnny Frank Griffin. Skeptical, Deason said he would have to talk to the witness himself before deciding. One evening shortly thereafter, Deason arrived at Sheriff Lamar Murphy's house and questioned a twenty-seven-year-old construction worker, Cecil Edward Padgett, about what he saw in Phenix City on the night of June 18. After the interrogation, which lasted most of the night, Deason agreed to prosecute the Albert Patterson murder cases.[54]

10
Watermelon Party

All three key witnesses for the state [Cecil Padgett, James Taylor,
and Bill Littleton] were thinking about a watermelon party, the
$10,000 reward offered by the state for the conviction of Albert
Patterson's killer.

Roderick Beddow Sr., March 9, 1955

In the weeks before the trial, both prosecutors and defense attorneys
scrambled to prepare their cases. Although Sykes had his three indictments, the attorney general's staff never let up on obtaining more
evidence. Toward the top of its most-wanted list was former assistant
police chief Buddy Jowers, who had disappeared on August 5 with
another Phenix City policeman, Dewey Chestnut. Chestnut had returned in October, telling investigators that he and Jowers had traveled as far as New Mexico before Chestnut decided to return home.
Jowers hadn't said much to Chestnut about the killing, but what he
did say intrigued investigators: "I know too damn much about the
killing and wish I didn't know it." Such a statement, along with the
RBA's insistence that Jowers had put Albert Fuller in the hospital for
causing the Phenix City cleanup, convinced investigators that Jowers
knew something substantial about the murder, something that made
him believe Fuller was responsible for the current state of affairs in
Phenix City.[1]

In late December, MacDonald Gallion received word that Jowers
had been seen around Odessa, Texas. A National Guard airplane delivered Gallion to Odessa, where he almost immediately spotted Jow-

ers in a car parked on a downtown street. Gallion simply walked up
to the car, leaned into the window, and asked, "Don't you think it's
about time you came home?" Jowers agreed, uneventfully. As the two
boarded the National Guard plane for the trip back to Alabama, it
was obvious to Gallion that Jowers had never flown before. It happened that this was not a good time to be initiated. Halfway through
the flight, smoke began pouring out of the cockpit's instrument panel
and filled the cabin. Gallion was concerned, but Jowers was terrified.
Fortunately, the plane was able to make an emergency landing in Mississippi without serious incident. Gallion called Governor Persons to
tell him of the problem, and the governor kindly offered to send another plane. Although respectful of his old friend's current position,
Gallion let loose a string of expletives, the upshot of which was, "Absolutely not!" Persons instead dispatched an Alabama Highway Patrol
car to transport them to Phenix City.[2]

Meanwhile, in Birmingham, Cecil Deason spent two weeks feverishly
digesting the reams of documentation that Sykes had collected over
the previous seven months in his attempt to develop a comprehensive
presentation for the trial jury. On January 31 he requested a two-week
delay so that he could interview witnesses and more fully examine the
pile of evidence, telling Judge McElroy that it was "physically and mentally impossible" to prepare a case before February 14. Although defense counsels had earlier sought a trial delay, they now objected.
McElroy agreed, saying that he could not grant a continuance simply
because the state had appointed a new prosecutor. The February 14
trial date would stand.[3]

The defense was in an even more harried position. In 1963, the
U.S. Supreme Court would rule in *Brady v. Maryland* that the state
must provide defense attorneys with any material that tended to ex-
culpate their client. In the winter of 1955, however, the *Brady* rule was
a long way off, and Deason wasn't going to volunteer the information.
To save time, Beddow and Rogers decided early on to pool their resources and share information. Contacting as many witnesses, policemen, deputies, and state investigators as they could, the defense attorneys usually met with indifference, sometimes with hostility. Thus
they were surprised when two of the I & I agents most closely associ-

ated with the case decided to cooperate fully. As a result, Fuller's and Ferrell's attorneys became almost as familiar with the state's planned testimony as Cecil Deason did. The only exceptions were James Taylor, who wouldn't talk, and the secret star witness whom Beddow and Rogers didn't know about yet.[4]

The day of the trial arrived. Fortunately, McElroy's courtroom, originally built as a small auditorium but converted to courtroom use years before, was the largest in the Jefferson County Courthouse. Anticipating huge crowds, court officials had made detailed seating arrangements. Front-row seats, both on the floor and in the balcony, belonged to the news media. McElroy had also reserved two sections for local attorneys who wanted to observe the trial. The middle section downstairs and most of the balcony were set aside for the general public on a first-come, first-seated basis.[5]

Spectators began crowding into the corridor shortly after 8:00 A.M., CST, a full hour before proceedings were scheduled to begin. Early arrivals included I & I investigators Ben Allen, Willie Painter, Claude Prier, and Robert Godwin, all of whom were habitually on time after years of courtroom appearances. Arch Ferrell arrived alone. Albert Fuller, now apparently fully recovered from his back injuries, followed a short while later, accompanied by his wife, Avon. Both defendants stood in the hallway and conferred with their attorneys. A few feet away, Attorney General John Patterson talked with friends from Phenix City. The prosecutors—Deason, Sykes, Gallion, Barton, and Caldwell—arrived as a group. Sykes, who had taken over a courthouse office and filled it with the reports and interview transcripts from the investigation, would spend much of his time during the trial lugging a huge briefcase between that office and the courtroom.

Two floors above, in another courtroom, Judge McElroy began jury selection. After the first round of exclusions, McElroy asked prosecutors and defense attorneys if they were ready to proceed. Beddow and Gwin declared themselves ready, as did Rogers and Redden. Deason, however, could not locate a witness vital to the prosecution. He asked for a delay until 4:00 CST, by which time he hoped to have more information. Beddow wanted more information now. Before the defense could agree to a delay, it would have to hear what the state expected to prove through the missing witness's testimony. Reluctantly, Deason identified him as James R. Taylor, a Columbus cab driver who would testify that he saw one of the defendants running from the scene of the crime. Somewhat sheepishly, Deason said that Taylor had last been seen headed for Mexico with four soldiers in his cab. McElroy deferred proceedings until the next day.

Frantic, Deason put out an all-points bulletin and swore out a fugitive warrant to bring in the FBI. At 9:30 P.M. CST, police in Niceville, Florida, spotted Taylor and pulled him over. Deason didn't get the full story until the Alabama Highway Patrol delivered Taylor overnight to Birmingham and placed him under Gallion's watchful eye. Taylor explained that the four soldiers had just received a ten-day pass and wanted to go to Mexico. He took them as far as Meridian, Mississippi, before they decided that Florida was more suitable. Realizing the hubbub his disappearance had caused only after he had checked in with his wife, Taylor tried to reach Deason in Birmingham but couldn't get through.[6]

The next morning, with Taylor in tow, Deason announced that the state was ready to continue. For weeks people had talked about whom Deason would try first, Ferrell or Fuller. Both defense counsels and the press believed it would be Ferrell, simply because he was the more prominent of the two. But Deason had other ideas. For one thing, the case against Fuller seemed stronger, not only because of the available evidence but also because Fuller was considered an easier target overall. He had recently been convicted of bribery and was about as sullied as he was going to get, while Ferrell was only under indictment for misdemeanor vote fraud. If Fuller were tried first, Circuit Solicitor Perry would gain more time to publicly tarnish Ferrell's reputation before his murder trial. Second, there was the momentum factor. Assuming the state had a better chance of convicting Fuller, conventional legal wisdom dictated that the stronger case go first with the hope that a guilty verdict in the first trial would influence the second.

Deason milked the suspense for all it was worth. Now, with the appropriate level of anticipation, he boomed out: "The state elects to try Albert Fuller first." There was audible surprise all around the courtroom. Rogers and Redden, fully expecting to make their opening statements momentarily, were completely stunned, but Ferrell stared straight ahead, expressionless. Fuller was obviously taken off guard and stiffened visibly. Then, shaking it off, he broke into a broad grin.[7]

Newspapermen noticed a distinct change in Fuller's demeanor since the previous summer. His usual scowls and menacing stares had been replaced with a permanent bland smile. Seemingly unconcerned with the preliminary proceedings, the former chief deputy sat in the spectator seats with his wife and strolled the corridors during recesses. During one of the breaks, Fuller casually glanced through the morning newspaper, skipping the front-page headlines concerning his capital murder trial. Observers had little doubt that his less threatening appearance was due to his attorneys' coaching. Yet on this first day Fuller had taken his laid-back look too far, wearing a cream-colored suit. In the dead of winter, the overall effect came off as flashy instead of subdued. Beddow and Gwin immediately instructed the former deputy sheriff to wear only "preacher's suits" of plain blue or brown.[8]

Ferrell, one day shy of his thirty-eighth birthday, was a completely different story. Dressed in a somber blue suit, he appeared totally serious, even grim. Choosing to sit at counsel's table, he ignored almost everyone but his close friends and attorneys. Unlike Fuller, who looked like he could have been watching a ballet recital, Ferrell hung on every word. When Judge McElroy asked if anyone in the courtroom was from Phenix City (meaning the prospective jurors), Ferrell dutifully raised his hand, eliciting a "Yes, I know that" smile from McElroy.

After a round of conferences on the morning of February 16, McElroy brought in the jury and invited the prosecution to make its opening statement. Deason continued to reveal as little as possible, simply reading the indictment to the jury. Beddow followed and was more enlightening. Fuller's defense would rest mostly on an "impregnable" alibi: "On behalf of this defendant I want to say that to each and every offense embraced in this indictment that . . . the defendant interposes a plea of not guilty. That plea, without any special mention, carries with it the plea of an alibi . . . that he was not there." So this was Fuller's defense strategy. The outcome of the trial would hinge on a single question: Was Fuller at the jail at the time Patterson was killed, or wasn't he? If Beddow could convince the jury to believe just one of his client's alibi witnesses, Fuller would be a free man.[9]

The state's first witness was Agnes Patterson. Her nine-minute tes-

timony was unemotional and to the point. Technically, the information she imparted during that short time was not particularly crucial.
From the prosecution's point of view, though, it was important that
jurors see for themselves that Albert Patterson was not just some judicial concept of "victim" but rather a real person with a wife, a family,
and a career. A real gap had occurred with his passing. Just as could
happen to any of them, Patterson headed off to work in the morning
and was dead by midnight. Deason could never convey this concept
better than with the simple appearance of Patterson's widow. Beddow
knew better than to cross-examine her.[10]

During the first full day of state testimony there was little contention between the prosecution and the defense. Deason produced
rather simple, factual testimony from police and other witnesses to
establish the facts of the murder. It wasn't until the second day that
he clashed with Beddow. Part of Deason's strategy of establishing
Fuller's motive was the contention that Patterson had been elected
on his pledge to clean up Phenix City and that Fuller, to keep that
from happening, had murdered him. Beddow and Gwin were worried
that Deason would use this as a vehicle to reveal all the vice accusations made against Fuller during the cleanup. Deason introduced the
subject through Leland Jones, who testified that he saw Patterson at
about 8:10 P.M. at his office and talked with him for about half an
hour. Then Deason asked, "Are you familiar with his campaign?" Beddow objected immediately. The state, he claimed, was trying to intro-
duce this line of questioning solely to prejudice the jury.[11]

McElroy overruled Beddow and allowed Deason to enter into evidence one of Patterson's campaign cards. Jones was followed by other
witnesses who saw Patterson either minutes before he died or just after
he was shot. In cross-examination, Beddow and Gwin were able to use
these witnesses to establish the fact that there were other persons in
the area who had as good an opportunity as Fuller to kill Patterson.
Part of their purpose was to show that any of these people, so far
unaccounted for by Sykes, could have been the real killer. More important, perhaps, was the suggestion that Sykes had run a shoddy investigation. If the jury was apt to believe that the investigation was
incomplete, then it was a small step to believing it had a faulty outcome: the indictment of the wrong man. The first opportunity came
with the testimony of Woodie Pope, who had met Patterson in the

post office sometime between 8:45 and 9:00. During cross-examination, Gwin had Pope tell the jury about the suspicious man he had
seen heading toward the Coulter Building soon after Patterson left
the post office.[12]

The defense strategy continued with the cross-examination of
Jimmy Sanders, called by the state to describe Patterson's death on
the Fifth Avenue sidewalk. Beddow wanted to know about the man,
yet unidentified, who walked through the gathering crowd minutes
after Patterson was gunned down. Sanders claimed that he pointed
out the man's photograph to state investigators but was never told
who he was. I & I agents had suggested that the man was either Fuller
or Ferrell, but Sanders was certain that it was not. At the time, Sanders
had been jailed for two days on a dubious charge while agents continued to question him.[13]

The story of Sanders's incarceration represented another defense
strategy to undermine the state's case: the at-all-costs compulsion on
the part of Sykes and his staff to incriminate Fuller, who was nowhere
near the scene, when they should have been tracking down other,
more promising suspects who *were* at the scene. The corollary to this
was that although Sanders didn't break under this kind of police pressure, it wouldn't be surprising if someone else did. The theme continued with Beddow's cross-examination of Hugh Buchanan, Sanders's
companion on the night of the murder. Buchanan said that state investigators constantly asked him if he had seen Fuller and Ferrell
around the Coulter Building, and they often reminded him of the
reward.[14]

The prosecution was growing increasingly uneasy at Beddow's
cross-examinations. It was uncanny how familiar he seemed to be with
witnesses' statements to investigators and the attorney general's staff.
Sometimes defense counsels were lucky in re-creating witness interviews, but when Beddow began reading verbatim excerpts from the
interview transcripts and investigator reports that Sykes had so jeal-
ously guarded over the past eight months, they knew someone on the
investigative staff had been talking—a lot. Those "someones," it turned
out, were I & I agents Ben Allen and W. L. Allen, who believed that
Sykes blew the case by concentrating on the wrong man—Fuller—
and had thus missed the opportunity to find the real murderer. Years
later, W. L. Allen would justify their actions by saying it was their duty

to tell the truth, when asked, but Beddow's possession of firsthand information indicated something beyond a refusal to lie. It appeared that the defense attorney had in hand full copies of a good portion of Sykes's files.[15]

Deason continued a parade of patrolmen, RBA members, and reporters to emphasize Phenix City gambling. RBA president Howard Pennington told of Patterson's private and public promises to utilize every available law enforcement agency to clean up the town once he took office. He also testified about the times he had personally witnessed gambling in Phenix City establishments over the years. According to him, gambling was never concealed. Pennington's appearance marked yet another strategy/counterstrategy in the trial. Like Sykes during the murder investigation, Deason relied on RBA members to provide firsthand testimony. Individually they were of unquestioned integrity, but Beddow, seeing the opportunity to brand the RBA as a group of misguided zealots, had anticipated this and began laying the groundwork for an attack based on the contention that the RBA had orchestrated Fuller's persecution.[16]

Having succeeded in inserting testimony to the effect that Fuller was a crooked cop, Deason now sought to go one step further. Calling state investigator Willie Painter to the stand, Deason asked about Painter's questions to Fuller and Fuller's responses in a January 7 interrogation: "Did he make a statement to you on that occasion with reference to taking graft from gamblers in Phenix City?" After McElroy overruled Beddow's objections, the jury heard Painter say that Fuller not only admitted receiving one-third of the take from Phenix City slot machine operations but that he was indeed guilty of the bribery charge brought by special prosecutors George Johnson and Bulley Fowler the previous autumn.

During cross-examination, Beddow had Painter confirm that Fuller had told him that Governor Persons's executive secretary, Vernon Merritt, had tipped him off regarding the highway patrol raid on Phenix City planned for June 18, 1954. Painter denied questioning Fuller about alleged Phenix City payoffs to the governor and his staff but admitted that "the subject came up." It was unclear what Beddow hoped to accomplish by this line of questioning, except to make the state pay a price. If the jury were to believe Fuller was a crook, it would have to believe that the governor and his staff were crooks, too.[17]

It was not until the fourth day of the trial that Deason produced the first witness who placed Fuller at the scene, former Phenix City cab driver Bill Littleton. One of the state's more controversial witnesses, Littleton had in 1949 run over a Fort Benning private outside the Square Dance Club on the outskirts of Phenix City, killing him instantly. After being arrested and jailed by Fuller, Littleton was released on $1,500 bond and went back to driving his taxi while he awaited trial. Littleton heard nothing more about it until National Guardsmen reopened the case in late 1954. He pleaded guilty to first-degree manslaughter and was sent to prison.

Dressed in prison garb, Littleton testified that on the night of June 18 he had driven a teenage girl to the Idle Hour Amusement Park in Phenix City. As he headed back to Columbus, he asked the dispatcher for the time and was told that it was 8:45. About five minutes later, Littleton saw Ferrell and Fuller standing in front of the Coulter Building. As he drove past, he tapped his horn and waved at the two. Ferrell even waved back. Deason had no more questions, but Beddow did, and for almost two hours he subjected Littleton to a relentless grilling.[18]

Except for his brief glimpse of Ferrell and Fuller, Littleton couldn't remember seeing anyone else that night, including any of his other fares. Reading from previous testimony, Beddow rattled off the names of almost everyone identified at the scene around the time of the murder. Littleton couldn't recall any of them. Most of Beddow's questions for the rest of the cross-examination concerned Littleton's contacts with state investigators and the attorney general's staff. Littleton denied having told two fellow inmates that he "would do anything in the world" to be released. Beddow ran through a list of about a half dozen other prisoners, asking Littleton if he had told them that he expected to be set free. Littleton denied having talked to each one but admitted that he neither testified before the grand jury nor talked to any officer before he was sent to prison on the manslaughter charge.[19]

Littleton's testimony placed Fuller in the area of the Coulter Building about fifteen minutes before Patterson was killed. The next step was to establish that Fuller was still in the immediate vicinity just after the murder. Deason called cab driver James Taylor to tell how he had come to Phenix City, heard the shots while waiting at the traffic light at Fifth Avenue, and then saw Fuller run from the direction of the Coulter Building, jump into a waiting car, and speed off.

This was a key moment in the trial. Beddow had to destroy Taylor's credibility, or Fuller could very well go to the electric chair. He first endeavored to show the "evolution" of Taylor as Fuller's accuser. To do so, Beddow brought up the fact that when Taylor first told his story to investigators in July, he couldn't identify the man he saw running:

> BEDDOW: Did you tell MacDonald Gallion that you didn't get a good look at his face?
> TAYLOR: I didn't get a good look at his face, I saw him from the side.
> BEDDOW: Didn't you tell Mr. Gallion that Fuller "filled the bill" as to build and size, but that you didn't get a good look at his face, and couldn't identify him?
> TAYLOR: I told him it was him.

Throughout the cross-examination, Beddow brought out the number of times Taylor had been interviewed by investigators, again suggesting an effort to pressure witnesses, but with a key difference: Taylor *did* name Fuller—eventually. Having established the possibility of inconsistent statements, Beddow addressed the court: "Your honor, we demand the statements which were allegedly taken down from this witness and demand that Bernard Sykes, Cecil Deason, and the prosecution produce them and turn them over to us." After reviewing the statements, McElroy ruled against Beddow.

Beddow also tried to bring up a Georgia murder case in which Taylor had told local authorities that he had seen the victim a few days before her murder riding around with two soldiers. Taylor had provided detailed descriptions of the soldiers and their car and even went so far as to point out different locations in and around Columbus, and even more distant towns, where he had seen the trio. When the body was found a few days later and the Muscogee County sheriff confronted Taylor with some contradictions in his earlier story, Taylor admitted that it was a hoax and that he had never seen the woman at any time. Beddow argued that the testimony should be allowed "to show that he [Taylor] is either the biggest prevaricator in the world or that he has delusions and hallucinations and likes to be identified with investigations of this kind." Deason objected, saying it was immaterial to the present case, and McElroy sustained the objection.[20]

Although Beddow had lost some key rulings from the court concerning Taylor, he had nevertheless raised a number of serious credibility issues during cross-examination, including the fact that the witness had not come forward until late and that even then he didn't identify Fuller right away. It was critical, then, for Deason to reestablish Taylor's credibility by introducing the "Albert Fuller did it" statement to show that he had indeed identified the defendant within minutes of the murder. On further cross-examination, Deason edged toward the statement by asking Taylor what happened after he left Chad's Rose Room. Beddow was immediately on his feet, and McElroy excused the jury and called counsel before him. Deason argued that the testimony should be allowed because Beddow had strongly suggested that Taylor's testimony came about only after he had heard about the $10,000 reward; the state deserved a chance to respond. McElroy ruled for Beddow, agreeing that such testimony would go far beyond what Taylor actually observed on the night of the murder. It was a strong blow to the prosecution. When the jurors returned, they heard Taylor admit that he had not identified Fuller to authorities as the man he saw running from the scene of the crime until after a reward was offered; they did not hear the state explain that he had said something to that effect to a co-worker only minutes after the murder.[21]

To contradict the expected testimony of Fuller's alibi witnesses, Deason called Phenix City policeman Walter Leon Sanders, who said he saw Fuller at the Sunny Lane Café at about 8:40, well after Fuller said he arrived at the jail. Sanders also recounted the mysterious destruction of the footprint he found behind the Coulter Building, a footprint he had told only Fuller about.[22] One of the first things Beddow did on cross-examination was bring out that Sanders was not actually a detective or patrolman at the time of the slaying but was merely assigned to checking parking meters. Pushed along by Beddow, Sanders provided more details about the ruined footprint, saying that it had not been totally erased but that it appeared as though someone had stepped into the print to alter the original impression. The question of why someone would make a minor alteration instead of completely erasing the print was left unanswered. Beddow then began emphasizing the differences between some of Sanders's earlier statements and his direct testimony minutes ago. There was a growing hum among the spectators as the exchange between Beddow and Sanders escalated. Finally, Sanders admitted that dirt could have trickled down into the footprint overnight.[23]

Although prosecutors had a motive—the idea that Fuller killed Patterson to avoid a Phenix City cleanup—it was no more specific to the defendant than to any other crooked local official. Deason's stronger point was that technical evidence placed Fuller at the scene. To unfold this aspect of the trial, Deason first called Wendell Sowell, the assistant state toxicologist, who described both his investigation of the murder scene and Patterson's autopsy early on June 19. Except for some early and often erroneous press reports, this was the first time the public had heard any details from the autopsy.[24]

Building on Sowell's testimony, Deason led National Guardsmen and state investigators through the chain of evidence regarding the bullets found in Fuller's home on October 12. Then he recalled Sowell to tell of the metallurgical similarities between one of those bullets and one taken from Patterson's body. There was not a lot Beddow could do except have Sowell admit that all other test results from Fuller's guns and bullets had come out negative. After the ballistics testimony, I & I agents Godwin, Williams, and Painter testified about the dusting of Patterson's car early on June 19, the fingerprinting of Fuller the following September, and Fuller's insistence throughout the investigation that he had never touched the car. Deason wrapped it up with FBI testimony demonstrating the similarities between the prints.[25]

One element of Deason's case that was confusing to many nonlegal spectators was the production of witnesses incriminating to Ferrell but not directly related to the prosecution of Fuller. This was due to a certain quirkiness in Alabama criminal law, not corrected until 1991, which made joint trials practically impossible. The resulting requirement to separately try defendants accused of the same crime placed an undue burden on prosecutors. If Deason were to convince the jury of Fuller's guilt, he also would have to convince it of Ferrell's guilt, even though Ferrell wasn't yet on trial. While there were obvious disadvantages—Ferrell's attorneys took notes throughout most of the trial—it also provided Deason with a dry run of Ferrell's upcoming trial, an opportunity to see what worked and what didn't.[26]

Deason called Russell County Courthouse custodian Quinnie Kelley to the stand. Kelley testified that shortly after hearing the gunshots, as he stood on the courthouse steps, he saw Ferrell come out of the post office driveway on Fifth Avenue, headed toward Fourteenth Street, and that he was standing by the flagpole in front of the post office when he lost sight of him.

Beddow got his turn at cross-examination. It was a somewhat awkward situation in that he was obliged to destroy testimony that did not directly incriminate his client, but it was an effective cross-examination, and, with George Rogers close by, it showed the close working relationship between Fuller's and Ferrell's attorneys. Beddow's questioning brought out the fact that Kelley had maintained for four months that he could not identify the man he saw coming from the direction of the murder scene, a man he only later identified as Ferrell. Beddow also insinuated that Kelley hated Fuller and Ferrell—especially Ferrell—because the circuit solicitor had blocked Kelley's attempts to obtain a pistol permit.[27]

Almost from the beginning of the trial, word had circulated among reporters that the state would produce a surprise witness who would send Fuller to the electric chair. Anticipation reached a climax on Friday, February 26, when Deason finally called Cecil Padgett to the stand. In appearance, Padgett made the perfect witness. With a dark tan set against a blue suit with matching tie, he looked like a movie star, yet Padgett possessed many Everyman qualities that the jurors could relate to or at least not feel intimidated by. He was obviously uneducated and just as obviously unconcerned about that fact. He was a manual laborer but carried that knowledge with pride and quiet dignity. He didn't show the slightest sign of nervousness or uncertainty. The overall impression he created was of a simple man with an important story to tell.

Even Deason acted as if Padgett were not a particularly important witness. As he began direct examination, his and Padgett's tones were subdued, even conversational, giving no indication of the explosion that was to come. Deason began by asking Padgett the most basic of questions: where he lived, where he worked. Then he moved on to the night of June 18. Padgett explained that he and his wife had eaten dinner at Choppy's Drive-in, in Columbus. They then drove past a couple of nearby movie theaters to see what was playing. Not interested in either the Bradley Theater or the Georgia Theater, the Padgetts crossed over to Phenix City and headed toward the Palace Theater, down Fifth Avenue from the Coulter Building.

At this point, Deason had the witness standing before a large map of the area around the murder scene. Padgett indicated that he parked his car, a 1939 Lincoln, in front of Bentley's Grocery, almost directly across from the alley in which Patterson's car was parked. Padgett got out alone, went across the street and up the ramp that went into the alley, turned right on the sidewalk, and walked to the Palace Theater, where he took a look at what was playing and the show times. After he left the theater, Padgett retraced his steps back to the Coulter Building.

DEASON: While you were walking back to the direction of the car, Mr. Padgett, did you see anyone?
PADGETT: Yes. When I got in front of Smitty's Grill, I did.
DEASON: Who did you see?
PADGETT: Mr. Fuller.
DEASON: Who else?
PADGETT: Mr. Patterson.
DEASON: Where were they when you saw them?
PADGETT: Between the entrance of the Coulter Building and Seymour's Dress Shop.
DEASON: Where did you cross the street to get in your car?
PADGETT: In front of the parking lot at the ramp.
DEASON: Now when you got across the street, was your car parked there?
PADGETT: Yes, sir.
DEASON: Was your wife there?
PADGETT: Yes.
DEASON: Did you hear anything as you got to your car?
PADGETT: Yes, sir.

DEASON: What did you hear?

PADGETT: I heard three shots.[28]

DEASON: When you heard three shots, what did you do?

PADGETT: I turned and stepped back and looked.

DEASON: What did you see?

PADGETT: I saw Mr. Fuller and—to the best of my judgment, Mr. Ferrell.

DEASON: What was this defendant doing at the time the shots were fired?

PADGETT: They were against the car.

DEASON: What did you see them do after the shots were fired?

PADGETT: They turned and run out the alley—I mean the parking lot behind.

DEASON: Are you positive that was Mr. Fuller?

PADGETT: Yes, sir.

DEASON: Answer Mr. Beddow's questions.

Padgett had been on the stand only five minutes, but his words electrified the courtroom. An audible gasp escaped the spectators, who were shocked that Deason had no more questions for him. Even Fuller and his attorneys seemed surprised. Unlike Johnny Frank Griffin, Padgett had seen not only the defendant but also, he believed, Arch Ferrell. His account matched the state's scenario almost perfectly, even for elements the jury was not allowed to hear. Later, in his analysis of the day's events, *Birmingham News* reporter Ed Strickland was ecstatic in telling how Padgett's testimony fell into place like the key piece of a seemingly unsolvable puzzle. The reporter now recalled a number of witnesses early in the investigation who said they had seen a young couple in front of the Coulter Building getting into an older-model car, leading Sykes and Gallion to appeal for them to come forward. Strickland now crowed, "The couple was, without a doubt, Padgett and his wife." And a number of witnesses, including Probate Judge Shannon Burch, had mentioned a car parked in front of the Coulter Building, along with a stake-body pickup truck parked nearby. "That old-model car was the 1939 Lincoln belonging to Padgett," Strickland continued. "The pickup truck belonged to Griffin, whom Padgett did not know." At one point in his testimony, Padgett mentioned that while on his way to the Palace Theater, a man passed him, but he couldn't remember anything particular about his appearance. Strickland felt sure that this man was none other than Johnny Frank Griffin.

But Strickland was either cheerleading the prosecution or engaging in wishful thinking. The pieces did *not* fit, and the puzzle was as unsolved as ever. It was true that witnesses had told investigators early on of a young couple close to the murder scene and that Sykes had on August 10 publicly appealed for their appearance. However, the couple was described as window-shopping, not very similar to Padgett's story, in which his wife never left the car. Furthermore, the couple in question was accounted for ten days after Sykes's appeal. As for Shannon Burch, the former probate judge did testify that he saw a large car in front of Bentley's, but on cross-examination Beddow had him clarify that it was not parked in the same place or at the same angle as Padgett described. And lastly, if both Griffin and Padgett were correct in their time elements, Padgett *could* have passed Griffin on the Fifth Avenue sidewalk, just as Strickland claimed. But Griffin, when specifically asked by Sykes before the grand jury, denied seeing anyone on the sidewalk—not didn't *recall,* but didn't *see.*[29]

Beddow had his work cut out for him, and he proceeded to grill the unflappable Mr. Padgett. Seeking to find some discrepancy in his testimony, Beddow had Padgett go through his day minute by minute. Padgett didn't make a single mistake. And for every question Beddow asked, Padgett was able to dig Fuller's grave a little deeper. When Beddow asked him if he saw either Fuller or Patterson make any violent moves toward the other, Padgett's answer was characteristic: "Not then."[30]

Padgett was followed on the stand by his wife, Edith, the state's forty-fourth and final witness. She didn't see the shooting because Cecil was blocking her view. During cross-examination, Edith proved as cool as her husband, sometimes berating Beddow for his repeated questions. Most of her responses consisted of "I don't know" or "I don't remember." At one point she told Beddow, "I don't remember, and if I tell you I don't remember, there's no use asking me again because I don't remember." After that, Deason announced he had no more witnesses, and the state rested.[31]

Fuller's defense team got busy. Beddow and Gwin rushed off to

Phenix City to find information, any information, on Padgett that could be used to attack his character. When court reconvened, Beddow and Gwin produced a number of witnesses to swear to Padgett's bad reputation and their inability to believe his sworn oath. Predictably, Beddow also established that Padgett was in debt, owing at least a thousand dollars, a sizable amount for a construction worker who brought home only about eighty-seven dollars weekly.[32]

Then came witnesses who denied that Padgett was at the scene at all. Steve Schermann and Pete Miller, two of the furniture movers, said they saw no car parked in front of Bentley's, as did city worker D. R. McLemore, who had passed the Coulter Building on his way home from the Boy Scout meeting at about 8:55 P.M. And, as Beddow pointed out, Padgett's car would have been hard to miss. His 1939 Lincoln measured seventeen and a half feet from bumper to bumper, while Fifth Avenue was only thirty-six feet wide.[33]

The defense also had to provide a logical explanation for the so-called getaway car described by Taylor and confirmed by a number of other state witnesses. Beddow called to the stand Sergeant Ray Eller and James McCain, a Columbus construction worker. Both testified that Eller's uncle had parked his car, a two-tone green Ford, in front of the First Federal Building on Fourteenth Street during the early evening and had picked it up at about 9:30. The contention was that if Taylor had seen the large, dark car, it would have been impossible for him to miss the Ford, yet Taylor swore that there were no other vehicles close by.[34]

Beddow also called Boy Scout officials James Layfield, Dan Carden, and George Pope to testify that they had chatted in front of the courthouse after the Boy Scout meeting from roughly 8:55 to 9:35. They didn't see Ferrell or Fuller cross Fourteenth Street; they didn't see or hear a car speed off from across the street at high speed; and they didn't see courthouse janitor Quinnie Kelley the whole time they stood on the courthouse steps.[35]

To attack the credibility of Bill Littleton, Beddow summoned Virginia Lange, Littleton's ex-girlfriend, who said that on the night of the murder Littleton came to the café in which she worked to tell her about Patterson's death but mentioned nothing about seeing Fuller or Ferrell. Fuller's attorneys also produced three of Littleton's fellow inmates who said that Littleton at one time or another had spoken of a parole-for-testimony deal.[36]

Since his indictment, Fuller had abandoned his claim that he had never touched Patterson's car. In his new story, Fuller recalled that during the initial investigation he had forcibly removed *Montgomery Advertiser* reporter Fred Andersen from the car. He had to steady himself against the vehicle as he did so lest he and Andersen fall to the ground. To support that contention, Beddow called to the stand another Phenix City cab driver, Lee Bankston, who confirmed that Fuller fell against Patterson's car while pulling away Andersen. Bankston was sure that Fuller hit the car with both hands.[37]

Beddow and Gwin also had to address the circumstantial evidence. Although previous testimony that Fuller was walking around with an empty holster after the murder proved nothing, it could have an effect on the jury, and Beddow had to dispel it. He had Probate Judge Burch say that he had often seen Fuller without a side arm in the fifteen years he had worked for the sheriff's department. In fact, Burch had, in his capacity as sheriff for six of those years, occasionally found it necessary to remind Fuller of regulations requiring him to remain armed while on duty. Burch was followed by former state highway patrolman Pat Mihelic, now Phenix City's police chief, who said essentially the same thing. Both men said that when Fuller did carry a side arm, it was almost always a .44, .45, or .357 caliber—anything but a .38, the kind used to kill Patterson.[38]

Fuller's first alibi witness was Ben Clark, the Russell County jailer. Of the seven alibi witnesses, Clark was in the best position to know if and when Fuller left the jail because Clark controlled the electronically locked door. He was sure that Fuller never left the jail from a little after dark until sometime before 9:30 when Clark let Fuller out on his way to the crime scene.[39]

Beddow next called highway patrolman George Phillips, considered the defense's big gun. Phillips had two things going for him as a believable witness: he was elderly and, as a visiting state patrolman, was not part of the regular jailhouse gang in Phenix City. He was positive that Fuller remained at the jail from the time he first saw him, about 8:25, until Fuller ran out upon hearing the news of Patterson's murder. And so Fuller's "impregnable alibi" continued to unfold through Sheriff Mathews, Robert Lee Smith, Curtis Deason, and Aaron Smith.[40]

Having laid the groundwork for Fuller's alibi, Beddow called the defendant to the stand. Dressed in a light tan suit, white shirt, and a yellow tie with tan trim, Fuller appeared relaxed, even casual, as Beddow took him through his testimony. Fuller had known Patterson for about fifteen years and considered him a personal friend. He had never harbored any ill will toward Patterson; nor, so far as he knew, did Patterson dislike him in any way. In fact, he was the only one at the courthouse who supported Patterson in the attorney general's race the previous spring. Fuller recounted his actions on June 18, saying it was one of those days that he had chosen to go unarmed. He definitely recalled Walter Sanders showing him the footprint behind the Coulter Building and leading state investigators to it in the morning. But here his account differed from Sanders's. Fuller testified that at that time, the print was in the same condition as when Sanders first showed it to him. There did not seem to be any attempt during the night to destroy it.

Now it came time to explain the fingerprints. Fuller said that at about 4 or 5 A.M., he saw Fred Andersen looking into Patterson's car. He asked him to step away, but Andersen either didn't hear him or ignored him. Fuller grabbed the reporter but lost his balance as he pulled him away and placed both hands on the car to break his fall. He denied ever telling state investigator Willie Painter that he had never touched the car.

Beddow questioned Fuller at length about the January 7 conversation with Painter. Fuller denied that he told Painter he had accepted bribes. What Fuller did remember was that Painter had said John Patterson knew that he, Fuller, hadn't killed his daddy but that he believed he knew who did or could find out. Painter further quoted John Patterson as saying that if Fuller would just put the finger on Arch Ferrell, Fuller's seven-year sentence for the bribery charge would be set aside and the murder charge would be dropped. At the time, Fuller protested to Painter that he knew "nothing in the world about Ferrell having something to do with the murder. I don't know who killed Mr. Patterson and I wish I could get up out of this bed and go help look for the man who killed Mr. Patterson." He assured Painter that if he knew who killed Patterson he would have offered that information long before his bribery trial or his indictment for murder.

And then came the climax of Fuller's testimony. Beddow, raising his voice slightly, asked, "I want you to tell that jury sitting there—did you kill Albert Patterson?" Fuller turned to face the jury: "No, sir, I did not."

BEDDOW: Do you know who did?

FULLER: No, sir. I do not.

BEDDOW: Were you at the Coulter Building, that is, the scene of the homicide, any time on the night of June 18 before Mr. Patterson was killed?

FULLER: No sir.

Under cross-examination by Deason, Fuller admitted that while he had supported Patterson, he did not vote for him. Deason also had Fuller indirectly contradict his own alibi by having Fuller admit that he heard no sirens while he and Sheriff Mathews were in the jailer's bedroom, even though Fuller had just said the windows were open— this in direct contrast to a number of previous witnesses who had testified that at least two emergency vehicles had roared by the courthouse on the way to the murder scene.

Fuller's testimony completed the defense's direct testimony, but there was still a ways to go before closing statements. It was now the time for rebuttal witnesses. For the state, this generally consisted of a parade of RBA members and sympathizers who testified to the bad reputation of Fuller and his alibi witnesses and their inability to believe anything they said, even under oath in a court of law. This included Mrs. Roberta Oakley, wife of a Centerville newspaper publisher, who swore that Patrolman George Phillips had told her the previous fall that he did not know of Fuller's whereabouts on the night of the murder and was drinking coffee with Arch Ferrell in a Phenix City café at the time shots were heard. Upon sur-rebuttal, however, Beddow recalled Phillips to say he had never met Ferrell until after the murder. Beddow also brought Highway Patrol chief Tom Carlisle and former Public Safety director L. B. Sullivan to swear to Phillips's good reputation and truthfulness.

The defense did the same for the state witnesses, especially Cecil Padgett. Ben and W. L. Allen could only shake their heads at the appearance of Padgett. Like Johnny Frank Griffin, he seemed to have been invisible to the established witnesses at the scene. Beddow called Ben Allen to the stand to say as much, but the question was disallowed, as was his testimony that he and W. L. Allen had written an official report to the attorney general's staff telling them that in their professional opinion, there was no viable case against Fuller.[41]

With rebuttal testimony completed, the prosecution began closing arguments. During the ninety-four-minute summation, Deason provided the state's version of what happened on the night of June 18, minute by minute and witness by witness. Using a pointer and the now-familiar map, he traced Fuller's alleged movements from the murder scene to the getaway car on Fourteenth Street, and from there toward Five Points, where he turned off onto Thirteenth Street and circled back around to the jail. Deason then analyzed the statements of Fuller's alibi witnesses. Although the state had heavily attacked the reputation of each through its own character witnesses, Deason now offered understanding, even charity. Maybe what each had said was true, except for one extremely crucial element: the time. None of the alibi witnesses could be absolutely certain what time it was when they observed Fuller; they could only guess. During their cross-examinations, Deason had brought this out quite well, even emphasizing a few contradictions among them.

In reviewing the testimony of Steve Schermann, the furniture mover who saw Patterson pointing to the left side of his chest as he rounded the corner of the Coulter Building, Deason asked rhetorically, "What was Mr. Patterson doing when he pointed to his chest? When he was pointing to his chest he was unable to speak and was trying to tell that the man who shot him wore a badge on his chest. That man [pointing to Fuller] wore a badge."

To defend Padgett, the state's star witness, Deason appealed to the Everyman: "The defense has left the inference that this man, because he owed a little money, would come up here and perjure himself. I'm willing to take your judgment about Padgett. I think you understand about him." What the jury was to understand was that Padgett was an average guy of average intelligence, a man who made a living with his hands. Without openly saying that Padgett was too dumb to make it up, Deason explained, "He couldn't possibly have fabricated the story which he told. He couldn't have told the story if he hadn't been there."

In the defense's closing arguments, Beddow and Gwin first reminded the jury of the heavy involvement of the RBA in the trial and their objective of cleaning up Phenix City. But Fuller, they explained, was charged with murder in this case—not gambling, not taking bribes, not any other crime. More importantly, the attorneys had to tear down the credibility of Littleton, Taylor, and Padgett, and this they did without mercy. Bill Littleton was "a miserable man." James Taylor had given his detailed description only after seeing Fuller for a "streamlined second." But it was Cecil Padgett, the state's star witness, for whom Beddow expressed the most contempt: "Where did Padgett come from? He was coined by Lamar Murphy. He was molded for the part he played in this case. He was conceived in sin. He was born of the woman in infamy. And I'm not talking about his mother, I'm talking about this case." All three witnesses were after the $10,000 reward. "It ought to be a capital felony to offer any such temptation to people like Littleton, Padgett, Taylor and others," Beddow said. And, he pointed out, it might be good to compare the likes of those three with Fuller's alibi witnesses, most of them lawmen: "If the state had as its witnesses Sheriff Mathews, Curtis Deason, George Phillips, Ben Clark, Aaron Smith, and Robert Lee Smith, and this defendant had as his alibi witnesses Padgett, Littleton, and Taylor, there would be no question of a conviction in this case."[42]

The jurors began deliberating at 6:30 P.M. CST on Thursday, March 10. After an hour and a half, they asked to be taken to their hotel. Deliberations picked up again the next morning, and by 1:30 CST they announced that they were ready with a verdict. Immediately the halls outside the courtroom were filled with a rush of people trying to get in, the whole scene brightly illuminated with television lights. Fuller and his attorneys, notified by telephone, arrived at about 2:00 CST. Security was extremely tight, with more than fifty deputies and police officers strategically placed in and around the courtroom, including at least ten in a semicircle around Fuller.

After everyone was seated, Judge McElroy signaled for the jurors to enter. After the foreman announced that they had reached a verdict, McElroy warned spectators, "If ever you have behaved, do so now." Fuller stood and gripped the arm of his chair as if to brace himself for what was coming: "We the jury find the defendant guilty of murder in the first degree as charged in the indictment . . . " Fuller leaned forward to hear whether the jury would let him live and showed visible relief as the foreman finished, " . . . and fix his punishment at life imprisonment." There was hardly a sound in the courtroom. Under McElroy's previous instructions, spectators remained in their seats, except for the reporters, who now made a mad dash for the doors. At twenty-three days, the trial had set a new record for a jury trial in Alabama.

About an hour later, Fuller and his wife emerged from Judge McElroy's chambers, to which they had retired after the verdict. Fuller's smile was still there, but now it seemed to be forced. A cordon of deputies accompanied him to the jail, located on the top floor. Meanwhile, outside the courtroom, Deason lit a fresh cigar, declared to reporters that he was satisfied with the verdict, and answered questions about Arch Ferrell's upcoming murder trial. He and MacDonald Gallion then went to inform John Patterson, waiting on another floor, of the verdict. His first question: How did Fuller react?[43]

11
Courageous and Honest Men

No man is ever acquitted at the bar of his own conscience.

John Patterson, May 4, 1955

For George Rogers and Drew Redden, Deason's decision to try Fuller first was a double-edged sword. There were advantages, obviously. First, it allowed them to observe the state's case firsthand. Faced with separately trying two defendants accused of the same crime, Deason provided Ferrell's attorneys with the blueprint of the case against their client. Second, there was a potential advantage in Fuller's receiving a verdict first, but only if it were acquittal. Otherwise, things could go considerably worse for Ferrell. On the negative side, the delay in Ferrell's murder trial now allowed Circuit Solicitor Perry to bring Ferrell up on the vote fraud charge first. Rogers and Redden had fought hard to have Ferrell face the murder charge first, and for good reason: if Ferrell were found guilty of vote fraud, Deason would be carrying the momentum into the murder trial and would certainly use the conviction to bolster a motive for Patterson's murder. Rogers and Redden held a deep suspicion that that was precisely why Perry was in such a hurry. This could, of course, work the opposite way if Ferrell beat the vote fraud charge, but considering how Ferrell's luck had been running since June 18, no one was willing to bet on it. And if Ferrell were found guilty of the murder charge, a misdemeanor conviction would be the least of his worries. Customarily, Ferrell's vote fraud trial would have been passed over until his murder trial was completed. About a week after Fuller's trial began, however, Perry succeeded in having it scheduled for March 7, making it very likely that Ferrell would be tried on the misdemeanor before facing the murder charge. Part of the purpose for this unorthodox procedure, Ferrell's attorneys believed, was to get them out of the Fuller courtroom.[1]

Yet Perry appeared to have second thoughts just before proceedings in Ferrell's vote fraud trial got under way. As Rogers and Redden were on their way to the courtroom, Perry, standing in the reception area of the circuit solicitor's office, asked Rogers, "Why don't we settle this case?" Rogers stopped long enough to ask how. "On a guilty plea," said Perry. "What would he get?" "Whatever the judge would give him," Perry replied. "That's a real bargain," said Rogers. Then he continued, seriously, "I won't even talk to him about that. If you want to promise him probation, I'll carry the message. I don't know what his response would be."[2] Allegedly, Perry subsequently brought up the possibility of a plea with John Patterson, who promptly vetoed any suggestion of a deal. There would be no compromise.[3]

Ferrell's vote fraud trial began on March 8, some three weeks into Fuller's murder trial. Perry had earlier refused the job of prosecutor in the murder trials, but it was hard to tell in opening arguments. He maintained that Patterson's pledge to clean up Phenix City was the motive not only for the Birmingham vote fraud but also for Patterson's murder. It was a brash move, asking a jury charged with settling a misdemeanor case to decide a capital murder question.[4]

Although Perry had a well-organized case, Ferrell's attorneys were able to shake many of the state witnesses. Red Porter's testimony was a huge disappointment for the state. Before the grand jury, Porter had testified that Ferrell had handed him $10,000 at a meeting with Phenix City gangsters not long after the May primary. During the trial, however, Porter couldn't remember who gave him the money, only that Ferrell was there when he received it. The state also underestimated Lamar Reid's vulnerability, or rather Rogers's ability to neutralize his effect. While most of Reid's testimony incriminated Garrett, there was plenty of trouble for Ferrell. The most damaging testimony concerned Ferrell's summation of the vote stealing around the state, his insistence that Reid go along with the 600-vote change in Jefferson

County, and his assurances that he and Garrett would handle any problems that might appear.[5]

Rogers and Redden were lucky in at least one respect. There was plenty of blame to go around, and Ferrell, when it came down to it, was only one of three involved. The attorneys now sought to shift the blame not only to Garrett but also to Reid. Rogers first had Reid confirm that the vote fraud was Garrett's idea, that it was Garrett who gave him the altered tally sheets, and that it was Reid himself who prepared the falsified certificate of results and then mailed it to the state committee. Seeking to further minimize Ferrell's involvement, Rogers had Reid confirm that throughout the vote fraud conversations in Birmingham, it was Garrett who did almost all the talking. Rogers also emphasized Reid's culpability, particularly his fruitless effort to cover his tracks after the vote fraud was discovered. Reid admitted that he lied to the local executive committee, to his attorney/brother-in-law Bruce White, to Solicitor Perry, and, while under oath, to the Jefferson County Grand Jury. In final arguments, Rogers characterized Ferrell as a simple county solicitor but depicted Reid, the chief accuser, as a spoiled little rich boy. With frequent references to Reid's home in the ritzy suburbs on the other side of Red Mountain and his vacation home in Florida, he asked the jury, "Can you take a man and utterly destroy him on the words of a man like Lamar Reid, a man born with a silver spoon in his mouth, a perjurer?"[6]

As the trial was winding down, news from the third floor threatened to influence the outcome. As Redden was making his closing remarks to the jury, Assistant Circuit Solicitor Bud Watson entered the courtroom and leaned over to whisper in Perry's ear: Fuller had just been convicted in the murder trial. Redden heard the remark, but apparently the jury had not. Raising his voice to drown out the ensuing exchange between Perry and Watson, Redden wrapped up his comments. As soon as Judge Wheeler completed his instructions to the jury, Rogers made a most unusual motion: could the jury be served its evening meal in the jury room instead of a local restaurant, as was customary? After a hurried conference, Judge Wheeler granted the unorthodox request, and the jury was ushered into the jury room to begin deliberations. It turned out to be a smart move. When Rogers and Redden finally left the courtroom, special edition newspapers with three-inch headlines proclaiming Fuller's conviction could be seen almost everywhere.[7]

Despite the strong defense, almost everyone, including Ferrell's attorneys, believed that Perry had convinced the jury. But after only two and a half hours of deliberation, some of that time spent eating dinner, the verdict was acquittal. Ferrell left the courtroom smiling, saying he was "innocent of the charge against me in the vote case, and I am innocent of the murder of Mr. Patterson." Apparently, Rogers and Redden were more successful with the jury than with the public. Most of the spectators expressed amazement at the outcome, and news offices were deluged with phone calls demanding an explanation. But, finally, Ferrell had won where it counted.[8]

The outcome was a tremendous blow to the murder case against Ferrell, which relied to a large extent on the proposition that Ferrell killed Patterson because the latter had threatened to expose the vote fraud, not only in Birmingham but all over the state. Now the defense could answer any suggestion of vote fraud during Ferrell's murder trial with one word: acquittal. Instead of delivering the vote fraud conviction that Deason planned to use as proof of Ferrell's motive for murdering Patterson, the jury left him with a handful of ashes.

Solicitor Perry did not take the defeat well. The day after the acquittal, Rogers and Redden were livid to find on the front page of the *Birmingham News* a skewed version of the earlier plea-bargain negotiations, saying that Ferrell's attorneys had offered a guilty plea in exchange for a $500 fine. In addition to committing the impropriety of disclosing conversations with defense counsel, Perry had deliberately, they believed, tried to poison public opinion before the murder trial. When Rogers and Redden confronted the solicitor at his home, Perry denied having leaked the information.[9] Three weeks later, Judge Wheeler, while charging another grand jury, complained about "trial juries who do not respect their oaths [to] decide cases on the evidence presented." Solicitor Perry agreed emphatically with Wheeler: "I know, and people on the street know, you were speaking of the Ferrell case. . . . And if there ever was a miscarriage of justice, it was that case. I blame the jury." Ferrell's attorneys were not about to allow those remarks to pass unchallenged. Claiming that Perry's and

Wheeler's publicized remarks made a fair trial impossible, Rogers and Redden again asked for a delay. Judge McElroy admitted that the publicity was poorly timed but said that any question of prejudice due to pretrial publicity could be disposed of during jury selection.[10]

Jury selection began on April 18, with testimony commencing two days later. In contrast to the huge crowds that attended the beginning of the Fuller trial, only eighteen spectators were on hand when Deason read the indictment to the jury. The lack of interest was due in part to the necessary duplication of the Fuller trial. Hoping he had discovered the winning formula, Deason for the most part called the same witnesses in the same order. An additional factor was that Rogers and Redden were more subdued in their courtroom performance than Beddow and Gwin, providing little of the drama that characterized Fuller's trial. It was as predictable as a summer rerun on television. Littleton, Kelley, and Padgett told the same stories they had told during the Fuller trial, the defense made the same objections and asked the same questions during cross-examination, and McElroy made the same rulings.[11]

There were few surprises, and one of the more memorable ones occurred outside the courtroom. One day during the lunch recess, the jurors were on their way back to the courtroom when thirty-year-old Joe Smith, a dairy farmer from Shelby County who was in the courthouse on business unrelated to the trial, hailed one of the jurors, a former classmate. Smith asked if he was on a jury, to which the juror answered affirmatively. Over his shoulder, Smith flippantly closed the conversation with the remark, "Hang 'em." Five jurors heard the comment, as well as bailiff Morris Oden and Chief Deputy Wilton Hogan.

Returning to the courtroom, Oden described the exchange to Judge McElroy, who was not amused. He ordered Hogan to track Smith down and bring him into court, where McElroy cited the stunned man with contempt. He then collared two unsuspecting attorneys to act as prosecutor and Smith's defense counsel. An ad hoc hearing began forthwith. The jurors who heard the remark told McElroy that they were under the impression that it was offered in jest with no insidious intent. Smith quickly confirmed that opinion by agreeing the remark was "stupid and idiotic." His attorney admitted that while Smith's act did in fact constitute contempt of court, he had made no effort to improperly influence the outcome of the trial. McElroy readily agreed and dismissed the charge. But now there was an even bigger problem. Ferrell's lawyers now moved for a mistrial, not because five jurors had heard the remark, but because McElroy had allowed the full jury to sit through Smith's contempt hearing, potentially prejudicing all twelve jurors. McElroy dismissed the motion but emphasized to the jury that the contempt charge had been instituted by him, not the state or the defense. Then he had them swear collectively that the incident would not affect their consideration of the case.[12]

Despite the repetition of witnesses from Fuller's trial, a distinct change in the nature of the testimony began to emerge midway through Deason's questions. For Fuller the emphasis had been on technical evidence, but with Ferrell the focus was on the more intangible components of motive and intent. In Fuller's trial, Deason was forced to use the rather vague assumption that Fuller, like every other crooked Russell County law enforcement officer, had a lot to lose if Patterson took office as attorney general. This was true for Ferrell, too, but the defendant's relationship with the victim had a different character. Ferrell truly hated Albert Patterson and had often said so. Deason used every example he could find.

Kenneth Cooper, circuit solicitor for Baldwin County, told the court about a statewide meeting, called by Si Garrett shortly before the June 1 Democratic runoff victory, to discuss the recent *Brown v. Board of Education* ruling by the U.S. Supreme Court. Although the morning session had indeed been taken up with the segregation topic, the afternoon consisted of a political pep rally with Ferrell urging his fellow solicitors to support Lee Porter for attorney general. Cooper quoted Ferrell as saying, "That Goddamned son of a bitch Albert Patterson is not going to take the attorney general's office."[13]

State toxicologist Wendell Sowell went over his expert testimony on the forensic evidence and added an observation not solicited during the Fuller trial: at the autopsy, Ferrell was extremely nervous. Associated Press reporter Rex Thomas testified that he overheard Ferrell say in the days after the murder that he was glad Patterson was dead. Edwin Strickland also testified, saying that at the Sunday-night dinner at the CoCo Club, Ferrell had said he "did not like the son of a bitch [Patterson] and was glad he was dead." Normally, Strickland would have made a credible witness—he had stayed in Phenix City longer than Sykes—but he had taken his Phenix City experiences and put them in a book, *Phenix City: The Wickedest City in America,* coauthored by Gene Wortsman of the *Birmingham Post-Herald.* Initially scheduled for release less than a month before Ferrell's trial began, the popular book was heavily critical of the Phenix City and Russell County political hierarchy, including Ferrell. Rogers now used Strickland's new-found fame against him, asking the reporter if he had ever said that if Fuller and Ferrell were convicted, it would probably increase book sales. Strickland denied it, but the jury understood the suggestion.[14]

Although Ferrell had just been acquitted for vote fraud, Deason used the vote fraud motive anyway, although not as directly as he had originally planned. Instead, he recast it as one component of the larger, overall argument that Ferrell and others were so intent on keeping Patterson out of office that they first tried to buy the election; when that didn't work they attempted to steal it; finally, with no other options, they killed Patterson. As soon as Deason brought up the subject of vote fraud, Ferrell's lawyers objected on the ground that the matter had already been disposed of in court. McElroy overruled them, and Rogers and Redden found themselves defending Ferrell for vote fraud all over again. Porter and Reid repeated their testimony, and Ferrell's attorneys replayed their defense.[15]

Quinnie Kelley testified and repeated his story about seeing Ferrell "half-walking, half-running" from the scene of the crime. Rogers and Redden picked away at his testimony, item by item. The first point was the distance involved, 257 feet, nearly the length of a football field. In addition, there was at least one physical discrepancy. Kelley testified that as he watched Ferrell move south on Fifth Avenue and west on Fourteenth Street, Kelley himself was also in motion around the court-house at the same pace. If that were so, asked Ferrell's attorneys, how was it that Ferrell walked a total of 155 feet while at the same time Kelley covered only 104 feet? Then, of course, the defense attacked Kelley's overall credibility. They pointed out that Kelley took a full four months to identify Ferrell and that he had left his job as a janitor shortly after that when Lamar Murphy invited him to become a deputy sheriff. Rogers also tried to reveal that Ferrell, as circuit solicitor, had opposed Kelley's efforts to obtain a pistol permit because he was afraid Kelley might shoot some kids who constantly played on the courthouse lawn and were a source of constant irritation for Kelley. That line of questioning was dropped because of state objections.[16]

After the state rested, Rogers lined up a number of witnesses to rip into Kelley's testimony. State investigator John Williams testified that he first talked to Kelley on June 24. At that time, Kelley said he didn't recognize the man heading up Fifth Avenue because the distance was too great. It was not until October 26 that Kelley identified the man as Ferrell. I & I agent Ben Allen also testified, outlining the discrepancies between Kelley's current testimony and what he had told investigators over the summer and fall. The defense also called to the stand a neighbor of Kelley's, Mrs. Hortense Tiller (the same Mrs. Tiller who had testified during Fuller's trial about seeing a large car racing down Third Avenue shortly before she heard the sirens). Although Kelley had earlier testified that he had told no one except investigators about what he had seen, Mrs. Tiller said that about two weeks after the murder Kelley had told her that just after the shooting he had seen a man come from between two buildings and get in a red or maroon car but that it was too dark to tell who it was.[17]

Rogers and Redden then went after Bill Littleton. As in Fuller's trial, Littleton's ex-girlfriend, Virginia Lange, testified that Littleton never mentioned seeing Fuller or Ferrell at the Coulter Building before the murder. In addition, Ferrell's lawyers pointed out a major discrepancy between Littleton's testimony and that of the two Southern Bell operators who handled Ferrell's long-distance phone calls on June 18. The state had earlier suggested that Ferrell's alibi telephone call, made at 8:57, could have been made from another location because the operator had not called back to verify Ferrell's location, as she did during his earlier phone calls, made between 8:36 and 8:51. Given that the state implicitly conceded that Ferrell was in his office until at least 8:51, how was it that Littleton saw Ferrell in front of the Coulter Building at about 8:50?[18]

Cecil Padgett's testimony, theoretically, was easier to contradict, since Padgett claimed he was standing in the middle of Fifth Avenue at the time of the shooting. In contrast to the situation with Littleton, the gunshots turned all eyes in Padgett's direction. One witness well situated to testify on the matter was Mrs. Bentley, the owner of the grocery store across from the Coulter Building. She said that when she closed the front door a few minutes after 9:00, no car was parked in front. On cross-examination, however, Deason succeeded in having her express some uncertainty. After a while, she clammed up: "You done asked me enough questions," she said, and shook her fist at Deason as she left the stand. Mrs. Bentley was followed by Jimmy Sanders, who told of running to Patterson just after he fell to the sidewalk. Sanders did not see a car across the street in front of Bentley's store, nor did he see anyone standing in the street. The same went for Sanders's buddy, Hugh Buchanan, who, like Sanders, had looked down the street and saw Patterson's body on the sidewalk but did not see Padgett or his car.[19]

To establish Ferrell's alibi, Rogers had to counter the state's contention that it was not Ferrell who made the critical phone call to Birmingham at 8:57 but rather an unknown accomplice making the call for him. Frank Long, the man who answered the telephone call at the Redmont, testified that the man who asked to speak to Garrett shortly before the murder was, in his "best considered judgment," Arch Ferrell. Long was followed on the stand by Retha Edmundson (formerly Retha Harris), the long-distance operator who handled Ferrell's two courthouse calls on the night of the murder. She agreed that the voice of the party making the second telephone call sounded the same as the one who had placed the first call.[20]

Rogers called Ferrell to the witness stand, where the defendant gave a detailed account of his movements on June 18 and a point-by-point denial of the testimony of Littleton, Kelley, and Padgett. Rogers led Ferrell to the scale map of the murder scene and pointed to the alley next to the Coulter Building. He now asked his client point-blank if either he or Albert Fuller was there when Patterson was killed. Slowly and emphatically, Ferrell replied, "I certainly was not present and I do not know about Mr. Fuller being present. No, sir, I was not there." Rogers now instructed him, "Tell this jury whether or not you fired those shots or were present."

FERRELL: No, sir.
ROGERS: Did you have anything to do with that matter?
FERRELL: No, sir.
ROGERS: Do you know who did it?
FERRELL: No, sir.

On cross-examination, Deason began by asking Ferrell about gambling conditions during his tenure as Russell County circuit solicitor. Ferrell said he had no knowledge of open gambling in Phenix City, but he admitted that the National Guard had confiscated a large number of gaming devices during the cleanup. Deason asked Ferrell to identify a number of Phenix City racketeers, by now familiar names from the newspapers and trials: Shepherd, Matthews, Davis, Revel, McCollister, Myrick, Abney, Gullatte, Cook, Roney, Billingsley, and Fuller. Ferrell allowed that he knew each one but said he had never asked any of them to support Lee Porter. He should have been more on his guard. Deason was reading a roster of the racketeers who had contributed to Porter's campaign—the same list Sykes had confronted him with the previous July. Now Deason had it, and the prosecutor sprang the trap. Waving the paper in front of Ferrell's face, he asked, "Have you seen this before?" "Yes, sir," Ferrell replied. After confirming his handwriting, Ferrell admitted that the list was the Phenix City racketeers he had just denied taking contributions from. Deason wanted to know what the figures next to each name signified. Ferrell said he had no idea, he had only copied it out of curiosity when he saw it in a Birmingham hotel room sometime after the May primary.

Deason followed this up with questions about Ferrell's actions on the day of the murder. After confirming that the window and shade to his office were open, Ferrell said he did not recall hearing any shots, sirens, or other unusual noises before he left his office at about 9:15. So it went for almost four hours. Ferrell remained unruffled throughout Deason's questioning; in fact, his eagerness to answer got him into trouble with his own lawyers, who admonished him on more than one occasion to wait until they had an opportunity to object before he answered.[21]

The final witness for the defense was Lamar Reid, who admitted that he had said on the day the murder trial began that he didn't believe Ferrell knew about the 600-vote change that occurred in the Jefferson County totals. To make sure that the jury didn't miss Ferrell's vote fraud acquittal, Ferrell's lawyers closed their case by simply reading Judge Wheeler's official order clearing him of the charges. With that, the defense rested.[22]

After rebuttal testimony, Deason immediately began his final arguments to the jury. In a touch of unintended drama, an emergency vehicle's siren on the street below started up just as Deason began a chilling description of the murder. Calling the defendant a "vicious killer," Deason argued that Ferrell killed Patterson only after other efforts had failed to keep him from becoming attorney general. Emphasizing statements attributed to Ferrell that Patterson would never become attorney general, that he and Garrett would see to it, Deason pointed to the grim-faced Ferrell and shouted, "Well, he saw to it that Albert Patterson wasn't the attorney general, didn't he?" With some incredulity in his voice, Deason asked the jury, "Can you imagine a man, can you imagine a man in your wildest imagination, who would get up before twelve men and deny to you that there was open gambling in Phenix City? You know that he wasn't telling the truth." He ridiculed Ferrell's denial of any involvement with the attempt to steal the election from Patterson: "He came here [Birmingham] with one purpose and one purpose alone. That purpose was to steal votes." Deason called attention to the testimony of two reporters who said they had heard Ferrell say he was glad Patterson was dead. "What sort of a man are we dealing with?" asked Deason scornfully. "There he sits. The man who was going to see that Albert Patterson didn't become attorney general, the man who said he was glad he was dead." He demanded that Ferrell receive the death penalty and claimed that the state had more than met the burden of proving beyond a reasonable doubt that Ferrell was guilty. "The evidence justifies, the evidence demands, that this man be placed in the electric chair for killing Albert Patterson. Do your duty and the State of Alabama will be satisfied."

After Deason's shouting, Rogers's and Redden's measured summary seemed quiet. They first reminded the jury that Ferrell was on trial for murder, not for vote fraud, and asked the jury not to allow themselves to be "whipped into a froth of malice and prejudice." Beyond that, they found it difficult to believe the state's case and expected that the jury would, too. Citing numerous contradictions among witnesses, particularly Littleton, Kelley, and Padgett, Ferrell's attorneys painted a picture of an incoherent and conflicting case against their client.[23]

The jurors began deliberating on Tuesday, May 3. By noon the next day, they hadn't reached a verdict. Then, about 3:30 CST, Sheriff Holt

McDowell entered the courtroom with a force of deputies and police officers. Ferrell came from the rear of the courtroom, where he had been sitting with his wife and other family members. As he and his attorneys took their seats at a table facing the jury, a half dozen officers surrounded him. Other officers stationed themselves at doors and other strategic positions throughout the courtroom. Within minutes, the number of spectators in the courtroom doubled, reaching about 150. After warning all those present against any demonstration regardless of the verdict, McElroy called for the jury. Before the foreman read the verdict, he produced a statement for the court: "We have put our whole heart in this and prayed for guidance. We offer this verdict with apologies to no one." After a brief pause, he continued, "We, the jury, find the defendant not guilty." In the press gallery, reporters Rex Thomas of the Associated Press and Ray Jenkins of the *Columbus Ledger* couldn't believe their ears. They had sat through both trials and were certain that Ferrell would be convicted just as Fuller had.[24] Throughout the courtroom there was a collective gasp, but Ferrell, still facing the jury, maintained his poker face. Except for some glistening around the eyes, he gave no sign of emotion as Chief Deputy Hogan escorted him through the courtroom to McElroy's chambers. Leaving the spectator seats, Madeline hurried to catch up with her husband and his attorneys.

About twenty minutes later, Ferrell reappeared to read a statement: "Twelve courageous and honest men have confirmed my innocence which I personally have always known. I am deeply grateful for the justice I have received." Cornered by another group of reporters, Madeline commented only that "today is a beautiful day," the same words she had used to test the courtroom public-address system during her testimony. Attorney General John Patterson was not present when the verdict was announced. He later issued a statement thanking prosecutors for their work and offered this observation: "Those of us who seek redress for the wrongs done us may console ourselves with this thought. No man is ever acquitted at the bar of his own conscience."[25]

12
Legacy

We hope that someday they [the children of Phenix City] will
rise up and throw off this ugly reputation that our town has had
for the past one hundred years.

Hugh Bentley, 1955

They [the people of Phenix City] will never live it down. Not in a
million years.

John Patterson, 1994

For all practical purposes, Arch Ferrell's trial jury acquitted Si Garrett,
too. How could the state reasonably argue that Garrett aided and abetted Ferrell in the murder of Albert Patterson after Ferrell had been
found not guilty? It was a moot question for John Patterson and the
attorney general's office while Garrett remained untouchable in a
Galveston psychiatric ward for five months. Then, on October 10,
1955, Garrett suddenly appeared at the Russell County jail with his
attorney, Rod Beddow, and declared that he was innocent of the murder charges, fully recovered from his illness, and ready to fight the
accusations against him.[1]

Garrett's return posed a problem for Patterson, who, now that Ferrell had been acquitted, was not particularly eager to bring Garrett
to trial. Caught off guard, the state agreed to Garrett's release on
$12,500 bond rather than reveal what evidence it had to keep him in
jail. But Patterson wasn't willing to let Garrett get away clean, either.
Murder might be almost impossible to prove, but insanity wasn't. Although the courts had denied Emmett Perry's attempt to have Garrett
submit to a lunacy examination in the vote fraud case, Patterson now
tried a similar ploy with the murder charge. Avoiding Section 428 of

the Alabama Criminal Code's Title 15, the provision that the state supreme court had earlier ruled did not apply to Garrett, Patterson instead brought to Judge McElroy's attention Section 425, a seldom-used passage directing circuit judges to order a mental examination for capital crime defendants if there were "reasonable grounds to believe that such defendant was insane at the time of the offense, or presently." Simultaneously, Patterson provided Judge McElroy with a statement from the director of Bryce State Hospital, J. S. Tarwater, who indeed expressed doubt as to Garrett's sanity. McElroy refused Patterson's request to send Garrett directly to the state psychiatric hospital, but he did schedule a hearing on the matter.[2]

At the hearing, held one week later in Phenix City, the state argued that the law was clear; McElroy had no choice but to order Garrett to the state hospital for a full psychiatric examination. Garrett's attorneys maintained that there was no reason for a mental exam because Garrett was completely recovered from his previous illness and in any case would never plead insanity as a defense. Instead of making an issue of Garrett's sanity, however, Beddow argued that the law prosecutors referred to was unconstitutional because it would deprive Garrett of his freedom without due process of law. Basically, it was an alteration of Beddow's previous argument against Perry's attempt to have Garrett examined after his vote fraud arrest. In that case, the state supreme court ruled that the purpose of the law ceased to exist once the defendant was out of jail. Beddow took that logic one step further to argue that the timing of the petition was immaterial. The state had agreed to let Garrett out on bail, and forcing him to submit to a sanity hearing would unconstitutionally deprive him of his liberty. On November 25, Judge McElroy agreed with Garrett's attorneys, but because the issue involved constitutionality, he invited a state supreme court appeal to settle the question.[3]

Even as the attorney general's office was sparring with Beddow on the issue of Garrett's sanity, it was also having to ward off Beddow's attempts to win a new trial for Albert Fuller. Beddow and Gwin had appealed Fuller's conviction, eventually putting forth some ninety-three grounds for a new trial. Most were based on alleged procedural errors on the part of Judge McElroy, such as improperly instructing the jury, allowing improper state testimony, or not allowing proper defense testimony. More interesting from the standpoint of the murder investigation, however, were Beddow's claims that previously unavailable testimony, particularly from Ferrell had his lawyers allowed him to testify, would have produced an acquittal. Now that Ferrell had been acquitted, of course, Rogers and Redden had no objection to having Ferrell take the stand.[4]

Beddow had also been able to produce some fairly substantial statements, also previously unavailable, to contradict testimony from three of the state's key witnesses. The first was from Mrs. C. W. Bentley, the owner of the grocery store across from the alley in which Patterson was murdered. As a witness in Fuller's trial, she had been cagey in letting either prosecutors or defense attorneys know what she had seen on the night of the murder. She was more forthcoming in Ferrell's trial, testifying that when she latched the door and turned the light off at precisely 9:00, there was no car parked in front of her store. When she looked out five minutes later at the sound of the shots, the parking places out front were still empty. She was also certain that no car went down Fifteenth Street, which bordered the north side of the store, because two of her doors were open on that side. Her statement directly contradicted Cecil and Edith Padgett's recollection that they had parked in front of Bentley's minutes before the shooting and then drove east on Fifteenth Street directly after.[5]

Supporting Mrs. Bentley's version of events was Robert J. Waters, who lived on Broad Street, one block west of Fifth Avenue. He said that he had left home sometime between 7:30 and 8:00 on the night of June 18 to go to the Golden Rule Barbecue, located on Third Avenue. He had walked south on Broad, east on Fourteenth Street, north on Fifth Avenue past the Coulter Building, and then east again on Fifteenth Street. At the restaurant he drank coffee and talked with friends for about an hour. Then, around 9:00, he left and headed home. As Waters started up Fifteenth Street again, this time heading west, he heard the gunshots but didn't think much about them. He was almost to the Fifth Avenue intersection when he remembered that he had forgotten to pick up the barbecue he had ordered to take home. Waters turned around and walked back to the restaurant. The whole time he was on Fifteenth Street, probably a full ten minutes after the shots were fired, Waters didn't see anyone, and that was precisely Beddow's point. It further contradicted Padgett's claim that he and his wife immediately left the area as soon as they heard the shots and headed back toward Columbus via Fifteenth Street.[6]

To further discredit state witness Bill Littleton, the Phenix City cab driver who testified that he saw Fuller and Ferrell standing in front of the Coulter Building about fifteen minutes before the murder, Beddow produced the statement of W. E. Wages of Phenix City. Wages said that a few days after the murder he was sitting at a local gas station reading a newspaper when Littleton stopped by. Jokingly, Wages asked Littleton when he was going to collect the reward in the Patterson case. Littleton said he knew nothing about a reward, and Wages pointed out the article which stated that Governor Persons had authorized $5,000 for information leading to the arrest and conviction of Patterson's murderer. A few weeks later, Wages claimed, Littleton contacted him and offered to split the reward money if Wages would support a story that he and another had concocted.[7]

Then there was the statement of fifteen-year-old Freda Ann Miller of Columbus, Georgia. She said that on the night of the murder she had caught a cab at about 8:35 to take her to Idle Hour Park in Phenix City. It was around 9:10 when the cabbie dropped her off, handing her his business card as he drove off. Miss Miller was sure that the driver was James Radius Taylor, the man who had testified that he saw Fuller running from the direction of the murder scene less than five minutes after he heard the shots at approximately 9:05.[8]

After considering the new testimony, Judge McElroy refused Fuller's petition for a new trial. He pointed out that Beddow and Gwin's spirited defense during the trial included several witnesses who contradicted James Taylor, Cecil Padgett, and Bill Littleton. The jury didn't believe them then, and there was little to indicate that one or two more would make any difference now. As for Ferrell's testimony, McElroy agreed with the state's contention that if Ferrell was where he said he was at the time of the murder, then obviously he could not have known if Fuller was at the murder scene or not. Beddow appealed the decision to the state supreme court.[9]

As prisoner number 67315 at Kilby State Penitentiary, Fuller worked first as a janitor and later in the prison cotton mill, making fifty cents every three weeks. He continued to insist on his innocence, hoping that one day "something will show up to prove to the public that I'm not guilty." Once or twice, it looked like Fuller's wish might be granted. On January 27, 1958, a suggestion of Fuller's innocence appeared in newspapers nationwide from an improbable source, syndicated columnist Dorothy Kilgallen's "Voice of Broadway." Kilgallen, a popular entertainment writer and permanent panelist on CBS's Sunday-night game show *What's My Line?*, had written, "City Desks might check with Special Investigator Bernard B. Spindel. He's reported to have evidence to prove that the chief deputy of Phenix City, who was given a life sentence for the murder of Alabama Attorney General Patterson, actually is innocent—and the real slayer is a gambler well known in those parts." Kilgallen's comment was only the most publicized facet of a bizarre series of events in which Fuller's quest for freedom became intertwined, first, with leftover Phenix City underworld maneuvering, and second, in Alabama electoral politics. In the end, it convinced state authorities of Fuller's guilt more than ever.[10]

One of John Patterson's biggest worries during his years as attorney general was that the state supreme court would grant Fuller a new trial. If that happened, Patterson would have to make sure that the evidence in a second trial was even stronger than in the first. As a result, Fuller's conviction hardly slowed down the state's effort to tie him to Patterson's murder. After months of investigation, however, it appeared that there was nothing new. About the only person remaining who could conceivably provide new information was "Head" Revel, one of Phenix City's top gangsters, who had fled town soon after Patterson's murder. That fact by itself was cause for attention from Sykes's investigators, who put out a fugitive warrant on Revel as soon as he was indicted by the Russell County Grand Jury on some fifty vice charges. Their suspicions were heightened by Hoyt Shepherd, who, in his heart-to-heart with MacDonald Gallion in the summer of 1954, had said that if anyone knew the details of Fuller's involvement in Patterson's murder, it would be Revel. The attorney general's staff let it be known that it would try to reduce the numerous cleanup charges against Revel if he would turn himself in. On June 18, 1956, two years to the day after Patterson was murdered, Revel drove up to the county jail and honked his horn until the jailer opened the gate. In his subsequent interrogation, Revel pleaded his innocence to Sheriff Murphy and attorney general staff members.[11]

Although investigators were convinced of Revel's innocence, they let him continue to believe that Fuller was incriminating him. The scam worked so well that Revel hired two New York detectives, one of them the Mr. Spindel named in Kilgallen's column, to make sure that the evidence against Fuller would preclude any suggestion of Revel's involvement. However, for reasons unexplained, the detectives had a change of heart after they reached Phenix City, dropped Revel as their client, and began working for those interested in making Fuller a free man. The identity of these new clients has never been revealed, but they were not motivated by the desire to right any injustice against Fuller. Instead, their purpose in clearing Fuller was simply to put an end to John Patterson's political career.[12]

In his three years as attorney general, Patterson and the Folsom administration had clashed over a number of issues, but none was charged with as much political acrimony as Patterson's attacks on the administration's shady dealings with favored contractors. Capitalizing on increasing anti-Folsom sentiment throughout the state, Patterson took up the fight for good government in the summer of 1956 and filed injunctions against some of the more questionable state contracts. His war with the Folsom administration continued through 1956 and 1957 and involved large state contractors as well as petty misspending in the Governor's Mansion Fund. Although the court actions were politically popular, Patterson was threatening powerful men. The last thing they wanted was for him to be governor after Folsom left office, but by early 1958 that's exactly where things were headed.

One way to dampen Patterson's political currency, these men calculated, was to prove that Fuller, one of the men whom John Patterson was absolutely sure killed his father, was innocent. This explains the turnaround of the two private detectives originally hired by Revel. Patterson began his own investigation and soon discovered that both detectives had had run-ins with the law. As luck would have it, not long after the attempt to smear Patterson became public, a federal grand jury in New York indicted Spindel for illegally wiretapping the Teamsters' Union Headquarters in Detroit, along with Jimmy Hoffa, the Midwest leader of the Teamsters. With Spindel's indictment and unfavorable press attention, the private effort to clear Fuller collapsed. The man hurt the worst in this debacle was, of course, Fuller, who probably was unaware of the forces raging around him.[13]

In the meantime, Revel continued to search for a way to prove that Fuller was the killer. He soon got his chance. One of Revel's former employees, Johnny Benefield, had gained considerable fame around Phenix City for his safecracking skills. Benefield, like Revel, had fled Phenix City soon after the murder. By late 1958 he was serving time in a Columbia, South Carolina, jail. Although Benefield faced relatively minor charges, local authorities had led him to believe that he was in more trouble than he actually was. In a panic, Benefield told police that he wanted to talk to Alabama authorities about Patterson's murder. When Assistant Attorney General Noel Baker arrived, Benefield said that he had some significant information concerning Albert Fuller and Patterson's murder but would tell it all only if Revel told him in person that it was OK. On New Year's Day 1959, John Patterson, accompanied by Assistant Attorneys General Baker and Joe Robertson, picked up Revel in Phenix City and drove to Columbia to hear the "true story" of Patterson's murder.[14]

Benefield told them the following story: on the day of Patterson's murder, Fuller contacted Benefield and asked for an untraceable handgun. It just so happened that a few weeks before, Benefield had cracked a safe in Georgia that belonged to a railroad detective. Among the items taken was an unusual handgun, a .38-caliber firing mechanism mounted on a larger .44 frame. Fuller picked up the gun on the afternoon of June 18. Late that night, Fuller showed up at Benefield's home with the gun and asked him to cut it up. Benefield placed the pistol on the concrete floor of his garage and went to work with his blowtorch. The result was four unrecognizable globs of steel that Fuller took away wrapped in a gunny sack.[15]

Patterson and his staff were skeptical. Over the past four years there had been a dozen or so such stories, almost all from people who hoped to catch some sort of break from the police. When Patterson, Baker, and Robertson returned to Alabama, they took Benefield's suggestion and actually dug up the concrete in the spot that Benefield had indicated. They then sent the slab to the Alabama Department of Toxicology and Criminal Investigation's Mobile office, which housed a metallurgical laboratory. There, technicians confirmed the existence of metal alloys, consistent with those found in the manufacture of handguns, embedded in the concrete.[16]

Fuller never got a retrial. On February 12, 1959, the Alabama Supreme Court upheld the 1955 conviction. While the justices admitted that Fuller's lawyers had provided a "substantial" defense, it was not their policy to supplant a trial jury's verdict, even if they disagreed with it. As for the issue of new evidence, they ruled that Judge McElroy was in a better position than they were to determine if the evidence was strong enough to justify a new trial. Sentenced to life in prison with no prospect of a retrial, Fuller's only hope was parole. His earliest eligibility date would be 1965, ten years after his conviction. Fuller was careful to avoid any trouble while at Kilby, and the state parole board granted his application as soon as his ten years were up. One provision of his release, though, was that he never enter Phenix City again. He moved to Mobile and took a job with the city's Water Services System. While working in the spring of 1969, he fell from a ladder and suffered critical brain injuries. The parole board looked the other way when former Russell County sheriff Ralph Mathews agreed to let Fuller move back into his old apartment, which Mathews owned. Despite two operations, Fuller's health steadily declined, and he died on September 16, 1969.[17]

In October 1958, the Alabama Supreme Court upheld Judge McElroy's ruling on Garrett's sanity hearing. Patterson never brought Garrett to trial on the murder charge. Garrett returned to his family farm in Clarke County and never got involved in politics again. In July 1964 the state officially dropped the murder charge at the behest of Richmond Flowers, state attorney general in George Wallace's first administration. A week later, the vote fraud charge was dropped as well. Garrett died of a massive stroke in July 1967.[18]

Arch Ferrell returned to Phenix City, but he never gained the stature he held before June 18, 1954. Despite his acquittals in both the murder and vote fraud trials, the Alabama Bar Association, based on the vote fraud testimony of Lamar Reid and Red Porter, disbarred him in April 1956. For a while, Ferrell made a living as a salesman; then, in 1969, the state bar association reinstated him. He ran a successful law practice in Phenix City until his death in 1993, maintaining his innocence to the end.[19]

Perhaps the man most affected by the Albert Patterson murder investigation was John Patterson, who before June 18, 1954, wanted nothing more than to be a small-town lawyer with enough time for fishing. Instead, Patterson was thrust into politics, a profession he disdained and had, in fact, attempted to dissuade his father from entering. Ironically, he was a hugely popular attorney general, fighting loan sharks, desegregation, and corruption in the Folsom administration. He parlayed that momentum into a successful bid for governor in 1958, first defeating a host of other candidates in the primary, then George Wallace in the runoff, Wallace's only statewide electoral defeat. Upon leaving office in 1963, Patterson ran a lucrative law practice. In 1966, he failed in his reelection effort against Lurleen Wallace. Although he quit politics after Howell Heflin defeated him in the 1970 race for Alabama Supreme Court chief justice, fourteen years later Governor Wallace appointed him to a vacancy on the Alabama Court of Criminal Appeals, a post he won in his own right in subsequent elections. He retired in 1997 and lives on his farm in Tallapoosa County, not far from where his father was born.[20]

By far the most tragic figure to emerge from the Albert Patterson murder investigation was Cecil Padgett, the prosecution's star witness. Padgett reveled in his role of celebrity, but like many other instant heroes, he couldn't handle the inevitable loss of fame. After the reporters lost interest, Padgett was able to avoid obscurity only through the support of a grateful John Patterson, who, as he began his campaign for governor in early 1958, hired Padgett as his personal bodyguard. In this capacity Padgett, packing a gun, appeared everywhere with the popular candidate. When Patterson took office, he appointed Padgett as a state liquor agent, potentially a much more lucrative position than the listed pay scale indicated. Patterson also awarded Padgett with an honorary appointment to the governor's staff with the rank of lieutenant colonel in the National Guard.[21]

Despite the governor's help, Padgett began to fall apart. He quit his state liquor agent job after Phenix City's mayor accused him of trying to control the town's beer licenses; then he began drinking, constantly fighting with his wife, and sometimes calling newspaper reporters just to remind them who he was. Then Padgett began getting into real trouble. In June 1961, a superior court in Muscogee, Georgia, convicted him of larceny and sentenced him to six months in prison. In January 1962, Padgett was sentenced to three months in jail for passing worthless checks. Five months after that, he received a thirty-day term for contempt of court after failing to pay a $12 fine for public intoxication. By November 1963 he had divorced his wife and moved to California, where he remarried. The change of location failed to turn Padgett's luck around, and he constantly badgered Patterson with stories of illnesses, operations, lost wallets, and unreasonable landlords and employers, inevitably ending each letter with a loan request.[22]

During the summer of 1965, Padgett decided to return home. On September 11, a Southern Pacific Railroad worker found him alongside the tracks about nine miles west of Marfa, Texas. He died about three hours later at a local hospital. A local investigation determined that he had fallen out of a freight train and fractured his skull.[23]

Throughout the latter half of 1954, Phenix City was constantly in the public spotlight. The story of the murder and subsequent cleanup was compelling, and almost immediately it became clear what interpretations were acceptable to the RBA and other winners in the cleanup. On December 6, 1954, CBS's *Studio One* broadcast the play *Short Cut*. Starring Jackie Gleason as the Patterson-like Sam Wheeler, the play portrayed a politician from a small, corruption-filled southern town who is murdered after he turns against the mobsters he was once allied with. It is unknown where the writers received their inspiration, but the Albert Patterson character presented to the nation three days before the murder indictments were handed down was very much like the one described by local lawmen and gangsters in the first few days after the murder: an unscrupulous, arrogant, and lecherous politician who got what was coming to him.

Many in Phenix City found that interpretation totally unacceptable. During the next year, Mrs. Patterson, Hugh Bentley, and Patterson's former secretary, Mrs. Lucille Smith, each filed suit against CBS, Gleason, and the show's sponsor, Westinghouse, with requested damages totaling millions of dollars. While the plaintiffs admitted that neither they nor Albert Patterson was named outright in the production, they insisted that no one familiar with Phenix City would fail to recognize the characters as themselves. As a result, the telecast had publicly ridiculed each of them and damaged the reputation of Albert Patterson. Eventually, the suits were settled out of court for an undisclosed sum.[24]

The RBA expressed no complaints about the accuracy of the next

Phenix City chronicle. *Birmingham News* reporter Ed Strickland, who arrived in town the night of the murder and stayed until the trials were moved to Birmingham, saw early on the commercial potential of a book on the subject. He joined with another Birmingham reporter who had made a name covering the Birmingham vote fraud investigation, Gene Wortsman of the *Birmingham Post-Herald,* to write what Strickland considered an insider's view of the murder investigation and cleanup. For a book released only three months after the final indictments were handed down, *Phenix City: The Wickedest City in America* was surprisingly accurate, and no wonder. The two reporters drew material not only from their almost daily field reporting but also from the sensational yet supposedly confidential results of the National Guard's investigation of Phenix City's vice establishments and the gangsters who ran them.

General Hanna wanted a historical record of the National Guard's activities in Phenix City should such a situation ever arise again. Hanna asked Major Hershel Finney, in civilian life a sixth-grade Scottsboro schoolteacher, to write a comprehensive history of the guard's tenure in Phenix City. Halfway through the project, Finney, like Strickland, realized the manuscript's market potential and asked Hanna if he could use it to write a book. He even had a working title, "The Phenix City Story." General Hanna declined, saying the material was the property of the Alabama National Guard and was not to be used for publication. Despite the general's prohibition, however, the report somehow became the basis for *Wickedest City,* and Strickland and Wortsman found themselves coauthors of one of the best-selling books ever written about Alabama, thanks in large part to the thorough yet uncredited work of Major Finney.[25]

Nor did the RBA have anything critical to say about the movie that followed, Allied Artists' *The Phenix City Story,* a highly fictionalized account of Albert Patterson's campaign for attorney general and John Patterson's continuation of his father's cause. Perhaps one reason why Phenix City residents overlooked the film's inaccuracy was that it was filmed on location, allowing many of them brief roles as extras. Starring Richard Kiley (*On the Waterfront, The Blackboard Jungle*) as John Patterson, John McIntire (*Wagon Train*) as Albert Patterson, and Kathryn Grant (soon to be Mrs. Bing Crosby) as a fictional card dealer struggling with the morality of her position, the movie didn't make a martyr of Albert Patterson so much as it made a hero of John Patterson. Alabamians watched admiringly as the avenging son slugged it out (literally) with the gangsters who murdered his father, and then, with face bleeding and hair and clothes still disheveled after the brawl, screamed through the telephone line to the state capitol before an angry crowd:

> TO STATE CAPITOL: Now before you say no again, I want you to listen. You've got to listen.
> TO CROWD: You want this city cleaned up? Well, let the State Capitol hear the voice of Phenix City! Shout, so he can hear it!
> [*Loud and enthusiastic affirmative from the crowd*]
> TO STATE CAPITOL: Now, by tomorrow morning, when they hear about my father's death, you'll hear ten thousand times that sound! The voice of Alabama! Now will you send us help?
> [*Crowd shouts approval*]
> TO STATE CAPITOL: [*Quietly*] Thank you.
> TO CROWD: They're sending the militia. By tomorrow Phenix City will be under martial law.
> [*Crowd shouts approval*][26]

The public loved it, and even if most Alabamians recognized it as fiction, it was probably what they wanted to believe.

The Albert Patterson murder investigation remains incomplete in that, one way or another, justice was denied. The Russell County Grand Jury indicted three men for Patterson's murder, and depending on one's point of view, either two of them escaped punishment or one was punished unjustly. For the winners in the Glorious Cleanup, the only possible conclusion is the former. And, historically speaking, that has been the accepted interpretation outside Phenix City. Within Phenix City, however, the jury is still out.

Albert Patterson's murder changed Phenix City forever. The reform element has been in firm control since the cleanup, and the town, once treated as a pariah by the rest of Alabama, is as God-fearing and politically conservative as any other county seat in Alabama—perhaps even more, given the residents' sensitivity to its reputation. There have been other changes as well. The downtown area is practically deserted, the businesses having moved when the highway by-passes were constructed on the outskirts. Someone standing outside the Coulter Building today would find it difficult to believe that at one time the area was buzzing with activity. Further channeling traffic away from the former center of town is the recently constructed Thirteenth Street Bridge, a four-lane structure connecting Phenix City to Columbus. But underneath, largely unnoticed from above, the Chattahoochee River—deep, dark, and murky, like Albert Patterson's murder—flows as it always has.

Major Characters

Abney, J. D.
Described in *Wickedest City* as one of Phenix City's "second-string mobsters"; part owner of the Bama Club, Club Avalon, and New York Club.

Allen, Ben
Investigator for Alabama Department of Public Safety's Identification and Investigative Division assigned to the Albert Patterson homicide case.

Allen, Walter L.
Investigator for Alabama Department of Public Safety's Identification and Investigative Division assigned to the Albert Patterson homicide case.

Andersen, Fred
Managing editor of the *Montgomery Advertiser;* in his role as reporter he accompanied Attorney General Silas Garrett to Phenix City in the days after the murder.

Baker, Noel
Opelika attorney; friend and confidant of John Patterson; appointed by Patterson as assistant attorney general in January 1955.

Barton, Lee
Assistant attorney general sent to Phenix City by Attorney General Silas Garrett three days after Albert Patterson's murder to coordinate investigation.

Beddow, Roderick, Jr.
Son of Roderick Beddow Sr.; associate legal counsel in Albert Fuller's murder trial.

Beddow, Roderick, Sr.
Chief legal counsel in Albert Fuller's murder trial; also represented Silas Garrett in legal proceedings resulting from Garrett's indictments for vote fraud and murder; also represented several Phenix City businessmen indicted for vice charges.

Belcher, William

Phenix City attorney and 1954 nominee for one of two state representative seats from Russell County; nomination subsequently voided by state committee.

Benefield, Johnny

Described in *Wickedest City* as a safecracker; later implicated Albert Fuller in the murder of Albert Patterson.

Bentley, Hugh

Columbus, Georgia, sporting goods merchant who founded Russell Betterment Association in 1951; generally considered leader of Phenix City's reform movement.

Bentley, Ida (Mrs. C. W.)

Stepmother of Hugh Bentley; owner of Bentley's Grocery, located across the street from alley in which Albert Patterson was murdered.

Billingsley, E. L. "Buck"

Described in *Wickedest City* as one of Phenix City's "second-string mobsters"; operator of Ritz Café.

Bodecker, Fred

Birmingham private detective hired by Jefferson County Democratic Executive Committee to investigate discrepancies in Jefferson County's 1954 primary runoff returns.

Brassell, J. W. "Jabe"

Phenix City attorney and one of two state representatives from Russell County; made official complaint of vote fraud to state Democratic Executive Committee following his defeat in 1954 primary; subsequently reinstated by state committee.

Britton, Hugh

One of the founders of the Russell Betterment Association. Compiled much of the information used to indict the gangsters during the cleanup.

Buchanan, Hugh

Area resident who was at door of Smitty's Grill when Albert Patterson was murdered.

Burch, Shannon

Russell County probate judge; former Russell County sheriff; testified at murder trials of Albert Fuller and Arch Ferrell.

Caldwell, James

Phenix City attorney assigned by state Democratic Executive Committee to replace Arch Ferrell as Russell County circuit solicitor after Ferrell's 1954 nomination was voided.

Carmichael, Albert
  Alabama attorney general, 1947–51; appointed by Attorney General Silas Garrett as first assistant attorney general in 1951.
Chambers, Maurice
  Investigator for Alabama Department of Public Safety's Identification and Investigative Division assigned to the Albert Patterson homicide case.
Chestnut, Dewey
  One of the first Phenix City policemen to arrive at murder scene.
Clark, Ben
  Chief jailer at Russell County jail; alibi witness for Albert Fuller.
Cochran, Abbie
  Proprietor of Elite Café; was in café when Albert Patterson was murdered.
Cochran, John
  Husband of Abbie Cochran; was also in Elite Café when Albert Patterson was murdered.
Cole, Ben
  Phenix City attorney and one of two state representatives from Russell County; made official complaint of vote fraud to state Democratic Executive Committee following his defeat in 1954 primary but was not reinstated.
Coley, Oscar
  Investigator for Alabama Department of Public Safety's Identification and Investigative Division assigned to the Albert Patterson homicide case.
Cook, "Red"
  Described in *Wickedest City* as "the enforcer" for Phenix City mobsters; operated the Original Barbecue Lottery.
Coulter, Hilda
  Helped organize Russell Betterment Association Ladies' Auxiliary; clerk of the reformed Russell County Grand Jury.
Curtis, V. Cecil
  Phenix City attorney and 1954 nominee for one of two state representative seats from Russell County; nomination subsequently voided by state Democratic Executive Committee.
Daniel, Pal
  Phenix City police chief at the time Albert Patterson was murdered.
Davis, Godwin, Jr.
  Son of Godwin Davis Sr.

Davis, Godwin, Sr.

Described in *Wickedest City* as one of the "inner council" of Phenix City mobsters; along with two sons, owned and operated Davis Enterprises, a conglomerate of businesses that included the National Lottery Company, Davis Sporting Goods and Pawn Shop, Manhattan Café, and Silver Slipper Lounge.

Deason, Cecil

Assistant Jefferson County circuit solicitor; appointed special prosecutor in the Albert Fuller and Arch Ferrell murder trials.

Deason, Curtis

Alabama Alcohol Beverage Control officer; alibi witness for Albert Fuller.

Dees, Johnny

Russell County assistant jailer; alibi witness for Albert Fuller.

Elkins, James

Ambulance attendant for Colonial Funeral Home in Phenix City; delivered Patterson's body to Cobb Memorial Hospital.

Eller, Charles

Defense witness in Albert Fuller murder trial.

Elwer, James

One of three young furniture movers in or in front of Coulter Building when Albert Patterson was murdered.

Ennis, Raymond

Area resident who was standing in front of Palace Theater when Albert Patterson was murdered.

Ferrell, Archer "Arch" Bradford

Russell County circuit solicitor; one of three men indicted for Albert Patterson's murder.

Ferrell, Henry A.

Arch Ferrell's father; Seale attorney and former probate judge and state representative.

Ferrell, Madeline

Arch Ferrell's wife.

Ferrell, Pelham

Arch Ferrell's brother; Phenix City attorney who represented Albert Fuller in bribery trials.

Folsom, James "Big Jim"

Alabama governor, 1947–51; renominated in 1954 Democratic Party primary.

Fowler, Conrad "Bulley"

Circuit solicitor for Alabama's Eighteenth Circuit; assigned as special prosecutor in Phenix City cleanup.

Fulgham, Emmitt

Area resident who observed actions of Arch Ferrell at crime scene during initial investigation.

Fuller, Albert

Russell County chief deputy sheriff; one of three men indicted for Albert Patterson's murder.

Gallion, George MacDonald "Mac"

Montgomery attorney; lost attorney general nomination to Albert Patterson in the 1954 Democratic Party primary runoff; assigned by Governor Persons as state's legal representative in the Patterson homicide investigation; appointed by Attorney General John Patterson as first assistant attorney general, January 1955; Alabama attorney general, 1959–63, 1967–71.

Garrett, Silas "Si" Coma, III

Alabama attorney general, 1951–55; one of three men indicted for Albert Patterson's murder.

Gibson, Ross

Area resident who was behind Smitty's Grill when Albert Patterson was murdered.

Godwin, Robert

Investigator for Alabama Department of Public Safety's Identification and Investigative Division assigned to the Albert Patterson homicide case.

Grant, Marvin

Area resident who was behind Smitty's Grill when Albert Patterson was murdered.

Griffin, Johnny Frank

Area resident who testified to Russell County Grand Jury that he saw Albert Fuller walk with Albert Patterson into the alleyway seconds before Patterson was murdered.

Griffin, William

One of the first Phenix City policemen to arrive at murder scene.

Gwin, Robert

Associate legal counsel in Albert Fuller's murder trial.

Hanna, Walter "Crack"

Adjutant general of the Alabama National Guard; assigned by Governor Persons to keep order in Phenix City after Albert Patterson's murder.

Harden, H. C.

Described in *Wickedest City* as one of Phenix City's "second-string mobsters"; owned and operated the Skyline Club.

Hicks, Julius

Russell County circuit judge; superseded by Judge Walter Jones for Phenix City cleanup cases.

Holloway, Glenn

One of the first Phenix City policemen to arrive at murder scene.

Hoover, J. Edgar

Director of the Federal Bureau of Investigation.

Horne, Kenneth

Student at University of Alabama School of Law; hired by Attorney General Silas Garrett as a personal assistant; accompanied Garrett to Phenix City in the days after Albert Patterson's murder.

House, Maurice

Birmingham police detective assigned to the Albert Patterson homicide case.

Ingram, Bob

Montgomery Advertiser reporter who covered the Phenix City investigations and trials.

Jenkins, Ray

Columbus Ledger reporter who covered the Phenix City investigations and trials.

Johnson, George

Circuit solicitor for Alabama's Eighth Circuit; assigned as special prosecutor in Phenix City cleanup.

Johnson, Colonel J. T.

Chief of Alabama's Selective Service System during Governor Persons's administration.

Jones, Leland

Area resident who spoke to Albert Patterson less than an hour before Patterson was murdered.

Jones, Mrs. Leland

Wife of Leland Jones; remained in car parked in front of Coulter Building while Mr. Jones spoke to Albert Patterson.

Jowers, Buddy

Phenix City assistant police chief; allegedly beat Albert Fuller for causing the Phenix City cleanup.

Kelley, Quinnie
Area resident who claimed he saw Arch Ferrell moving away from murder scene seconds after Albert Patterson was shot.

King, Alta
Jefferson County circuit judge who presided over Jefferson County Grand Jury during Birmingham vote fraud investigation.

Kirkland, Jimmy
Area resident who passed by Coulter Building seconds before Albert Patterson was murdered.

Knowles, Dr. Clyde
Phenix City physician; assisted in Albert Patterson's autopsy.

Lange, Virginia
Girlfriend of state witness Bill Littleton; contradicted Littleton's testimony in murder trials.

Littleton, Bill
Witness in murder trials; cab driver who claimed he saw Arch Ferrell and Albert Fuller standing in front of the Coulter Building minutes before Albert Patterson was murdered.

Long, Frank
Head of state Young Democrats organization; attorney and Democratic Party activist allied with Jim Folsom; alibi witness for Arch Ferrell.

MacMurdo, Robert A.
Birmingham police detective assigned to the Albert Patterson homicide case.

Madison, Gordon
Assistant attorney general and former state senator; named as possible replacement for Albert Patterson; accompanied Bernard Sykes to Phenix City one week after Patterson's murder.

Martin, Logan
Alabama attorney general during the Girard cleanup of 1916.

Mathews, Ralph
Russell County sheriff; alibi witness for Albert Fuller.

Matthews, Jimmy
Business partner of Hoyt Shepherd; described in *Wickedest City* as member of Phenix City's "inner council" of gangsters.

McCollister, Stewart
Described in *Wickedest City* as one of Phenix City's "second-string mobsters"; operated, along with Clyde Yarbrough, the Yarbrough-McCollister Lottery; part owner of Yarbrough's Café, Bama Club,

Avalon Club, and New York Club; named in grand jury testimony as trying to buy votes in south Alabama for Lee Porter in days after primary runoff.

McDowell, Holt
Jefferson County sheriff; state witness in Arch Ferrell's vote fraud case.

McElroy, J. Russell
Circuit judge of Alabama's Tenth Judicial Circuit; assigned to preside at murder trials of Albert Fuller and Arch Ferrell.

Mihelic, Patrick
State highway patrolman; later appointed Phenix City police chief.

Miller, Bill
Owner of Tropical Trailer Court in Columbus; father of Leroy "Pete" Miller.

Miller, Leroy "Pete"
One of three young furniture movers in or in front of Coulter Building when Albert Patterson was murdered.

Moore, Robert R.
Fort Benning mess sergeant who told investigators he saw Arch Ferrell and Albert Patterson in alleyway next to Coulter Building on the evening Patterson was murdered.

Murphy, Lamar
Phenix City service station owner; appointed as Russell County sheriff during the Phenix City cleanup.

Myrick, Robert "Shorty"
Described in *Wickedest City* as one of Phenix City's "second-string mobsters."

Oden, Morris
Bailiff for Judge J. Russell McElroy during murder trials.

Padgett, Cecil Edward
Area resident who testified he was standing in street in front of Coulter Building alleyway when Albert Patterson was murdered.

Padgett, Edith
Wife of Cecil Padgett; area resident who testified she was sitting in car across street from Coulter Building when Albert Patterson was murdered.

Painter, Willie
Investigator for Alabama Department of Public Safety's Identification and Investigative Division assigned to the Albert Patterson homicide case.

Patterson, Agnes Benson
   Wife of Albert Patterson.
Patterson, Albert L.
   Phenix City attorney and Democratic Party nominee for state at-
   torney general.
Patterson, F. B.
   Supervisor for Southern Bell Telephone Company, Columbus Ex-
   change; provided technical information to investigators about the
   Arch Ferrell/Silas Garrett alibi telephone call.
Patterson, John Malcolm
   Law partner and eldest son of Albert Patterson; named as attorney
   general nominee by state Democratic Executive Committee to re-
   place his father; state attorney general, 1955–59; Alabama gover-
   nor, 1959–63.
Patterson, Mary Jo
   Wife of John Patterson.
Pennington, Howard
   President and founding member of the Russell Betterment Asso-
   ciation.
Perry, Emmett
   Jefferson County circuit solicitor; prosecutor in Arch Ferrell's vote
   fraud trial.
Persons, Gordon, Sr.
   Alabama governor, 1951–55.
Phillips, George
   Visiting highway patrolman (driver's license examiner) on the
   night of Albert Patterson's murder; alibi witness for Albert Fuller.
Pope, Woodie
   Area resident who saw Albert Patterson at post office less than an
   hour before he was murdered.
Porter, Lee "Red"
   Gadsden attorney; lost attorney general nomination to Albert Pat-
   terson in the 1954 Democratic Party primary runoff.
Powell, Leonard David
   Area resident who was in front of Smitty's Grill when Albert Pat-
   terson was murdered.
Prier, Claude
   Investigator for Alabama Department of Public Safety's Identifica-
   tion and Investigative Division assigned to the Albert Patterson
   homicide case.

Putnam, Jimmy
    City clerk for Phenix City; generally described as a friend of Arch
    Ferrell's.
Ratigan, Edward
    Birmingham policeman and National Guardsman assigned as
    Russell County jailer during the Phenix City cleanup.
Redden, Drew
    Associate legal counsel in Arch Ferrell's vote fraud trial and mur-
    der trial.
Reese, Elmer
    Phenix City commissioner, 1940–54; mayor, 1953–54; resigned office
    during cleanup while under indictment for willful neglect of duty.
Rehling, Dr. C. J.
    Director of Alabama Department of Toxicology and Criminal In-
    vestigation at the time of Albert Patterson's murder.
Reid, Amos Lamar
    Birmingham attorney and chairman of the Jefferson County
    Democratic Executive Committee; indicted, along with Arch Fer-
    rell and Silas Garrett, for vote fraud; state witness in Ferrell's vote
    fraud trial and murder trial.
Revel, C. O. "Head"
    Described in *Wickedest City* as one of the "inner council" of Phenix
    City mobsters; owner, along with George T. Davis, of the Bridge
    Grocery, headquarters for Phenix City's largest lottery, the Metro-
    politan.
Reynolds, Morgan
    Clanton attorney and brother-in-law of John Patterson; at John Pat-
    terson's request, arrived in Phenix City shortly after Albert Patter-
    son's murder.
Robertson, Joe
    Appointed by John Patterson as assistant attorney general, January
    1955.
Rogers, George
    Chief legal counsel in Arch Ferrell's vote fraud trial and murder
    trial.
Roney, W. C.
    Described in *Wickedest City* as one of Phenix City's "second-string
    mobsters"; owned, along with son, Lawrence, Yellow Front Café and
    514 Club.

Rosenthal, Albert
Birmingham attorney; one of Albert Patterson's campaign coordinators in Jefferson County; testified before Jefferson County Grand Jury investigating vote fraud.

Ryals, Fred
Eufaula resident who told investigators he was stopped at corner of Fifth Avenue and Fourteenth Street when Albert Patterson was murdered; later discredited.

Sanders, James
Area resident who was standing in front of Smitty's Grill when Albert Patterson was murdered.

Sanders, Walter Leon
Phenix City policeman who was present at crime scene investigation; state witness in Albert Fuller murder trial.

Sanks, Margaret
Area resident who had passed by Coulter Building minutes before Albert Patterson was murdered.

Schermann, Steve
One of three young furniture movers in or in front of Coulter Building when Albert Patterson was murdered.

Shanklin, Gordon
Federal Bureau of Investigation special agent stationed at Mobile office; contacted by Governor Persons about possible FBI involvement in Albert Patterson murder investigation.

Shepherd, John Hoyt
Generally described as the "godfather" of Phenix City gangsters; did not directly control any vice operations at the time of Albert Patterson's murder.

Sivak, Dr. George
Phenix City physician who had an office on upper floor of Coulter Building.

Smelley, Joe
Chief of Alabama Department of Public Safety's Identification and Investigative Division.

Smith, Aaron
Russell County deputy sheriff; alibi witness for Albert Fuller.

Smith, Joe
Phenix City attorney; represented, with Pelham Ferrell, Albert Fuller in bribery trials.

Smith, Lucille
Albert Patterson's secretary at the time Patterson was murdered.

Smith, Maury Drane
Assistant attorney general assigned to the Albert Patterson homicide case.

Smith, Robert Lee
Brother of Aaron Smith; alibi witness for Albert Fuller.

Sowell, Wendell, Sr.
Assistant state toxicologist for the Alabama Department of Toxicology and Criminal Investigation; performed, with Dr. Clyde Knowles, autopsy on Albert Patterson's body; state witness in murder trials.

Stallworth, Clarke
Birmingham Post-Herald reporter who covered the Phenix City investigations and trials.

Strickland, Edwin
Birmingham News reporter who covered the Phenix City investigations and trials; coauthored, with Gene Wortsman, *Phenix City: The Wickedest City in America*.

Sullivan, L. B.
Director of the Alabama Department of Public Safety.

Sykes, Bernard
Assistant attorney general under Silas Garrett; appointed acting attorney general one week after Albert Patterson's murder; directed state investigation of the homicide.

Taylor, James Radius
Area resident who testified he was at the corner of Fifth Avenue and Fourteenth Street when Albert Patterson was murdered.

Tharp, Hubert
Area resident who was in Bentley's Grocery, located across from Coulter Building, when Albert Patterson was murdered.

Thomas, Rex
Reporter for Associated Press's Montgomery bureau who covered the Phenix City investigations and trials.

Tiller, Hortense
Area resident who lived in proximity of Russell County Courthouse; state witness in Albert Fuller murder trial; defense rebuttal witness in Arch Ferrell murder trial.

Warren, Jack
> Alabama National Guard officer; appointed sheriff of Russell County during martial rule.

Wheeler, Robert
> Jefferson County circuit judge who presided over Arch Ferrell's vote fraud trial.

White, Bruce
> Lamar Reid's brother-in-law and legal counsel.

White, John
> State highway patrolman who accompanied Attorney General Silas Garrett to Phenix City three days after Albert Patterson's murder.

Williams, John, Jr.
> Investigator for Alabama Department of Public Safety's Identification and Investigative Division assigned to the Albert Patterson homicide case.

Wortsman, Gene
> *Birmingham Post-Herald* reporter who covered the Birmingham vote fraud investigation; coauthored, with Ed Strickland, *Phenix City: The Wickedest City in America*.

Young, James
> Area resident who observed actions of Arch Ferrell at crime scene during initial investigation.

Notes

ABBREVIATIONS

ADAH   Alabama Department of Archives and History, Montgomery
ADFS   Alabama Department of Forensic Sciences, Auburn
ADPS   Alabama Department of Public Safety, Montgomery
APCF   Albert Patterson Case Files, ADAH
AP-FBI Albert L. Patterson FBI Investigative Files, BPL
BPL   Birmingham Public Library, Archives and Manuscripts Department

PREFACE

1. Wilbur J. Cash, *The Mind of the South* (New York: Random House, 1941), 48.

CHAPTER 1

1. "Conference with State Investigators," June 26, 1954, Barton's Briefing Book, APCF; Edwin Strickland and Gene Wortsman, *Phenix City: The Wickedest City in America* (Birmingham: Vulcan Press, 1955), 10; *Montgomery Advertiser,* June 20, 1954.

2. Emmett Perry, "The Story behind Phenix City: The Struggle for Law in a Modern Sodom," *American Bar Association Journal* 42 (December 1956): 1149; Strickland and Wortsman, *Phenix City,* 11.

3. Strickland and Wortsman, *Phenix City,* 1.

4. Russell County Historical Commission, *History of Russell County* (Dallas: National Sharegraphics, 1982), C67–C69.

5. Ibid.; Strickland and Wortsman, *Phenix City,* 8.

6. Harold S. Coulter, *A People Courageous: A History of Phenix City, Alabama* (Columbus, Ga.: Howard Printing Co., 1976), 104.

7. Russell County Historical Commission, *History of Russell County,* C67–C69.

8. Ibid.

9. Coulter, *A People Courageous,* 262–69.

10. Ibid., 272–81; Strickland and Wortsman, *Phenix City,* 195; *Huntsville*

Times, July 23, 1954; Hershel Finney, "Alabama National Guard—Phenix City History," draft typescript, n.d., Finney Family Private Collection [hereinafter cited as Finney, "Phenix City History"].

11. Strickland and Wortsman, *Phenix City*, 195–96.

12. W. D. McGlasson, "Phenix City 1954: Putting Out the Flames of Corruption," *National Guard*, June 1981, 13; Perry, "The Story behind Phenix City," 1147; Strickland and Wortsman, *Phenix City*, 196; Russell County Historical Commission, *History of Russell County*, C67–C69.

13. William Campbell MacLean IV, "From the Ashes: Phenix City, Alabama, and Its Struggle with Memory" (master's thesis, Emory University, 1995), 66; John Patterson with Furman Bisher, "I'll Get the Gangs That Killed My Father!" *Saturday Evening Post*, November 27, 1954, 60; Perry, "The Story behind Phenix City," 1147; Strickland and Wortsman, *Phenix City*, 64, 206–7.

14. MacLean, "From the Ashes," 76–79; Strickland and Wortsman, *Phenix City*, 73.

15. Strickland and Wortsman, *Phenix City*, 69; McGlasson, "Phenix City 1954," 13; Finney, "Phenix City History"; *Huntsville Times*, July 23, 1954.

16. Strickland and Wortsman, *Phenix City*, 1–2, 196–99; "Crime: The Odds Were Right," *Time*, June 28, 1954, 22; *Atlanta Constitution*, November 29, 1983; McGlasson, "Phenix City 1954," 8.

17. V. O. Key Jr., *Southern Politics in State and Nation* (New York: Vintage Books, 1949), 52–55; Strickland and Wortsman, *Phenix City*, 2.

18. The four governors were William D. Brandon in 1922, Bibb Graves in 1934, Chauncey Sparks in 1942, and Jim Folsom in 1954.

19. Alexander Heard and Donald G. Strong, *Southern Primaries and Elections, 1920–1949* (Tuscaloosa: University of Alabama Press, 1950), 10–14; [Alabama] Democratic Executive Committee, *Official Election Returns, Democratic Primaries, Alabama, 1918 and 1920* (Montgomery: Brown Printing Co., 1920), 9; Ed Packard, Alabama Elections Division, Office of the Secretary of State, e-mail to author re: 1950 and 1954 Alabama Democratic Primaries, March 28, 2001.

20. Patterson, "I'll Get the Gangs!" 64; Strickland and Wortsman, *Phenix City*, 2, 70–71, 76, 114–30, 205; Finney, "Phenix City History"; Finney, "Crime and Vice Operations," in ibid.; John Patterson, *Messages and Addresses of John Patterson, Governor of Alabama, 1959–1963; Attorney General of Alabama, 1955–1959* (Montgomery: Brown Printing Co., 1963), xiii.

21. Strickland and Wortsman, *Phenix City*, 71, 206–11; Finney, "Organization and Personalities," in "Phenix City History."

22. Katharine Hillyer and Katharine Best, "The Angry Women of Phenix City," *McCall's*, September 1955, 62.

23. Strickland and Wortsman, *Phenix City*, 185, 212; MacLean, "From the Ashes," 116.

24. Patterson, "I'll Get the Gangs!" 60; Douglas Cater, "The Wide-Open Town on the Chattahoochee," *Reporter*, February 24, 1955, 22–27.

25. There is some disagreement about Patterson's date of birth. His student record at the University of Alabama and his driver's license list the date as January 27, 1894, and John Patterson lists that date in "I'll Get the Gangs!" However, Patterson's tombstone at New Site and the memorial statue on the grounds of the state capitol give the date as 1897. State newspapers from the era provide dates of anywhere between 1891 and 1897.

26. Patterson, "I'll Get the Gangs!" 60; *Birmingham News,* June 19, 1954; *Montgomery Advertiser,* June 19, 1954; "Albert Patterson Biography," n.d. [hereinafter cited as "Albert Patterson Biography"], "Albert L. Patterson—personal" folder, John Patterson Papers, ADAH; Patterson, *Messages and Addresses,* xiii, 152.

27. *Birmingham News,* June 19, 1954, February 17, 1955; "Albert Patterson Biography."

28. "Albert Patterson Biography"; Patterson, "I'll Get the Gangs!" 60.

29. "Albert Patterson Biography"; Patterson, "I'll Get the Gangs!" 60; *Birmingham News,* June 19, 1954.

30. *Birmingham News,* June 14, 1954; Ruth Cole, interview by author, Birmingham, January 9, 1998.

31. University of Alabama Student Records.

32. *Birmingham News,* June 19, 1954; Cole, interview; "Albert Patterson Biography"; Patterson, *Messages and Addresses,* xiii.

33. Cole, interview; Patterson, *Messages and Addresses,* xiii.

34. *Birmingham News,* February 17, 1955.

35. Ibid.; Patterson, "I'll Get the Gangs!" 60; "Albert Patterson Biography"; *Montgomery Advertiser,* October 25, 1954.

36. *Columbus Ledger,* July 1, 1954; Patterson, "I'll Get the Gangs!" 62.

37. Patterson, "I'll Get the Gangs!" 62; Strickland and Wortsman, *Phenix City,* 132.

38. *Columbus Ledger,* June 19, 1954; *Montgomery Advertiser,* June 19, 1954; *Opelika Daily News,* May 31, 1954; "Albert Patterson Biography"; Hilda Coulter, interview by author, Phenix City, November 30, 1995; Patterson, "I'll Get the Gangs!" 60.

39. Margaret Anne Barnes, *The Tragedy and the Triumph of Phenix City, Alabama* (Macon, Ga.: Mercer University Press, 1998), 75–76; Alabama, *Journals of the Senate of State of Alabama, Organizational Session of 1947* (Birmingham: Birmingham Printing Co., 1948), 18–21.

40. Barnes, *Tragedy and Triumph,* 75–76; Alabama, *Journals of the Senate,* 18–21; *Birmingham News,* December 10, 1954; *Birmingham Post-Herald,* April 18, 1955; Patterson, "I'll Get the Gangs!" 64.

41. Burt Corant to James Folsom, March 20, June 11, 1949, "Senators" folder, Governor James Folsom Papers, ADAH; Patterson, "I'll Get the Gangs!"

60; George E. Sims, *The Little Man's Big Friend: James E. Folsom in Alabama Politics, 1946–1958* (Tuscaloosa: University of Alabama Press, 1985), 138; Thomas Gilliam, "The Second Folsom Administration: The Destruction of Alabama Liberalism, 1954–1958" (Ph.D. diss., Auburn University, 1975), 87; *Opelika Daily News*, February 13, 14, 1949; Strickland and Wortsman, *Phenix City*, 21.

42. MacLean, "From the Ashes," 75–76, 127–28; Ed Strickland, interview by author, Montgomery, October 7, 1994; Strickland and Wortsman, *Phenix City*, 63–65; Finney, "Phenix City History."

43. Cater, "Wide-Open Town," 23; *Birmingham News*, December 10, 1954, April 18, 1955; *Columbus Ledger-Enquirer*, September 18, 1949; *Columbus Ledger*, July 1, 1954; *Birmingham Post-Herald*, December 10, 1954; American Legion Department of Alabama, *A History of the American Legion and American Legion Auxiliary in Alabama, 1948–1975* (Birmingham: Birmingham Publishing Co., 1978), 59.

44. Strickland, interview; *Birmingham Post-Herald*, April 18, 1955.

45. Bernard Sykes, memorandum for record, September 7, 1954, "D" folder, APCF; Acting Selective Service System State Director Colonel J. T. Johnson to Gordon Persons, October 29, 1951, and Johnson to Vernon Merritt, October 9, 1951, "Selective Service" folder, Governor Gordon Persons Papers, ADAH; notes [re: James Godwin Davis], n.d., Barton's Briefing Book, APCF.

46. Vernon Merritt to Colonel J. T. Johnson, October 16, 1951, "Selective Service" folder, Persons Papers.

47. Patterson, "I'll Get the Gangs!" 63; Strickland and Wortsman, *Phenix City*, 188–89.

48. *Birmingham News*, January 12, 1955; Hillyer and Best, "The Angry Women of Phenix City," 56, 62.

49. MacLean, "From the Ashes," 84; Hillyer and Best, "The Angry Women of Phenix City," 52, 56; Strickland and Wortsman, *Phenix City*, 191.

50. MacLean, "From the Ashes," 88–90; Patterson, "I'll Get the Gangs!" 64.

51. Patterson, "I'll Get the Gangs!" 62–63; Strickland and Wortsman, *Phenix City*, 192; Coulter, interview.

52. Strickland and Wortsman, *Phenix City*, 177–78.

53. MacLean, "From the Ashes," 96.

54. Gordon Persons Jr., interview by author, Gulf Shores, Ala., May 29, 1996.

55. Hillyer and Best, "The Angry Women of Phenix City," 58; Strickland and Wortsman, *Phenix City*, 150, 192; MacLean, "From the Ashes," 96–98; Patterson, "I'll Get the Gangs!" 63.

56. Strickland and Wortsman, *Phenix City*, 190–91; MacLean, "From the Ashes," 99–100.

57. MacLean, "From the Ashes," 99–102; Finney, "Phenix City History."

58. Patterson, "I'll Get the Gangs!" 64; Hillyer and Best, "The Angry Women of Phenix City," 66; *Birmingham News,* February 22, 1955; "Testimony of Howard Pennington," *Fuller v. State,* Supreme Court of Alabama, February 12, 1959, 6 Div. 917, ADAH [hereinafter cited as *Fuller v. State,* ADAH].

CHAPTER 2

1. Gilliam, "The Second Folsom Administration," 88.

2. David L. Martin, *Alabama's State and Local Governments* (Tuscaloosa: University of Alabama Press, 1975), 108; Strickland and Wortsman, *Phenix City,* 16.

3. MacDonald Gallion, interview by author, Montgomery, August 19, 1990; Alabama, *Code of Alabama 1940* (St. Paul, Minn.: West, 1941), 13:229.

4. *Montgomery Advertiser,* February 23, 1936, February 22, 1942, February 3, 1946, January 23, 1947; *(Montgomery) Alabama Journal,* February 18, 1942; *Birmingham News,* July 25, 1942.

5. Cater, "Wide-Open Town," 23.

6. *Mobile Press,* December 17, 1953, March 16, 1954; *Mobile Register,* March 16, 1954.

7. *Mobile Register,* November 26, 1953; *Mobile Press,* April 27, 1950; *(Montgomery) Alabama Journal,* October 13, 1948.

8. *Montgomery Advertiser,* May 23, 1954; *Mobile Press,* April 26, 1950.

9. *Montgomery Advertiser,* July 10, 1954; MacDonald Gallion, interview by author, Montgomery, November 10, 1994.

10. Williams and Painter to Sykes, memorandum, July 21, 1954, Investigators' Book, APCF.

11. Patterson, *Messages and Addresses,* xiii–xiv.

12. *Montgomery Advertiser,* May 3, 1954.

13. Strickland and Wortsman, *Phenix City,* 153; *Birmingham News,* April 9, 1955.

14. Strickland and Wortsman, *Phenix City,* 143; MacDonald Gallion, interviews by author, Montgomery, November 10, 1994, September 1, 1999.

15. *Montgomery Advertiser,* May 7, 1954; *Opelika Daily News,* May 31, 1954; Strickland and Wortsman, *Phenix City,* 153.

16. Strickland and Wortsman, *Phenix City,* 57, 94, 97, 155; Finney, "Crime and Vice Operations" and "Organization and Personalities," in "Phenix City History"; Barton to Sykes re: $26,000 contribution to Lee (Red) Porter's campaign by Phenix City machine, memorandum, July 28, 1954, Barton's Briefing Book, APCF; *Birmingham News,* April 23, 1955; interview with Godwin Davis, July 22, 1954, Dictaphone Book #5, APCF.

17. Strickland and Wortsman, *Phenix City,* 154; *Montgomery Advertiser,* May 28, 1954; *Opelika Daily News,* May 31, 1954; *Birmingham News,* April 9, 1955; Barton to Sykes re: $26,000 contribution to Lee (Red) Porter's campaign by

Phenix City machine, memorandum, July 28, 1954, Barton's Briefing Book, APCF.

18. Strickland and Wortsman, *Phenix City*, 154–55; Barton to Sykes re: $26,000 contribution to Lee (Red) Porter's campaign by Phenix City machine, memorandum, July 28, 1954, Barton's Briefing Book, APCF.

19. Strickland and Wortsman, *Phenix City*, 155; *Birmingham News*, April 23, 27, 1955.

20. *Birmingham Post-Herald*, July 24, 1954.

21. Strickland and Wortsman, *Phenix City*, 156; *Birmingham Post-Herald*, June 2–4, 1954.

22. Strickland and Wortsman, *Phenix City*, 151–58; "Testimony of Frank Porter" and "Testimony of Preston Hornsby," *Proceedings of the Russell County Grand Jury*, vol. 2, APCF [hereinafter cited as *Russell County Grand Jury*, APCF].

23. Strickland and Wortsman, *Phenix City*, 228–29.

24. *Birmingham News*, March 8, 9, 1955.

25. Strickland and Wortsman, *Phenix City*, 241.

26. Ibid., 229, 241; *Birmingham News*, March 9, 1955.

27. Strickland and Wortsman, *Phenix City*, 241–43; *Birmingham News*, March 9, 10, 1955.

28. *Birmingham News*, March 9, 1955.

29. Strickland and Wortsman, *Phenix City*, 143, 231; "Testimony of Albert Rosenthal," *Russell County Grand Jury*, vol. 7, APCF; *Birmingham Post-Herald*, June 10, 1954; Strickland, interview.

30. "Testimony of Ed Strickland," *Russell County Grand Jury*, vol. 4, APCF; Strickland, interview; Perry, "The Story behind Phenix City," 1148; Strickland and Wortsman, *Phenix City*, 231.

31. *Birmingham Post-Herald*, June 10, 11, 1954; Smith to Sykes re: interview with Neil Metcalf, memorandum, August 6, 1954, Barton's Briefing Book, APCF.

32. Strickland and Wortsman, *Phenix City*, 156–60; MacLean, "From the Ashes," 18; *Huntsville Times*, June 15, 16, 1954; interview with Godwin Davis, July 22, 1954, Dictaphone Book #5, APCF.

33. *Birmingham News*, March 8, May 5, 1955; Barton to Sykes re: Garrett's meeting with Lamar Reid and Bruce White in Selma on 6/12/54, memorandum, August 20, 1954, Barton's Briefing Book, APCF; Strickland and Wortsman, *Phenix City*, 234.

34. Strickland and Wortsman, *Phenix City*, 231–32.

35. *Birmingham News*, March 10, 13, 1955; Strickland and Wortsman, *Phenix City*, 233.

36. Strickland and Wortsman, *Phenix City*, 235–36.

37. Ibid., 159; Barton to Sykes re: $26,000 contribution to Lee (Red) Por-

ter's campaign by Phenix City machine, memorandum, July 28, 1954, Barton's Briefing Book, APCF.

38. Smith to Sykes re: interview with Gordon Madison, Charlie Pinkston, Albert Rosenthal, Murray Battles, James E. Folsom, Fuller Kimbrell, Victor Gold, Leo Wilett, and James Jolly, memorandum, n.d., Barton's Briefing Book, APCF; notes [re: Howard Pennington and John Luttrell], June 27, 1954, ibid.; Strickland and Wortsman, *Phenix City*, 160; "Statement of Mrs. Lucille Smith," n.d., unmarked folder, APCF.

39. *Birmingham Post-Herald*, July 7, 1954; Strickland and Wortsman, *Phenix City*, 161; Smith to Sykes re: interview with Neil Metcalf, memorandum, August 6, 1954, Barton's Briefing Book, APCF; "Testimony of Albert Rosenthal," *Russell County Grand Jury*, vol. 7, APCF.

40. "Statement of Grace Curry Oliver," June 24, 1954, Investigators' Book, APCF; *Columbus Enquirer*, June 19, 1954; *Columbus Ledger*, June 19, 1954; MacMurdo and House to Sykes re: Mr. Patterson's activities shortly before his death, memorandum, August 11, 1954, Investigators' Book, APCF; Cater, "Wide-Open Town," 21.

CHAPTER 3

1. "Statement by Oscar R. Coley," July 15, 1954, Investigators' Book, APCF; MacMurdo and House to Sykes re: Mr. Patterson's activities shortly before his death, memorandum, August 11, 1954, ibid.; Painter to Sykes re: Mr. Albert L. Patterson's actions 6/18/54, memorandum, August 19, 1954, ibid.; *Columbus Ledger*, June 19, 1954.

2. Painter to Sykes re: Mr. Albert L. Patterson's actions, 6/18/54, memorandum, August 19, 1954, Investigators' Book, APCF; MacMurdo and House to Sykes re: Mr. Patterson's activities shortly before his death, memorandum, August 11, 1954, ibid.; interview with Lucille Smith, July 15, 1954, Dictaphone Book #6, APCF; "Testimony of Reuben Newton," *Russell County Grand Jury*, vol. 1, APCF.

3. Central standard time. Unlike the rest of Alabama, Phenix City is in the eastern time zone. Unless otherwise specified, all times given here are eastern standard time.

4. "Statement of Oscar R. Coley," July 15, 1954, Investigators' Book, APCF; Painter to Sykes re: Mr. Albert L. Patterson's actions, 6/18/54, memorandum, August 19, 1954, ibid.; MacMurdo and House to Sykes re: Mr. Patterson's activities shortly before his death, memorandum, August 11, 1954, ibid.; "Testimony of Reuben Newton," *Russell County Grand Jury*, vol. 1, APCF.

5. Painter to Sykes re: Mr. Albert L. Patterson's actions, 6/18/54, memorandum, August 19, 1954, Investigators' Book, APCF.

6. Ibid.; Conrad "Bulley" Fowler, interview by author, Tuscaloosa, Ala.,

July 13, 1994; Smith to Sykes re: interview with Gordon Madison et al., memorandum, n.d., Barton's Briefing Book, APCF; "Testimony of Albert Rosenthal," *Russell County Grand Jury*, vol. 7, APCF.

7. Painter to Sykes re: Mr. Albert L. Patterson's actions, 6/18/54, memorandum, August 19, 1954, Investigators' Book, APCF; "Testimony of Mac Brassell," *Russell County Grand Jury*, vol. 1, APCF.

8. Phillips to Sykes re: Actions of Albert L. Patterson 6/18/54, memorandum, n.d., Investigators' Book, APCF.

9. Ibid.

10. Later, Edmondson would mention that a man came in right after Patterson, sat at a booth facing away from him, and ordered a small soft drink. He disappeared soon after Patterson left, leaving a dime for the cola he didn't drink. See ibid.

11. Painter to Sykes re: Mr. Albert L. Patterson's actions, 6/18/54, August 19, 1954, ibid.

12. Finney, "Phenix City History"; *Birmingham Post-Herald*, December 10, 1954; *Birmingham News*, December 10, 1954; Strickland and Wortsman, *Phenix City*, 221; Cater, "Wide-Open Town," 23.

13. *Birmingham Post-Herald*, December 10, 1954; *Birmingham News*, December 10, 1954; Finney, "Phenix City History."

14. *Birmingham News*, March 5, 1955; Painter to Sykes re: Albert Fuller's activities . . . , memorandum, August 27, 1954, Investigators' Book, APCF; Prier and Godwin to Sykes re: Albert Fuller, memorandum, September 13, 1954, ibid.; "Testimony of Ralph Mathews" and "Testimony of Albert Fuller," *Fuller v. State*, ADAH.

15. Painter to Sykes re: Albert Fuller's activities . . . , memorandum, August 27, 1954, Investigators' Book, APCF; Prier and Godwin to Sykes re: Albert Fuller, memorandum, September 13, 1954, ibid.

16. *Birmingham News*, March 3–5, 1955; Painter to Sykes re: Albert Fuller's activities . . . , memorandum, August 27, 1954, Investigators' Book, APCF; Prier and Godwin to Sykes re: Albert Fuller, memorandum, September 13, 1954, ibid.

17. *Birmingham News*, March 5, 1955; Painter, MacMurdo, and House to Sykes re: statement of Ben Clark, memorandum, September 28, 1954, Investigators' Book, APCF; MacMurdo, House, and Painter to Sykes re: Robert Lee Smith, memorandum, September 25, 1954, ibid.; Prier to Sykes re: Robert Lee Smith, memorandum, July 29, 1954, ibid.; MacMurdo and House to Sykes re: Sheriff Ralph Mathews, memorandum, n.d., ibid.; Prier and Godwin to Sykes re: Albert Fuller, memorandum, September 13, 1954, ibid.; MacMurdo and House to Sykes re: Aaron Smith, memorandum, September 27, 1954, ibid.

18. Interview with Arch Ferrell, July 9, 1954, Dictaphone Book #1, APCF

[hereinafter cited as Ferrell interview, APCF]; Prier and Godwin to Sykes re: report on Arch Ferrell, memorandum, September 9, 1954, Investigators' Book, APCF; Strickland and Wortsman, *Phenix City*, 160.

19. Ferrell interview, APCF.

20. Ibid.; Prier and Godwin to Sykes re: report on Arch Ferrell, memorandum, September 9, 1954, Investigators' Book, APCF.

21. Ferrell interview, APCF; *Birmingham News*, April 29, 1955; Prier and Godwin to Sykes re: report on Arch Ferrell, September 9, 1954, Investigators' Book, APCF.

22. "Testimony of Silas Garrett," June 18, 1954, *Proceedings of the Jefferson County Grand Jury*, "Garrett" folder, APCF; "Testimony of Fred Andersen," July 1, 1954, "Emmett Perry—Grand Jury" folder, APCF; note, n.d., "Garrett" folder, APCF; MacMurdo and House to Sykes re: Si Garrett, 6/18/54, August 23, 1954, Investigators' Book, APCF; *Birmingham Post-Herald*, June 18, 1954; interview with Dorothy Johnson, August 17, 1954, Dictaphone Book #3, APCF.

23. MacMurdo, Smith, House, and W. L. Allen to Sykes re: Lee Porter, August 8, 1954, Investigators' Book, APCF; Smith to Sykes re: interview with Gordon Madison, et al., memorandum, n.d., Barton's Briefing Book, APCF; Strickland and Wortsman, *Phenix City*, 162.

24. When he was first questioned, Wortsman told investigators that he did not talk to Ferrell until the next day. "Testimony of Gene Wortsman," *Russell County Grand Jury*, vol. 5, APCF; Sykes re: telephone call from Gene Wortsman to Arch Ferrell, 6/18/54, memorandum for record, November 18, 1954, Barton's Briefing Book II, APCF.

25. Strickland and Wortsman, *Phenix City*, 237; "Testimony of Silas Garrett," June 18, 1954, *Proceedings of the Jefferson County Grand Jury*, "Garrett" folder, APCF.

26. "Notes on Conference," June 25, 1954, Barton's Briefing Book, APCF; Strickland and Wortsman, *Phenix City*, 237; Smith to Sykes re: interview with Gordon Madison et al., memorandum, n.d., Barton's Briefing Book, APCF; *Birmingham News*, March 3, 1955.

27. *Birmingham Post-Herald*, June 24, 1954; Cater, "Wide-Open Town," 22.

28. Barton to Sykes re: Mrs. Leland Jones, memorandum, August 23, 1954, Barton's Briefing Book, APCF; Painter to Sykes re: Albert Patterson's actions 6/18/54, memorandum, August 19, 1954, Investigators' Book, APCF; "Conference with State Investigators," June 26, 1954, Barton's Briefing Book, APCF; notes re: Mr. and Mrs. Leland Jones, July 1, 1954, ibid.; "Testimony of Leland Jones," *Russell County Grand Jury*, vol. 1, APCF.

29. Godwin and Williams re: Woodie Pope interview, memorandum, June 21, 1954, Barton's Briefing Book, APCF; W. L. Allen and Ben Allen to Sykes re: Homicide [Woodie Pope], August 30, 1954, Investigators' Book, APCF;

Birmingham News, February 17, 1955; "Testimony of Woodie Pope," *Russell County Grand Jury,* vol. 1, APCF.

30. Godwin and Chambers re: Margaret Sanks interview, memorandum, June 22, 1954, Investigators' Book, APCF; W. L. Allen and Ben Allen to Sykes re: Patterson Homicide [Abbie Cochran], memorandum, August 27, 1954, ibid.; Barton to Sykes re: Margaret Sanks, memorandum, July 28, 1954, Barton's Briefing Book, APCF; "Testimony of Abbie Cochran," *Russell County Grand Jury,* vol. 1, APCF.

31. Interview with Maggie Thaxton, July 9, 1954, Dictaphone Book #6, APCF.

32. Godwin and Chambers re: James Elwer interview, memorandum, June 25, 1954, Investigators' Book, APCF; Godwin and Chambers re: Steve Schermann, memorandum, June 25, 1954, ibid.; W. L. Allen and Ben Allen to Sykes re: Steve Sherman [*sic*], August 27, 1954, ibid.; "Testimony of Steve Schermann," *Russell County Grand Jury,* vol. 1, APCF.

33. One wonders why Patterson, with his handicap, went through the trouble of walking *back* upstairs after getting his mail. Some have suggested that he didn't—that he went directly to his car and that the furniture movers heard someone else on the stairs.

34. Godwin and Chambers re: James Elwer interview, memorandum, June 25, 1954, Investigators' Book, APCF; Godwin and Chambers re: Steve Schermann, memorandum, June 25, 1954, ibid.; W. L. Allen and Ben Allen to Sykes re: Steve Sherman [*sic*], August 27, 1954, ibid.; "Testimony of Steve Schermann," *Russell County Grand Jury,* vol. 1, APCF.

35. Godwin and Williams re: Hugh Buchanan interview, memorandum, June 22, 1954, Investigators' Book, APCF; Godwin and Painter re: Jimmy Sanders interview, memorandum, June 29, 1954, ibid.; notes re: Howard Pennington, July 1, 1954, Barton's Briefing Book, APCF; "Testimony of Jimmy Sanders" and "Testimony of Hugh Buchanan," *Russell County Grand Jury,* vol. 1, APCF.

36. Godwin and Chambers re: Hugh Buchanan interview, memorandum, June 22, 1954, Investigators' Book, APCF; Godwin and Painter re: Jimmy Sanders interview, memorandum, June 29, 1954, ibid.; Godwin and Chambers re: Jimmy Kirkland interview, memorandum, June 23, 1954, ibid.; James Kirkland, interview by author, Phenix City, April 10, 1996; interview with Jimmy Kirkland, August 23, 1954, Dictaphone Book #6, APCF.

37. Gallion and Barton to Sykes re: Leonard David Powell, memorandum, July 23, 1954, Investigators' Book, APCF; W. L. Allen and Ben Allen to Sykes re: L. D. Powell, August 27, 1954, ibid.; interviews with Leonard David Powell, July 23, 1954, Milton Lindsey, August 2, 1954, and Mrs. Milton Lindsey, July 23, 1954, all in Dictaphone Book #6, APCF; "Testimony of Leonard David Powell," *Russell County Grand Jury,* vol. 1, APCF.

38. "Testimony of Steve Schermann," *Fuller v. State,* ADAH; W. L. Allen and Ben Allen to Sykes re: Stefan Sherman [*sic*], memorandum, August 27, 1954, Investigators' Book, APCF; "Testimony of Steve Schermann," *Russell County Grand Jury,* vol. 1, APCF.

39. Godwin and Williams re: James Kent, memorandum, June 20, 1954, Investigators' Book, APCF; Godwin and Chambers re: Mrs. Abbie Cochran interview, memorandum, June 22, 1954, ibid.; Ben Allen and W. L. Allen to Sykes re: Homicide, memorandum, August 30, 1954, ibid.; "Testimony of Abbie Cochran," *Fuller v. State,* ADAH; W. L. Allen and Ben Allen to Sykes re: Patterson Homicide [Abbie Cochran], August 27, 1954, Investigators' Book, APCF; notes [re: copy of Griffin and Chestnut's notes from 6/18/54], July 14, 1954, Barton's Briefing Book, APCF; "Testimony of Mrs. C. W. Bentley" and "Testimony of Hubert Tharp," *Russell County Grand Jury,* vol. 1, APCF.

40. Godwin and Chambers re: Hugh Buchanan interview, memorandum, June 22, 1954, Investigators' Book, APCF; Barton to Sykes re: Leonard David Powell, July 23, 1954, Barton's Briefing Book, APCF; W. L. Allen and Ben Allen to Sykes re: L. D. Powell, memorandum, August 27, 1954, Investigators' Book, APCF; James Sanders, interview by author, Phenix City, June 11, 1995; *Huntsville Times,* April 28, 1955; interviews with Leonard David Powell, July 23, 1954, Milton Lindsey, August 2, 1954, Mrs. Milton Lindsey, July 23, 1954, and Jimmy Kirkland, August 23, 1954, all in Dictaphone Book #6, APCF; "Testimony of Mrs. C. W. Bentley," "Testimony of Leonard David Powell," and "Testimony of Hugh Buchanan," *Russell County Grand Jury,* vol. 1, APCF.

41. Interview with Ross Gibson, September 13, 1954, Dictaphone Book #4, APCF; Godwin and Williams re: Marvin Grant, memorandum, June 20, 1954, Investigators' Book, APCF; Williams to Sykes re: Ross Lamuel Gibson, memorandum, June 19, 1954, ibid.; *Columbus Enquirer,* June 19, 1954; "Testimony of Marvin Grant," *Russell County Grand Jury,* vol. 1, APCF.

42. Godwin and Chambers re: Margaret Sanks interview, memorandum, June 22, 1954, Investigators' Book, APCF; Barton to Sykes re: Margaret Sanks, memorandum, July 28, 1954, Barton's Briefing Book, APCF; Godwin and Prier to Sykes re: Floyd Waites, memorandum, September 11, 1954, Investigators' Book, APCF.

43. Interview with Raymond Ennis, July 30, 1954, Dictaphone Book #4, APCF; "Testimony of Raymond Ennis," *Russell County Grand Jury,* vol. 1, APCF; House and MacMurdo to Sykes re: Mr. Ennis, memorandum, August 4, 1954, Investigators' Book, APCF; Barton to Sykes re: Raymond Eugene Ennis, August 12, 1954, Barton's Briefing Book, APCF; *Birmingham News,* February 19, 1955.

44. Holmes to Sykes re: Tucker story—David Mobley, memorandum, n.d., Investigators' Book, APCF.

45. Prier to Sykes re: Hortense Tiller, memorandum, November 23, 1954, ibid.; interview with Hortense Tiller, July 18, 1954, Dictaphone Book #6, APCF; "Testimony of Mrs. Hortense Tiller," *Fuller v. State*, ADAH.

46. Godwin and Coley re: James Elkins, memorandum, June 27, 1954, Investigators' Book, APCF; Godwin and Painter re: John Leslie, memorandum, June 28, 1954, ibid.; Painter, House and MacMurdo to Sykes re: interview with Tom Scroggins, memorandum, September 29, 1954, ibid.

47. *Columbus Ledger,* June 19, 1954.

CHAPTER 4

1. "Notes on Conference," June 25, 1954, Barton's Briefing Book, APCF; Stanley Atkins to M. H. House [re: 6/18/54 telephone call to Si Garrett], August 24, 1954, Barton's Briefing Book II, APCF.

2. "Notes on Conference," June 25, 1954, Barton's Briefing Book, APCF.

3. Prier and Godwin to Sykes re: report on Arch Ferrell, memorandum, September 9, 1954, Investigators' Book, APCF; Ferrell interview, APCF.

4. Prier and Godwin to Sykes re: report on Arch Ferrell, memorandum, September 9, 1954, Investigators' Book, APCF; Ferrell interview, APCF.

5. Prier to Sykes re: Robert Lee Smith, memorandum, July 29, 1954, ibid.; MacMurdo and House re: Sheriff Ralph Mathews, memorandum, August 11, 1954, ibid.; Prier and Godwin to Sykes re: Albert Fuller, memorandum, September 13, 1954, ibid.; "Testimony of Ralph Mathews" and "Testimony of George Phillips," *Fuller v. State,* ADAH; *Birmingham News,* March 5, 1955.

6. MacMurdo and House re: Sheriff Ralph Mathews, memorandum, August 11, 1954, Investigators' Book, APCF; Prier and Godwin to Sykes re: Albert Fuller, memorandum, September 13, 1954, ibid.; *Birmingham News,* March 5, 1955.

7. "Testimony of Ralph Mathews," *Russell County Grand Jury,* vol. 4, APCF; Godwin and Prier re: Pat Mihelic, memorandum, September 11, 1954, Investigators' Book, APCF.

8. Barton to Sykes re: telephone calls to Mrs. Carl J. Rehling, wife of state toxicologist, memorandum, August 11, 1954, Barton's Briefing Book, APCF.

9. Painter to Sykes re: Lee (Red) Porter, memorandum, July 31, 1954, Investigators' Book, APCF; MacMurdo, Smith, House, and W. L. Allen re: Lee Porter, memorandum, August 8, 1954, ibid.

10. Wendell Sowell Jr., interview by author, Hanceville, Ala., May 4, 1998; C. L. Rabren, interview by author, Auburn, Ala., December 10, 1997; "Testimony of Wendell Sowell," *Russell County Grand Jury,* vol. 2, APCF; Wendell Sowell, "Narrative Account," n.d., Case 54-14662 (Albert Patterson Homicide File), ADFS; *Birmingham News,* February 18, 1955.

11. "Testimony of Wendell Sowell," *Russell County Grand Jury,* vol. 2, APCF;

Barton to Sykes re: telephone calls to Mrs. Carl J. Rehling, wife of state toxicologist, memorandum, August 11, 1954, Barton's Briefing Book, APCF; MacMurdo and House to Sykes re: Sheriff Ralph Mathews, memorandum, August 11, 1954, Investigators' Book, APCF; Sowell, "Narrative Account," Case 54-14662, ADFS.

12. Ferrell interview, APCF; MacMurdo and House to Sykes re: Sheriff Ralph Mathews, memorandum, August 11, 1954, Investigators' Book, APCF.

13. "Testimony of Wendell Sowell," *Russell County Grand Jury*, vol. 2, APCF; Sowell, "Narrative Account," Case 54-14662, ADFS; Ferrell interview, APCF; *Birmingham News*, February 23, 1955.

14. Barton to Sykes re: alibi of "Ashie" Roberts, memorandum, n.d., Barton's Briefing Book, APCF; Ferrell interview, APCF; Painter to Sykes re: location of Patterson murder car in alley by Coulter Building early morning 6/19/54, memorandum, November 9, 1954, "P" folder, APCF.

15. MacMurdo, House, and Gallion to Sykes re: Leon Sanders, memorandum, August 10, 1954, Investigators' Book, APCF; Painter, MacMurdo, and House to Sykes re: Glenn Holloway, memorandum, September 23, 1954, ibid.; Painter, MacMurdo, and House to Sykes re: Houston Ragsdale, memorandum, September 23, 1954, ibid.; *Birmingham News*, February 19, March 5, 1955.

16. Ben Allen and MacMurdo to Sykes re: Leroy Miller, memorandum, November 12, 1954, Reinterview Book, APCF; Smith to Sykes re: Leroy Miller, memorandum, July 19, 1954, "Maury Smith" folder, APCF; Steve Franklin, interview by author, Phenix City, June 20, 1996.

17. Godwin and Coley [re: James Elkins], memorandum, June 27, 1954, Investigators' Book, APCF; *Montgomery Advertiser*, June 20, 1954.

18. Painter to Sykes re: Albert Fuller's activities, memorandum, August 27, 1954, Investigators' Book, APCF; Prier to Sykes re: Albert Fuller with no pistol on night of 6/18, memorandum, October 15, 1954, ibid.; Prier to Sykes re: Howard Pennington, memorandum, October 15, 1954, ibid.; Prier to Sykes re: David Morris, memorandum, October 15, 1954, ibid.; *Birmingham News*, February 23, 24, 1955.

19. *Huntsville Times*, May 2, 2002; Williams and Painter to Sykes re: Sherman F. Sylvia, memorandum, n.d., Investigators' Book, APCF; "Testimony of Morgan Reynolds," *Russell County Grand Jury*, vol. 7, APCF.

20. *Huntsville Times*, May 2, 2002; MacMurdo and House to Sykes re: Aaron Smith, memorandum, September 27, 1954, Investigators' Book, APCF; MacMurdo, House, and Painter to Sykes re: Robert Lee Smith, memorandum, September 25, 1954, ibid.

21. *Columbus Enquirer*, June 19, 1954; *Huntsville Times*, May 2, 2002; Prier to Sykes [re: Morgan Reynolds], memorandum, September 29, 1954, Investigators' Book, APCF.

22. Barton to Sykes re: J. W. ("Jabe") Brassell's attempt to call Governor

Gordon Persons, memorandum, August 12, 1954, Barton's Briefing Book, APCF; *Montgomery Advertiser,* June 19, 1954.

23. Years later, Shanklin would gain notoriety among Kennedy assassination buffs as the FBI supervisor in Dallas who, after Lee Harvey Oswald was arrested, ordered the destruction of a handwritten note Oswald had written to the bureau two weeks before Kennedy was killed.

24. *Montgomery Advertiser,* June 19, 1954; MacMurdo and House to Sykes re: Sheriff Ralph Mathews, memorandum, August 11, 1954, Investigators' Book, APCF; Price to Rosen, memorandum, June 19, 1954, Sanders to Belmont, memorandum, June 19, 1954, and Gordon Shanklin to J. Edgar Hoover, telegram, June 19, 1954, all in AP-FBI.

25. *Columbus Enquirer,* July 16, 1954; *Mobile Register,* May 6, 8, 1951; *Montgomery Advertiser,* June 3, 1951.

26. Strickland and Wortsman, *Phenix City,* 254; Finney, "Narrative Account," in "Phenix City History."

27. Strickland and Wortsman, *Phenix City,* 254.

28. Finney, "Narrative Account," in "Phenix City History"; McGlasson, "Phenix City 1954," 10; Strickland and Wortsman, *Phenix City,* 254–55.

29. "Notes on Conference," June 25, 1954, Barton's Briefing Book, APCF.

30. Initial press reports misidentified this "bullet" as a .25 caliber. See *Montgomery Advertiser* and *Columbus Enquirer,* June 19, 1954.

31. "Notes on Conference," June 25, 1954, Barton's Briefing Book, APCF; Sowell, "Narrative Account," Case 54-14662, ADFS; "Testimony of Wendell Sowell," *Russell County Grand Jury,* vol. 2, APCF; Painter to Sykes re: interview with Dr. Clyde Knowles, memorandum, n.d., "P" folder, APCF; Ferrell interview, APCF.

32. Sowell, "Narrative Account," Case 54-14662, ADFS.

33. Prier and Godwin to Sykes re: Albert Fuller, memorandum, September 13, 1954, Investigators' Book, APCF; Ferrell interview, APCF; Sowell, "Narrative Account," Case 54-14662, ADFS.

34. Sowell, "Narrative Account," Case 54-14662, ADFS; Ferrell interview, APCF; "Notes on Conference with State Investigators," June 26, 1954, Barton's Briefing Book, APCF; Prier to Sykes [re: Morgan Reynolds], memorandum, September 29, 1954, Investigators' Book, APCF.

35. "Notes on Conference with Investigators," June 26, 1954, Barton's Briefing Book, APCF; Sowell, "Narrative Account," Case 54-14662, ADFS; Wendell Sowell re: Autopsy Report, memorandum to file, June 21, 1954, ibid.; Godwin and Coley re: James W. McGehee interview, memorandum, June 27, 1954, Investigators' Book, APCF; Barton to Sykes re: 6/21/54 interview, Pal Daniel, August 19, 1954, Barton's Briefing Book, APCF.

36. Ferrell interview, APCF.

37. Wendell Sowell re: Autopsy Report, memorandum to file, June 21, 1954, Case 54-14662, ADFS; Ferrell interview, APCF.

38. Wendell Sowell re: Autopsy Report, memorandum to file, June 21, 1954, Case 54-14662, ADFS; Ferrell interview, APCF; "Notes on Conference with Investigators," June 25, 1954, Barton's Briefing Book, APCF.

39. Sowell, "Narrative Account," Case 54-14662, ADFS; MacMurdo, House, and Gallion to Sykes re: Leon Sanders, memorandum, August 10, 1954, Investigators' Book, APCF; "Notes on Conference," June 25, 1954, Barton's Briefing Book, APCF; Ferrell interview, APCF; *Birmingham News,* February 19, 20, 1955.

CHAPTER 5

1. Ferrell interview, APCF; Sowell, "Narrative Account," Case 54-14662, ADFS.

2. Ferrell interview, APCF; Sowell, "Narrative Account," Case 54-14662, ADFS.

3. Ferrell interview, APCF; Sowell, "Narrative Account," Case 54-14662, ADFS; Prier to Sykes re: Emmett C. Fulgham, memorandum, October 15, 1954, Investigators' Book, APCF.

4. Strickland and Wortsman, *Phenix City,* 255; McGlasson, "Phenix City 1954," 10; Finney, "Narrative Account," in "Phenix City History."

5. *Columbus Ledger,* June 22, 1954; "Resolution," June 19, 1954, "RBA" folder, APCF.

6. *Opelika Daily News,* June 22, 1954; *Montgomery Advertiser,* June 22, 1954.

7. *Huntsville Times,* June 20, 1954; *Fort Benning Bayonet,* July 1, 1954; *Montgomery Advertiser,* June 20, 1954.

8. Finney, "Narrative Account," in "Phenix City History"; Strickland and Wortsman, *Phenix City,* 255–56; McGlasson, "Phenix City 1954," 10.

9. Prier and Godwin to Sykes re: report on Arch Ferrell, memorandum, September 9, 1954, Investigators' Book, APCF; "Notes on Conference," June 25, 1954, and "Conference with State Investigators, June 26, 1954, Barton's Briefing Book, APCF.

10. *Huntsville Times,* June 20, 1954.

11. Barnes, *Tragedy and Triumph,* 204; MacLean, "From the Ashes," 27–28.

12. Gordon Shanklin to J. Edgar Hoover, telegram, June 18, 1954, AP-FBI.

13. Gordon Shanklin to J. Edgar Hoover, telegram, June 19, 1954, ibid.

14. Ibid.

15. MacMurdo, Smith, House, and W. L. Allen to Sykes re: Lee Porter, August 8, 1954, Investigators' Book, APCF; "Notes on Conference," June 25, 1954, Barton's Briefing Book, APCF.

16. As reprinted in "Crime—Politics, Incorporated," *Alabama: The News Magazine of the Deep South,* June 25, 1954, 4.

17. Ibid.

18. *Columbus Ledger,* June 19, 1954.

19. As reprinted in the *Huntsville Times,* June 20, 1954.

20. *Mobile Press-Register,* June 21, 1954.

21. *Huntsville Times,* June 20, 1954.

22. *Mobile Press-Register,* June 22, 1954.

23. As reprinted in the *Huntsville Times,* June 20, 1954.

24. *Montgomery Advertiser,* July 23, 1954.

25. *Mobile Press-Register,* June 21, 1954.

26. Strickland and Wortsman, *Phenix City,* 238.

27. Strickland and Wortsman, *Phenix City,* 238; Sandra Baxley Taylor, *Faulkner: Jimmy, That Is* (Huntsville, Ala.: Strode Publishers, 1984), 108; *Huntsville Times,* June 28, 1954; *Montgomery Advertiser,* June 27, July 10, 1954.

28. Patterson, "I'll Get the Gangs!" 60.

29. Patterson, "I'll Get the Gangs!" 60; *Montgomery Advertiser,* June 21, 1954; Albert P. Brewer, interview by author, Birmingham, August 28, 1990.

30. "Testimony of Fred Andersen," July 1, 1954, "Emmett Perry—Grand Jury" folder, APCF; "Notes on Conference," June 25, 1954, Barton's Briefing Book, APCF.

31. *Montgomery Advertiser,* June 22, 1954; Ferrell interview, APCF; "Testimony of Fred Andersen," July 1, 1954, "Emmett Perry—Grand Jury" folder, APCF.

32. "Testimony of Fred Andersen," July 1, 1954, "Emmett Perry—Grand Jury" folder, APCF.

33. Ibid.

34. Ibid.; Pagan Six to Pagan Five re: Visit to Phenix City on June 20, 1954, by Attorney General Si Garrett, memorandum, June 28, 1954, "Si Garrett" folder, APCF.

35. "Testimony of Fred Andersen," July 1, 1954, "Emmett Perry—Grand Jury" folder, APCF; Prier and Godwin to Sykes re: report on Arch Ferrell, memorandum, September 9, 1954, Investigators' Book, APCF.

36. Ferrell interview, APCF; "Testimony of Fred Andersen," July 1, 1954, "Emmett Perry—Grand Jury" folder, APCF.

37. J. Edgar Hoover to Tolson, Nichols, Boardman, and Tamm, memorandum, June 21, 1954, AP-FBI.

38. Barton to Sykes re: Ferrell's two alibi telephone calls from Phenix City to Frank Long Jr. in Birmingham, memorandum, August 10, 1954, Barton's Briefing Book, APCF.

39. *Columbus Enquirer,* June 21, 1954; *Columbus Ledger,* June 21, 1954; Ferrell interview, APCF.

40. *Columbus Ledger,* June 22, 1954.

41. *Montgomery Advertiser,* June 23, July 10, 1954.

42. Maury Smith, interview by author, Montgomery, September 13, 1994.

43. Barton to Sykes [re: 6/21/54 interview with Pal Daniel], memoran-

dum, August 19, 1954, Barton's Briefing Book, APCF; Maury Smith, interview by author, Montgomery, January 10, 1995.

44. "Notes on Conference," June 25, 1954, Barton's Briefing Book, APCF.

45. Ibid.; "Testimony of Fred Andersen," July 1, 1954, "Emmett Perry—Grand Jury" folder, APCF.

46. "Testimony of Fred Andersen," July 1, 1954, "Emmett Perry—Grand Jury" folder, APCF.

47. Smith, interview, September 13, 1994.

48. Ibid.; Maury Smith, interview by author, Montgomery, September 20, 1994.

49. *Montgomery Advertiser*, July 10, 1954; *Birmingham Post-Herald*, June 25, July 15, 1954.

50. Smith, interviews, September 13, 20, 1994.

51. "Testimony of Fred Andersen," July 1, 1954, "Emmett Perry—Grand Jury" folder, APCF; *Montgomery Advertiser*, December 19, 1954.

52. "Testimony of Fred Andersen," July 1, 1954, "Emmett Perry—Grand Jury" folder, APCF; *Montgomery Advertiser*, December 19, 1954.

53. *Montgomery Advertiser*, December 19, 1954.

54. Ibid.

55. Ibid.; Cater, "Wide-Open Town," 24.

56. *Montgomery Advertiser*, December 19, 1954; Cater, "Wide-Open Town," 24.

57. *Montgomery Advertiser*, December 19, 1954.

58. "Testimony of John White," *Russell County Grand Jury*, vol. 7, APCF; Bob Ingram, interview by author, Montgomery, March 15, 1996; *Montgomery Advertiser*, September 19, 1954; "Notes on Conference," June 25, 1954, Barton's Briefing Book, APCF.

59. *Montgomery Advertiser*, December 19, 1954; "Testimony of Fred Andersen," July 1, 1954, "Emmett Perry—Grand Jury" folder, APCF.

60. *Montgomery Advertiser*, December 19, 1954; Ferrell interview, APCF; "Notes on Conference," June 25, 1954, and memorandum [re: Kenneth Horne], n.d., Barton's Briefing Book, APCF; "Testimony of Fred Andersen," July 1, 1954, "Emmett Perry—Grand Jury" folder, APCF; "Testimony of John White," *Russell County Grand Jury*, vol. 7, APCF.

61. *Montgomery Advertiser*, December 19, 1954; "Testimony of John White," *Russell County Grand Jury*, vol. 7, APCF.

62. "Testimony of John White," *Russell County Grand Jury*, vol. 7, APCF; "Testimony of Fred Andersen," July 1, 1954, "Emmett Perry—Grand Jury" folder, APCF.

63. Patterson, "I'll Get the Gangs!" 60; *Huntsville Times*, May 2, 2002; *Hartselle Enquirer*, April 4, 2002.

64. *Columbus Ledger*, June 22, 1954.

65. Godwin and Chambers re: William Miller, memorandum, June 25, 1954, Investigators' Book, APCF.

66. *Huntsville Times,* June 21, 1954; *Montgomery Advertiser,* June 22, 1954.

67. "Notes on Conference," June 25, 1954, Barton's Briefing Book, APCF; Strickland and Wortsman, *Phenix City,* 238–40; *Birmingham Post-Herald,* June 24, 1954.

CHAPTER 6

1. *Montgomery Advertiser,* June 25, 1954; *Opelika Daily News,* June 25, 1954; *Birmingham Post-Herald,* June 25, 1954.

2. *Montgomery Advertiser,* July 8, 1954; *Birmingham Post-Herald,* June 25, 1954; *Columbus Enquirer,* June 24, 1954; *Birmingham Post-Herald,* June 24, 1954; Ray Jenkins, interview by author, Baltimore, Md., February 29, 1996.

3. C. B. Nichols to Mr. Tolson, June 24, 1954, and J. Edgar Hoover to Bernard Sykes, June 28, 1954, AP-FBI; *Birmingham Post-Herald,* June 25, 1954.

4. *Birmingham News,* June 27, 1954; Bernard Sykes to Arch Ferrell, June 25, 1954, "Arch Ferrell" folder, APCF; *Montgomery Advertiser,* June 27, 1954.

5. "Notes on Conference," June 25, 1954, Barton's Briefing Book, APCF; *Columbus Ledger,* June 21, 1954.

6. "Notes on Conference," June 25, 1954, Barton's Briefing Book, APCF.

7. Ibid.; Sowell re: Laboratory examination of bullets, memorandum to file, 3 July 1954, Case 54-14662, ADFS; FBI Laboratory to Dr. C. J. Rehling re: Albert Patterson murder, memorandum, June 24, 1954, ibid.

8. "Notes on Conference," June 25, 1954, Barton's Briefing Book, APCF; *Huntsville Times,* June 20, 1954.

9. "Notes on Conference," June 25, 1954, Barton's Briefing Book, APCF.

10. Ibid.

11. "Conference with State Investigators," June 26, 1954, Barton's Briefing Book, APCF.

12. Notes [re: Maurice Patterson], June 26, 1954, ibid.

13. Notes [re: Howard Pennington and John Luttrell], June 27, 1954, ibid.

14. Ibid.

15. Ibid.

16. "Conference with State Investigators," June 26, 1954, ibid.; *Birmingham Post-Herald,* June 25, 1954; *Montgomery Advertiser,* June 30, 1954; Sykes [re: Jim Pruitt alibi], memorandum for record, 8 September 1954, Investigators' Book, APCF; MacMurdo and House to Sykes re: John Pruitt alibi, memorandum, September 8, 1954, ibid.

17. Notes [re: Hugh Britton], June 28, 1954, Barton's Briefing Book, APCF.

18. Notes [re: James Godwin Davis Jr.], June 28, 1954, ibid.; Barton to Sykes re: Albert L. Patterson as Member of Russell County Draft Board, memorandum, September 1, 1954, Barton's Briefing Book II, APCF.

19. Notes, June 27, 1954, Barton's Briefing Book, APCF.

20. Barton to Sykes, memorandum, July 28, 1954, ibid.

21. "Crime—Politics, Incorporated," 3; *Mobile Press-Register,* June 27, 1954.

22. *Montgomery Advertiser,* June 27, August 6, 1954; *Huntsville Times,* June 28, July 1, 1954.

23. *Huntsville Times,* June 30–July 2, 1954.

24. Ibid., July 1, 1954; Bob Ingram, interview by author, Montgomery, September 4, 1990.

25. MacDonald Gallion, interviews by author, Montgomery, November 10, 1994, March 6, 1998.

26. Gallion, interviews, November 10, 1994, March 6, 1998.

27. Gordon Persons to Sykes re: John Patterson, telegram, July 2, 1954, "Governor" folder, APCF.

28. *Montgomery Advertiser,* June 29, 1954; *Birmingham News,* June 29, 1954.

29. *Montgomery Advertiser,* June 29, 1954; *Birmingham News,* June 26, 29, 1954.

30. *Montgomery Advertiser,* June 29, 1954; *Birmingham News,* June 26, 29, 1954; Jones School of Law web page, www.faulkner.edu.

31. *Montgomery Advertiser,* July 26, 1954.

32. Ibid., June 28, July 6, 11, 1954; *Huntsville Times,* July 1, 1954.

33. *Montgomery Advertiser,* July 1, 1954; *Birmingham Post-Herald,* July 1, 1954.

34. "Notes on Conference," June 25, 1954, Barton's Briefing Book, APCF.

35. Interview with [Patterson's former secretary], July 2, 1954, Dictaphone Book #4, APCF.

36. Williams and Painter to Sykes, memorandum, n.d., Investigators' Book, APCF.

37. "Testimony of Fred Andersen," July 1, 1954, "Emmett Perry—Grand Jury" folder, APCF.

38. *Montgomery Advertiser,* July 10, 1954.

39. "History of the Investigative and Identification Division," September 19, 1974, Public Information and Education Unit, ADPS [hereinafter cited as "History of the I & I"]; Major Jerry Shoemaker, ADPS, interview by author, Montgomery, June 30, 1998; Major John Cloud, ADPS, interview by author, Montgomery, May 14, 1998; Walter L. Allen, interview by author, Montgomery, October 21, 1994.

40. "Testimony of Willie Painter," *Fuller v. State,* ADAH; *Birmingham Post-Herald,* December 15, 1954; Cloud, interview.

41. Lieutenant John Williams III, ADPS, interview by author, June 30, 1998; "Testimony of John Williams," *Russell County Grand Jury,* vol. 4, APCF; ADPS, Public Information and Education Unit, to author, December 7, 1998; "Testimony of Robert Godwin," *Fuller v. State,* ADAH.

42. "History of the I & I"; Shoemaker, interview, June 30, 1998; ADPS, Public Information and Education Unit, to author, December 7, 1998.

43. Allen, interview; ADPS, Public Information and Education Unit, to author, December 7, 1998.

44. ADPS, Public Information and Education Unit, to author, December 7, 1998.

45. Ibid.; Major Jerry Shoemaker, ADPS, interview by author, Montgomery, September 14, 1998; Allen, interview.

46. Strickland and Wortsman, *Phenix City*, 12, 223, 225; *Birmingham News,* December 10, 1954; Noel Baker, interview by author, Opelika, Ala., August 1, 1994.

47. *Montgomery Advertiser,* July 8, 1954.

48. "Testimony of Morgan Reynolds" and "Testimony of Willie Painter," *Russell County Grand Jury,* vol. 7, APCF; "Notes on Conference," June 25, 1954, Barton's Briefing Book, APCF.

49. MacDonald Gallion, interview by author, Montgomery, December 30, 1994.

50. Sykes re: report of Smith and Sykes on Trip to see Emmett Perry, 9/16/54, memorandum for record, September 17, 1954, Barton's Briefing Book II, APCF; Perry to Sykes [re: Jefferson Grand Jury witnesses], July 28, 1954, and Perry to Sykes [re: Jefferson Grand Jury transcripts], memorandum, September 22, 1954, "Emmett Perry—Grand Jury" folder, APCF.

51. Strickland and Wortsman, *Phenix City,* 14; *Montgomery Advertiser,* July 6, 10, 1954; Fowler, interview.

52. Ferrell interview, APCF.

53. Ibid.; notes [re: Kenneth Horne], n.d., Barton's Briefing Book, APCF.

54. Ferrell interview, APCF; *Birmingham Post-Herald,* July 10, 1954.

55. Painter to Sykes re: Albert Fuller's activities, memorandum, August 27, 1954, Investigators' Book, APCF; Prier to Sykes re: Albert Fuller with no pistol on night of 6/18, memorandum, October 15, 1954, ibid.

56. Strickland and Wortsman, *Phenix City,* 223; Finney, "Narrative Account," in "Phenix City History"; Coulter, interview; Barton re: Albert Fuller, memorandum for file, n.d., "Albert Fuller" folder, APCF.

57. *Montgomery Advertiser,* July 11, 1954.

58. Ibid., July 7, 12, 13, 1954; Alabama Supreme Court, *Ex parte* Garrett, December 16, 1964, 76 So. 2d 681; *Los Angeles Times,* July 13, 1954.

59. *Montgomery Advertiser,* July 13, 1954; *Los Angeles Times,* July 13, 1954.

60. *Montgomery Advertiser,* July 15–17, 1954; "Accident Report," Mississippi State Highway Safety Patrol, July 16, 1954, "Garrett" folder, APCF.

CHAPTER 7

1. Strickland and Wortsman, *Phenix City,* 14; *Mobile Press-Register,* July 17, 18, 1954; *Montgomery Advertiser,* July 18, 1954.

2. Smelley to Phillips, Godwin, Painter, and W. L. Allen, July 20, 1954, "Investigators" folder, APCF.

3. *Montgomery Advertiser,* July 15, October 3, 1954.

4. Allen, interview.

5. Walter Stone to Gordon Persons [re: Lee Barton], n.d., "Phenix City Investigation (Albert Patterson Murder)" folder, Persons Papers; N. P. Callahan to Mr. Mohr, July 6, 1954, AP-FBI.

6. Sykes [re: Ben Allen], memorandum, n.d., "Investigators" folder, APCF; ADPS, Department of Public Education and Information Unit, to author, December 7, 1998; Shoemaker, interview, June 30, 1998.

7. Maury Smith, interview by author, Montgomery, January 25, 2000; Tim MacMurdo, interview by author, Huntsville, Ala., September 22, 1999; Birmingham Police Department, Records Division, letter to author, February 9, 2000.

8. Claude Prier, interview by author, Mobile, Ala., July 2, 1998; Sykes to L. B. Sullivan [re: Claude Prier], memorandum, September 10, 1954, "Investigators" folder, APCF; Cloud, interview; Shoemaker, interview, June 30, 1998; "History of the I & I"; "Claude S. Prier Is New Executive Director," *Alabama Police Journal*, Spring 1979, 17.

9. *Montgomery Advertiser*, July 9, 1954.

10. House and MacMurdo to Sykes re: Mr. Ennis, memorandum, August 4, 1954, Investigators' Book, APCF; Barton to Sykes re: Raymond Eugene Ennis, August 12, 1954, Barton's Briefing Book, APCF; *Birmingham News*, February 19, 1955.

11. Interview with Gordon Terry, July 8, 1954, Dictaphone Book #5, APCF; Prier and MacMurdo to Sykes re: Lullella Colbert, memorandum, November 20, 1954, Reinterview Book, APCF.

12. Allen, interview; "Conference with State Investigators," June 26, 1954, Barton's Briefing Book, APCF; Godwin and Chambers re: Jimmy Kirkland interview, memorandum, 23 June 1954, Investigators' Book, APCF.

13. Allen, interview.

14. Godwin and Painter re: Jimmy Sanders interview, memorandum, June 29, 1954, Investigators' Book, APCF; notes [re: Howard Pennington], July 1, 1954, Barton's Briefing Book, APCF.

15. Prier and Godwin to Sykes re: report on Arch Ferrell, memorandum, September 9, 1954, Investigators' Book, APCF; *Birmingham News*, 18 February, April 28, 1954.

16. Barton to Sykes [re: James Ray Taylor], memorandum, June 19, 1954. "Taylor" folder, APCF.

17. Finney, "Narrative Account," in "Phenix City History"; Strickland and Wortsman, *Phenix City*, 73, 259.

18. McGlasson, "Phenix City 1954," 111; Strickland and Wortsman, *Phenix City*, 259–60; *Columbus Ledger-Enquirer*, August 15, 1954; Smith, interview, September 13, 1994.

19. Strickland and Wortsman, *Phenix City*, 14–15; *Columbus Ledger-Enquirer*, August 15, 1954; McGlasson, "Phenix City 1954," 11; *Montgomery Advertiser*,

July 23, 1954; Alabama Supreme Court Associate Justice Preston Clayton to Gordon Persons, June 26, 1954, "Phenix City Investigation (Albert Patterson Murder)" folder, Persons Papers.

20. *Montgomery Advertiser*, July 23, 1954; McGlasson, "Phenix City 1954," 11, 12; Strickland and Wortsman, *Phenix City*, 251–53.

21. *Columbus Ledger-Enquirer*, August 15, 1954; Ed Ratigan, interview by author, Birmingham, March 26, 1995; Sowell to file re: Albert L. Patterson, memorandum, August 27, 1954, Case 54-14662, ADFS.

22. Strickland and Wortsman, *Phenix City*, 73–74, 263; McGlasson, "Phenix City 1954," 12; *Montgomery Advertiser*, July 25, 1954; *Columbus Ledger-Enquirer*, August 15, 1954; Finney, "Narrative Account," in "Phenix City History."

23. Subcommittee on Elections, State Democratic Executive Committee of Alabama, "Final Decree," July 15, 1954, "Phenix City Investigation (Albert Patterson Murder)" folder, Persons Papers.

24. *Montgomery Advertiser*, July 29–August 3, August 6, 14–15, 28, 1954; Finney, "Narrative Account," in "Phenix City History"; Subcommittee on Elections, State Democratic Executive Committee of Alabama, "Final Decree," July 15, 1954, "Phenix City Investigation (Albert Patterson Murder)" folder, Persons Papers; Strickland and Wortsman, *Phenix City*, 278.

25. Strickland and Wortsman, *Phenix City*, 15; Smith, interview, September 13, 1994; *Montgomery Advertiser*, July 13, 1954.

26. Gallion, MacMurdo, and House to Sykes re: New Information: James R. Taylor, memorandum, July 26, 1954, Investigators' Book, APCF.

27. Ibid.

28. Interview with Colonel George Berry, Warrant Officer James Manger, and Albert Freemen, July 15, 1954, Dictaphone Book #5, APCF.

29. Barton to Sykes re: Army Lieutenant en route to Chad's Rose Room, memorandum, July 26, 1954, Barton's Briefing Book, APCF; Strickland and Wortsman, *Phenix City*, 15; *Montgomery Advertiser*, July 28, 1954.

30. Painter to Sykes re: Fred Ryals, memorandum, July 30, 1954, Investigators' Book, APCF; interview with Fred Ryals, August 3, 1954, Dictaphone Book #5, APCF.

31. Painter to Sykes re: Fred Ryals, memorandum, July 30, 1954, Investigators' Book, APCF; interview with Fred Ryals, August 3, 1954, Dictaphone Book #5, APCF.

32. Ben Allen to Sykes re: Homicide, memorandum, August 30, 1954, Investigators' Book, APCF.

33. Painter to Sykes re: Albert Fuller's activities . . . , memorandum, August 27, 1954, ibid.

34. Ben Allen to Sykes re: Homicide, memorandum, August 30, 1954, ibid.; W. L. Allen and Ben Allen to Sykes re: Homicide, August 30, 1954, ibid.

35. W. L. Allen and Ben Allen to Sykes re: Homicide, memorandum, Au-

gust 30, 1954, ibid.; Painter to Sykes re: Albert Fuller's activities . . . , memorandum, August 27, 1954, ibid.

36. Barton to Sykes re: Margaret Sanks, memorandum, July 28, 1954, Barton's Briefing Book, APCF.

37. "Testimony of Fred Andersen," July 1, 1954, "Emmett Perry—Grand Jury" folder, APCF.

38. Baker, interview; Smith, interview, September 13, 1994; *Columbus Ledger*, June 19, 1954.

39. Sykes to Smith re: General Assignment, memorandum, August 14, 1954, "Investigators" folder, APCF.

40. "Testimony of Albert Rosenthal," *Russell County Grand Jury*, vol. 7, APCF; Smith to Sykes re: interview with Gordon Madison et al., memorandum, n.d., Barton's Briefing Book, APCF; notes [re: Howard Pennington and John Luttrell], June 27, 1954, ibid.; Barton to Sykes re: Patterson's purpose to appear before the Jefferson County Grand Jury, memorandum, August 10, 1954, ibid.; Sykes to John Patterson [re: Addis Green], memorandum, September 20, 1954, Barton's Briefing Book II, APCF; Sykes to Allens [re: Addis Green and $15,000], memorandum, September 22, 1954, ibid.; MacMurdo and House to Sykes re: Joe S. Eddins, memorandum, August 23, 1954, Investigators' Book, APCF; Smith, interview, September 13, 1994.

41. Prier to Sykes [re: Howard Pennington], memorandum, October 28, 1954, Investigators' Book, APCF.

42. MacMurdo and House to Sykes re: Besse June Miller, memorandum, July 23, 1954, ibid.; Prier and Godwin to Sykes [re: Mrs. Mildred Wall interview], memorandum, August 24, 1954, ibid.

43. Porter had not reported the sums on his campaign disclosure forms. MacMurdo and House to Sykes re: interview with Lamar A. Reid, memorandum, August 6, 1954, ibid.; Smith to Sykes re: trip to Birmingham, Gadsden and Waynesboro, 8/2 3/54, August 6, 1954, ibid.

44. Smith to Sykes re: trip to Birmingham, Gadsden and Waynesboro, 8/2–3/54, August 6, 1954, ibid.; MacMurdo and House to Sykes re: Si Garrett, memorandum, August 8, 1954, ibid.

45. Barton to Sykes re: Arch Ferrell's telephone alibi, memorandum, August 9, 1954, Barton's Briefing Book, APCF.

46. Barton to Sykes re: Arch Ferrell's two long-distance conversations with Frank Long Jr. and Si Garrett on the night of the murder, memorandum, August 12, 1954, ibid.; Barton to Sykes re: telephone calls made from pay phone in Smitty's Grill on night of murder, August 2, 1954, ibid.

47. Barton to Sykes re: Arch Ferrell's telephone alibi, August 9, 1954, ibid.

48. Prier to Sykes re: Sergeant Robert R. Moore, memorandum, October 16, 1954, Investigators' Book, APCF.

49. Ibid.

50. Memorandums in "Investigators" folder, APCF: Sykes to Painter re:

General Assignment, August 14, 1954; Sykes to Ben Allen and W. L. Allen re: General Assignment, August 14, 1954; Sykes to MacMurdo and House re: General Assignment, August 14, 1954; Sykes to Godwin and Prier re: General Assignment, August 14, 1954; Sykes to Smith re: General Assignment, August 14, 1954; Sykes to Gallion re: General Assignment, August 14, 1954; and Sykes to Barton re: General Assignment, August 14, 1954.

CHAPTER 8

1. Gordon Persons to John Patterson [re: Phenix City investigation], September 21, 1954, "Gordon Persons" folder, John Patterson Papers; John Patterson to Gordon Persons [re: Phenix City investigation], September 25, 1954, ibid.

2. MacDonald Gallion, interviews by author, Montgomery, October 11, 1994, September 1, 1999.

3. Ibid.; Gallion to Sykes re: information coming from the confidential source, memorandum, August 11, 1954, Investigators' Book, APCF.

4. Strickland and Wortsman, *Phenix City*, 220–22; *Birmingham News*, February 16, 1955.

5. *Birmingham News*, February 16, 1955.

6. Jenkins, interview.

7. Painter to Sykes re: fingerprints, memorandum, 24 November 1954, "Albert Fuller" folder, APCF; Hoover to Tolson [re: telephone call to Governor Gordon Persons], memorandum, 23 September 1954, AP-FBI; *Birmingham News*, 19 February 1955.

8. Allen, interview.

9. Finney, "Chronology," in "Phenix City History"; *Montgomery Advertiser*, 28 August 1954; Strickland and Wortsman, *Phenix City*, 227, 269–70.

10. *Montgomery Advertiser*, 29 July 1954; Jenkins, interview; Steve Franklin, interview, July 21, 1997.

11. "Statement of Johnny Frank Griffin," September 25, 1954, "Albert Fuller" folder, APCF.

12. Sykes [re: Johnny Frank Griffin interview], memorandum for record, October 11, 1954, Barton's Briefing Book II, APCF.

13. Painter to Sykes re: Albert Fuller's activities . . . , August 27, 1954, Investigators' Book, APCF; Painter, MacMurdo, and House to Sykes re: Albert Fuller alibi, October 5, 1954, ibid.

14. Painter, MacMurdo, and House to Sykes re: Albert Fuller alibi, October 5, 1954, ibid.

15. Ibid.

16. Ibid.; "Testimony of Albert Fuller," *Fuller v. State*, ADAH.

17. Painter, MacMurdo, and House to Sykes re: Albert Fuller alibi, memorandum, October 5, 1954, Investigators' Book, APCF.

18. Memorandums, Gallion and Barton to Sykes re: Leonard David Powell, July 23, 1954, W. L. Allen and Ben Allen to Sykes re: L. D. Powell, August 27, 1954, W. L. Allen and Ben Allen to Sykes re: Mrs. Doris Lindsey, August 27, 1954, Godwin and Chambers re: Jimmy Kirkland, June 23, 1954, and Godwin and Painter re: Jimmy Sanders, June 29, 1954, all in ibid.; *Birmingham News*, April 28, 1955; "Affidavit of Mrs. Bentley," June 2, 1955, New Trial Hearing, *Fuller v. State*, ADAH; notes re: Howard Pennington and John Luttrell, July 27, 1954, Barton's Briefing Book, APCF.

19. Sykes [re: Johnny Frank Griffin], memorandum for record, October 11, 1954, Barton's Briefing Book II, APCF; Prier to Sykes re: Johnny Frank Griffin, memorandum, October 26, 1954, Investigators' Book, APCF; "Arrest record," n.d., "Johnny Frank Griffin" folder, APCF.

20. Sykes [re: Johnny Frank Griffin], memorandum for record, October 11, 1954, Barton's Briefing Book II, APCF; Prier to Sykes re: Johnny Frank Griffin, memorandum, October 26, 1954, Investigators' Book, APCF; "Arrest record," n.d., "Johnny Frank Griffin" folder, APCF; "Bryce's Admission Form," April 24, 1941, "Johnny Frank Griffin" folder, APCF; Prier to Sykes re: Johnny Frank Griffin, memorandum, October 26, 1954, Investigators' Book, APCF.

21. Painter to Sykes [re: Fred Ryals], memorandum, October 6, 1954, and House to Sykes re: James Ray Taylor, memorandum, October 7, 1954, Investigators' Book, APCF; Smith to Sykes re: Fred Ryals, memorandum, October 27, 1954, Barton's Briefing Book II, APCF.

22. Sowell re: Comparison of bullets, memorandum to file, August 3, 1954, Case 54-14662, ADFS; *Montgomery Advertiser*, August 8, 1954; Sowell to Rehling, memorandum, February 14, 1955, and Sowell re: Albert L. Patterson, memorandum to file, August 27, 1954, Case 54-14662, ADFS; Barton to W. L. Allen re: Colt Revolver, .38 Cobra, July 28, 1954, Barton's Briefing Book, APCF; Gallion to Rehling re: test bullets, memorandum, August 20, 1954, "Pistol" folder, APCF.

23. *Birmingham News*, February 22, 1955; "Case Log," n.d., Case 54-14662, ADFS; Sowell re: Examination of physical evidence, memorandum to file, October 30, 1954, ibid.; Sowell re: Case 54-14662, Albert L. Patterson, memorandum to file, October 30, 1954, ibid.; Rehling to Sykes re: Case 54-14662, Albert L. Patterson, memorandum, November 1, 1954, ibid.

24. Smith, interview, September 13, 1994.

25. *Montgomery Advertiser*, November 10, 11, 1954; *Birmingham News*, February 16, 1955; Strickland and Wortsman, *Phenix City*, 136–40.

26. *Montgomery Advertiser*, November 11, 1954; *Birmingham News*, February 16, 1955; Sowell re: Laboratory Examination of Physical Evidence, memorandum to file, November 24, 1954, Case 54-14662, ADFS; Rehling to Sykes re: Case 54-14662, Albert L. Patterson, memorandum, November 24, 1954, ibid.

27. *Birmingham Post-Herald*, November 10, 1954; *Montgomery Advertiser*, November 11, 1954; Sowell re: Laboratory Examination of Physical Evidence,

memorandum to file, November 24, 1954, Case 54-14662, ADFS; Rehling to Sykes re: Case 54-14662, Albert L. Patterson, memorandum, November 24, 1954, ibid.; Smith, interview, September 13, 1994.

28. Williams and Smelley to Sykes [re: Quinnie Kelley], memorandum, July 21, 1954, Investigators' Book, APCF; Fowler, interview; "Testimony of John Williams," *Fuller v. State*, ADAH.

29. *Birmingham News*, April 27, 1955; Fowler, interview.

30. Notes, June 28, 1954, Barton's Briefing Book, APCF.

31. Prier and Godwin to Sykes re: report on Arch Ferrell, memorandum, September 9, 1954, Investigators' Book, APCF; Prier to Sykes re: John Luttrell, memorandum, October 15, 1954, ibid.; Prier to Sykes re: Emmett L. Fulgham, October 16, 1954, ibid.; Prier to Sykes re: James L. Young, October 15, 1954, ibid..

32. *Birmingham News*, December 10, 1954; notes [re: Margaret Sanks], July 28, 1954, Barton's Briefing Book, APCF.

33. Jenkins, interview; *Huntsville Times*, May 2, 2002; Barnes, *Tragedy and Triumph*, 281, 293-96; MacLean, "From the Ashes," 21.

34. Allen, interview; Jenkins, interview; notes re: Howard Pennington and John Luttrell, June 27, 1954, Barton's Briefing Book, APCF; Barton to Sykes re: Rufus Massey, memorandum, August 18, 1954, ibid.

35. Prier and Godwin to Sykes re: report on Arch Ferrell, memorandum, September 9, 1954, Investigators' Book, APCF.

36. MacMurdo and House to Sykes re: Si Garrett, 6/18/54, memorandum, August 23, 1954, Investigators' Book, APCF.

37. *State ex rel. Martin, Attorney General v. John B. Tully, Circuit Judge*, Alabama Supreme Court, 1894, 15 So. 722; "Legal Brief," n.d., "Si Garrett" folder, APCF.

CHAPTER 9

1. *Montgomery Advertiser*, August 3, September 4, 5, 7, October 9, November 4, 1954; *Birmingham News*, December 5, 1954, February 16, 1955; Strickland and Wortsman, *Phenix City*, 23, 96; Finney, "Chronology," in "Phenix City History"; "Statement of Ray McFall," n.d., and Prier and Godwin to Sykes re: Albert Fuller, memorandum, September 13, 1954, "Albert Fuller" folder, APCF.

2. *Montgomery Advertiser*, September 3, 7, October 3, 17, 1954; *Birmingham News*, February 22, 1955; Gallion, interviews, November 10, 1994, September 1, 1999.

3. *Birmingham News*, December 5, 1954; Jenkins, interview; Maury Smith, interview by author, Montgomery, September 9, 1994.

4. *Montgomery Advertiser*, November 16, 17, 1954; *Birmingham News*, January 20, 22, 1955; *Birmingham Post-Herald*, December 10, 1954.

5. *Montgomery Advertiser*, July 25, 1954.

6. Ibid., August 6, 1954; Sykes [re: Arch Ferrell's DUI arrest], memorandum for record, August 20, 1954, "B" folder, APCF; Barton to Sykes re: Caroll E. Bagby, memorandum, August 9, 1954, Barton's Briefing Book, APCF.

7. *Montgomery Advertiser*, August 7, 12, 1954.

8. Ibid., August 7, 12, 17, 1954; Johnson to Persons re: H. A. Ferrell, member, Russell County Local Board, August 31, 1954, "Selective Service" folder, Persons Papers.

9. *Montgomery Advertiser*, August 28, September 27, November 4, 14, 1954; *Birmingham News*, December 6, 1954.

10. *Montgomery Advertiser*, July 17, August 7, September 10–14, 17–18, 1954; *Birmingham News*, September 13, 1954.

11. *Montgomery Advertiser*, September 11–17, 1954; Alabama Supreme Court, *Ex parte* Garrett, December 16, 1954, 76 So. 2d 681; *Los Angeles Times*, July 13, 1954.

12. *Montgomery Advertiser*, September 25, 28, October 15, 1954; *Birmingham Post-Herald*, November 13, 1954; *Montgomery Advertiser*, November 13, 1954.

13. J. O. Sentell, "Roderick Beddow of the Birmingham Bar," *Alabama Lawyer* 31, no. 3 (1970): 343–44; *Birmingham News*, February 16, March 6, 1955; *Birmingham Post-Herald*, February 20, 1967.

14. *Birmingham News*, February 20, 1955.

15. Ibid., October 2, 6, 1954.

16. Ibid., October 7, 8, 12, 1954; Fowler, interview.

17. *Birmingham News*, October 8, 9, 12, 1954. Jones returned Johnson's compliment by providing a glowing tribute to the solicitor on October 25, 1954, in his weekly "Off the Bench" column in the *Montgomery Advertiser:* "Steadfast he stands in his place, proud representative of a great people, battling for law and decency with all courage and all fidelity. . . . Defendants and their henchmen . . . never awe him. The stage-like appearance of noted criminal defense lawyers, with all their big law books, their files of impressive-looking papers, and retinue of assistants, never fill him with panic."

18. *Montgomery Advertiser*, October 3, 21, 1954.

19. Ibid., October 21, 1954.

20. *Columbus Ledger*, November 1, 1954; *Montgomery Advertiser*, November 2, 1954; *Huntsville Times*, November 2, 1954; *Birmingham News*, November 7, 1954; Strickland and Wortsman, *Phenix City*, 16.

21. Fred Simpson, interview by author, Huntsville, Ala., April 17, 2000.

22. "Testimony of Sgt. Robert Moore," *Russell County Grand Jury*, vol. 5, APCF; *Montgomery Advertiser*, November 30, December 8, 1954; *Birmingham News*, February 10, 1955.

23. "Testimony of Raymond Ennis" and "Testimony of Hubert Tharpe," *Russell County Grand Jury*, vol. 1, APCF.

24. "Testimony of Johnny Frank Griffin," *Russell County Grand Jury*, vol. 3, APCF; Ratigan, interview.

25. *Montgomery Advertiser*, December 3, 4, 1954; "Testimony of John Patterson" and "Testimony of Claude Prier," *Russell County Grand Jury*, vols. 4 and 2, respectively, APCF. Coulter (interview) insists that she saw Griffin that afternoon and that he appeared to be completely sober.

26. *Birmingham News*, December 3, 5, 1954; *Montgomery Advertiser*, December 3, 1954; "Statement of Barbara Jean Parker," December 2, 1954, and "Statement of James D. Williams," December 11, 1954, Jack Warren Papers, BPL.

27. *Birmingham News*, December 4, 5, 1954.

28. Clarke Stallworth, interview by author, Birmingham, July 25, 1994. Griffin's untimely death has contributed to another Phenix City legend, namely, that if Griffin had testified during the trials, Ferrell would certainly have been convicted. In fact, however, Griffin never mentioned Ferrell in his statements to investigators and in his grand jury testimony. See *Russell County Grand Jury*, vol. 3, "Testimony of Johnny Frank Griffin."

29. *Birmingham News*, December 9, 1954; "Indictment," *Fuller v. State*, ADAH.

30. *Birmingham News*, December 9, 10, 1954.

31. Ibid., December 10, 1954; *Birmingham Post-Herald*, December 10, 15, 1954.

32. Shanklin to Hoover [re: request from Bernard Sykes], memorandum, December 12, 1954, AP-FBI.

33. *Birmingham News*, December 12, 14, 1954.

34. Alabama Supreme Court, *Ex parte* Garrett, December 16, 1954, 76 So. 2d 681; *Montgomery Advertiser*, December 17, 1954; *Birmingham News*, December 16, 1954.

35. *Montgomery Advertiser*, December 14, 15, 1954; "Testimony of Bob Gwin," Proceedings of Motion for a New Trial, *Fuller v. State*, ADAH.

36. *Birmingham News*, December 10, 14, 1954.

37. *Montgomery Advertiser*, December 15, 1954; Pat Boyd Rumore, *Lawyers in a New South City: A History of the Legal Profession in Alabama* (Birmingham: Associated Publishing Co., 2000), 104, 252; Drew Redden, interviews by author, Birmingham, August 16, 1994, August 21, 1997, April 10, 2000.

38. *Birmingham News*, December 16–18, 1954.

39. *Montgomery Advertiser*, December 8–9, 15, 1954; *Birmingham News*, December 9, 1954.

40. Jenkins, interview.

41. *Birmingham News*, December 23, 1954, February 16, 1955.

42. *Birmingham News*, December 23, 27–28, 1954.

43. Ibid., January 7, 9, 1955.

44. Ibid.

45. *Montgomery Advertiser,* August 15, December 30, 1954; *Birmingham News,* December 30, 1954; James Caldwell, interview by author, Lanett, Ala., August 25, 1994.

46. *Birmingham News,* January 7, 9, 1955.

47. Ibid.

48. Ibid., January 7, 20, 1955.

49. Ibid., January 12, 1955.

50. Ibid., January 13, 14, 1955.

51. *Montgomery Advertiser,* January 21, 1955; Redden, interview, August 16, 1994.

52. *Birmingham News,* January 21, 30, 1955.

53. Redden, interview, August 16, 1994.

54. MacDonald Gallion, interviews by author, Montgomery, September 1, December 30, 1994; *Birmingham News,* January 27, February 10, 1955; *Birmingham Post-Herald,* February 26, 1955.

CHAPTER 10

1. Prier to Sykes re: interview with Dewey Chestnut, memorandum, October 27, 1954, Investigators' Book, APCF; Coulter, interview.

2. Gallion, interview, March 6, 1998; *Birmingham News,* January 3, 1955.

3. *Birmingham News,* January 30, February 1, 16, 1955.

4. Ibid., February 28, 1955; Redden, interview, August 16, 1994; "Testimony of Bob Gwin," Proceedings of Motion for a New Trial, *Fuller v. State,* ADAH.

5. *Birmingham News,* February 15, 23, 1955.

6. Ibid., February 14, 15, 1955.

7. Ibid.; Redden, interview, August 16, 1994.

8. *Birmingham News,* February 16, 17, 25, 1955.

9. Ibid., February 15, 17, 1955.

10. Ibid., February 17, 1955; "Testimony of Agnes Patterson," *Fuller v. State,* ADAH.

11. "Testimony of Leland Jones," *Fuller v. State,* ADAH.

12. "Testimony of Woodie Pope," ibid.

13. *Birmingham News,* February 18, 1955; "Testimony of Jimmy Sanders, *Fuller v. State,* ADAH.

14. *Birmingham News,* February 19, 1955; "Testimony of Jimmy Sanders" and "Testimony of Hugh Buchanan," *Fuller v. State,* ADAH.

15. Allen, interview; *Birmingham News,* February 25, 1955.

16. *Birmingham News,* February 25, March 8, 1955; "Testimony of Howard Pennington," *Fuller v. State,* ADAH.

17. *Birmingham News,* February 24, 1955; "Testimony of Willie Painter," *Fuller v. State,* ADAH.

18. *Birmingham News*, February 18, 1955; "Testimony of Bill Littleton," *Fuller v. State*, ADAH.

19. *Birmingham News*, February 18, 25, 1955; "Testimony of Bill Littleton," *Fuller v. State*, ADAH.

20. *Birmingham News*, February 20, 1955; "Testimony of James Taylor," *Fuller v. State*, ADAH.

21. *Birmingham News*, February 22, 23, 1955; "Testimony of James Taylor," *Fuller v. State*, ADAH.

22. There is no indication that Beddow was aware that at least three other policemen, including Buddy Jowers, had seen the footprint within an hour of the murder.

23. *Birmingham News*, February 19, 1955; "Testimony of Walter Leon Sanders," *Fuller v. State*, ADAH.

24. *Birmingham News*, February 18, 21, 24, 1955; "Testimony of Wendell Sowell," *Fuller v. State*, ADAH.

25. *Birmingham News*, February 19, 20, 22, 23, 1955; "Testimony of Wendell Sowell," "Testimony of Robert Godwin," "Testimony of John Williams," "Testimony of Willie Painter," and "Testimony of J. Everett Burke," *Fuller v. State*, ADAH.

26. Alabama Supreme Court, *Alabama Rules of Criminal Procedure, 1991*, ed. Hugh Maddox (Charlottesville, Va.: Michie, 1990), Rule 13.3, 94–108; Simpson, interview.

27. *Birmingham News*, February 24, 25, 1955; "Testimony of Quinnie Kelley," *Fuller v. State*, ADAH.

28. Although Wendell Sowell concluded that there were four shots, almost all the witnesses, including Padgett, testified that they heard three or fewer. This may have occurred because the echoes of the first shots distorted the sounds of the later ones, a common occurrence in a confined space like the Coulter Building alleyway.

29. *Birmingham News*, March 1, 1955; *Montgomery Advertiser*, August 11, 21, 1955; "Testimony of Johnny Frank Griffin," *Russell County Grand Jury*, vol. 3, APCF; "Testimony of Shannon Burch," *Fuller v. State*, ADAH.

30. *Birmingham News*, March 1, 1955; "Testimony of Cecil Padgett," *Fuller v. State*, ADAH.

31. *Birmingham News*, February 26–28, 1955; "Testimony of Edith Padgett," *Fuller v. State*, ADAH.

32. *Birmingham News*, February 28, March 2, 1955; "Testimony of R. T. Shirling," "Testimony of L. L. Brown," "Testimony of Davis E. Myers," "Testimony of Tom Corley," and "Testimony of Cecil Padgett," *Fuller v. State*, ADAH.

33. *Birmingham News*, March 1, 3, 1955; "Testimony of Steve Schermann," "Testimony of Leroy Miller," and "Testimony of D. R. McLemore," *Fuller v. State*, ADAH.

34. *Birmingham News,* March 1, 1955; "Testimony of Ray Eller" and "Testimony of James McCain," *Fuller v. State,* ADAH.

35. *Birmingham News,* March 3, 1955; "Testimony of James H. Layfield" and "Testimony of Matthew Daniel Carden," *Fuller v. State,* ADAH.

36. *Birmingham News,* March 2, 1955; "Testimony of Virginia Lange," "Testimony of Jack Forston," "Testimony of Ottis Shadrix," and "Testimony of Charles Dobbs," *Fuller v. State,* ADAH.

37. *Birmingham News,* March 2, 1955; "Testimony of Walter Lee Bankston," *Fuller v. State,* ADAH.

38. *Birmingham News,* February 24, March 3, 1955; "Testimony of Judge Shannon Burch" and "Testimony of Patrick H. Mihelic," *Fuller v. State,* ADAH.

39. *Birmingham News,* March 3, 1955; "Testimony of Ben Clark," *Fuller v. State,* ADAH.

40. *Birmingham News,* March 3, 1955; "Testimony of George Phillips," "Testimony of Ralph Mathews," "Testimony of Robert Lee Smith," "Testimony of Curtis Alexander Deason," and "Testimony of Aaron Smith," *Fuller v. State,* ADAH.

41. *Birmingham News,* March 5, 6, 8, 9, 1955; "Testimony of Mrs. Roberta Oakley," "Testimony of Albert Fuller," "Testimony of Ben Allen," *Fuller v. State,* ADAH; Allen, interview.

42. *Birmingham News,* March 11, 1955.

43. Ibid., March 11, 12, 1955.

CHAPTER 11

1. Redden, interview, August 16, 1994; *Birmingham News,* February 24, 1955.

2. Redden, interview, August 16, 1994.

3. *Birmingham News,* March 13, 1955.

4. Ibid., February 24, March 2–9, 1955.

5. Ibid., March 9, 1955.

6. Ibid., March 10, 12, 1955.

7. Redden, interview, August 16, 1994.

8. *Birmingham News,* March 12, 13, 1955.

9. Ibid., March 13, 1955; Redden, interview, August 16, 1994.

10. *Birmingham News,* April 7, 12, 14, 1955.

11. Ibid., April 20, 26, 1955; Jenkins, interview.

12. *Birmingham News,* April 22, 1955.

13. Ibid., April 23, 27, 1955.

14. Ibid., March 23, April 23, 26, 1955.

15. Ibid., April 23–25, 1955.

16. Ibid., April 27, 1955.

17. Ibid., April 27, 29, 1955.

18. Ibid., April 28, May 1, 1955.

19. Ibid., April 28, 1955.

20. Ibid., April 29, 30, 1955.

21. Ibid., April 30, May 1, 1955.

22. Ibid., May 1, 2, 1955.

23. Ibid., May 2–4, 1955; *Montgomery Advertiser*, May 3, 1955.

24. *Columbus Ledger-Enquirer*, May 5, 2002.

25. *Birmingham News*, May 3, 5, 1955.

CHAPTER 12

1. *Birmingham News*, February 20, 1955; *Huntsville Times*, October 11, 1955.

2. Alabama Supreme Court, *Ex parte State of Alabama, ex rel. John M. Patterson, Attorney General*, 4 Div. 874, October 9, 1958, 108 So. 2d, 448–54; *Huntsville Times*, October 12–13, 20–21, 1955; *Montgomery Advertiser*, October 20–21, 24–25, 1955, November 22, 1955.

3. Alabama Supreme Court, *Ex parte State of Alabama, ex rel. John M. Patterson, Attorney General*, 4 Div. 874, October 9, 1958, 108 So. 2d, 448–54; *Huntsville Times*, October 21, 25, 1955; *Montgomery Advertiser*, October 20–21, November 26, 1955.

4. "Brief and Argument of John Patterson, et al.," n.d., *Fuller v. State*, ADAH.

5. "Statement of Mrs. C. W. Bentley," June 2, 1955, New Trial Hearing, ibid.

6. "Statement of Robert Waters," June 4, 1955, New Trial Hearing, ibid.

7. "Statement of W. E. Wages," June 2, 1955, New Trial Hearing, ibid.

8. "Statement of Freda Ann Miller," March 24, 1955, New Trial Hearing, ibid.

9. *Mobile Press*, June 13, 1955; *Mobile Register*, June 13, 1955; *Birmingham News*, June 13, 1955; *Montgomery Advertiser*, June 16, 1955.

10. *Montgomery Advertiser*, July 22, 1955, June 17, 1956, February 3, 1958, June 18, 1960; *Montgomery Advertiser-Journal*, April 12, 1963.

11. *Montgomery Advertiser*, June 19, 1956; Baker, interview.

12. *Montgomery Advertiser*, February 3, 1958.

13. Ibid., February 7, 1958.

14. Baker, interview.

15. Ibid.

16. Ibid. This story is confirmed by C. L. Rabren, ADFS legal custodian of records, who recalls the memorandum from the metallurgical lab outlining the results of the analysis. In the late 1980s, Noel Baker requested the

memorandum for a newspaper article, but it was never found among the department's records.

17. *Fuller v. State; Birmingham Post-Herald,* July 6, 1965, September 17, 1969; *Birmingham News,* July 7, 1965; *Montgomery Advertiser-Journal,* July 20, 1965; *Montgomery Advertiser,* July 10, 1969; *Columbus Ledger,* September 17, 1969.

18. *(Montgomery) Alabama Journal,* July 27, 1967.

19. *Montgomery Advertiser,* April 21, 1956; *Columbus Ledger-Enquirer,* August 5, 1993.

20. Alabama governors web page, http://www.archives.state.al.us/govslist.

21. *Columbus Ledger,* September 14, 1965.

22. Cecil Padgett to John Patterson, June 10, 1964, February 11, May 11, 1965, "Cecil Padgett" folder, John Patterson Papers.

23. *Birmingham News,* September 13, 1965; *Birmingham Post-Herald,* September 13, 1965; *Columbus Ledger,* September 14, 1965; *Montgomery Advertiser,* September 14, 1965.

24. *Montgomery Advertiser,* November 29, December 8, 1955.

25. Rev. "Mack" Finney, interview by author, Huntsville, Ala., March 27, 1995; *Birmingham News,* September 8, 1954.

26. *The Phenix City Story,* Allied Artists, 1955.

Bibliography

PRIMARY SOURCES

Manuscript Sources

Alabama Department of Archives and History, Montgomery.
  Albert Patterson Case Files.
  Folsom, Governor James. Papers.
  Fuller v. State, Supreme Court of Alabama, February 12, 1959, 6 Div. 917.
  Patterson, John. Papers.
  Persons, Governor Gordon. Papers.
Alabama Department of Forensic Sciences, Auburn.
  Case 54-14662 (Albert Patterson Homicide File).
Alabama Department of Public Safety, Public Information and Education Unit, Montgomery
  "History of the Investigative and Identification Division," September 19, 1974.
Birmingham Public Library, Archives and Manuscripts Department.
  Albert L. Patterson FBI Investigative Files.
  Warren, Jack. Papers.
Finney Family Private Collection.
  Finney, Hershel. "Alabama National Guard—Phenix City History," draft typescript, n.d.

Court Cases

Ex parte Garrett. Alabama Supreme Court, 76 So. 2d (1954).
Ex parte State of Alabama, *ex rel*. John M. Patterson, Attorney General. Alabama Supreme Court, 108 So. 2d (1958).
Fuller v. State. Alabama Supreme Court, 113 So. 2d (1959).
State ex rel. Martin, Attorney General v. John B. Tully, Circuit Judge, Alabama Supreme Court, 15 So. (1894).

Newspapers

Birmingham (Ala.) News
Birmingham (Ala.) Post-Herald

Columbus (Ga.) Enquirer
Columbus (Ga.) Ledger
Huntsville (Ala.) Times
Mobile (Ala.) Press-Register
Montgomery (Ala.) Advertiser
Opelika (Ala.) Daily News

Subjects Interviewed by the Author

Allen, Walter L. Montgomery, Ala., October 21, 1994.

Baker, Noel. Opelika, Ala., August 1, 1994.

Brewer, Albert P. Birmingham, Ala., August 28, 1990.

Brown, Colonel James "Boxcar." Birmingham, Ala., March 17, 1995.

Caldwell, James. Lanett, Ala., August 25, 1994.

Cloud, Major John. Alabama Department of Public Safety. Montgomery, Ala., May 14, 1998.

Cole, Ruth. Birmingham, Ala., January 9, 1998.

Coulter, Hilda. Phenix City, Ala., November 30, 1994.

Finney, Rev. "Mack." Huntsville, Ala., March 27, 1995.

Fowler, Conrad "Bulley." Tuscaloosa, Ala., July 13, 1994.

Franklin, Captain Charles. Alabama Department of Public Safety. Montgomery, Ala., June 30, 1998.

Franklin, Steve. Phenix City, Ala., June 20, 1996, July 21, 1997.

Gallion, George MacDonald. Montgomery, Ala., August 19, 1990, September 1, October 11, November 10, December 30, 1994, March 6, 1998, September 1, 1999.

Gwin, Robert. Birmingham, Ala., October 16, 1997.

Howard, Gene. Jacksonville, Ala., October 21, 1990.

Ingram, Bob. Montgomery, Ala., September 4, 1990, March 15, 1996.

Jenkins, Ray. Baltimore, Md., February 8, 29, 1996.

Kimbrell, Fuller. Tuscaloosa, Ala., September 4, 1990.

Kirkland, James. Phenix City, Ala., April 10, 1996.

MacMurdo, Tim. Huntsville, Ala., September 22, 1999.

Mitchell, Carson. Phenix City, Ala., January 13, 1999.

Oden, Morris. Birmingham, Ala., November 17, 1994.

Patterson, John. Montgomery, Ala., October 23, 1990, October 21, 1994, January 9, 1995.

Persons, Gordon, Jr. Gulf Shores, Ala., May 29, 1996.

Prier, Claude. Mobile, Ala., July 2, 1998.

Rabren, C. L. Auburn, Ala., December 10, 1997.

Ratigan, Ed. Birmingham, Ala., March 26, 1995.

Redden, Drew. Birmingham, Ala., August 16, 1994, August 21, 1997, April 10, 2000.

Rinehart, Ted. Montgomery, Ala., November 10, 1994.

Robertson, Joe. Birmingham, Ala., October 2, 2000.

Sanders, James. Phenix City, Ala., June 11, 1995.

Shoemaker, Major Jerry. Alabama Department of Public Safety. Montgomery, Ala., June 30, September 14, 1998.

Simpson, Fred. Huntsville, Ala., April 17, 2000.

Smith, Maury. Montgomery, Ala., September 9, 13, 20, 1994, January 10, 25, 1995, January 25, 2000.

Sowell, Wendell, Jr. Hanceville, Ala., May 4, 1998.

Stallworth, Clarke. Birmingham, Ala., July 25, 1994.

Strickland, Ed. Montgomery, Ala., October 7, 1994.

Teague, Doris. Alabama Department of Public Safety. Montgomery, Ala., January 25, 2000.

Turney, Mrs. Norris. Hartselle, Ala., January 18, 1998.

Williams, Lieutenant John, III. Alabama Department of Public Safety. Montgomery, Ala., June 30, 1998.

SECONDARY SOURCES

Alabama. *Code of Alabama 1940*. St. Paul, Minn.: West, 1941.

——. *Journals of the Senate of State of Alabama, Organizational Session of 1947*. Birmingham: Birmingham Printing Co., 1948.

[Alabama] Democratic Executive Committee. *Official Election Returns, Democratic Primaries, Alabama, 1918 and 1920*. Montgomery: Brown Printing Co., 1920.

Alabama Supreme Court. *Alabama Rules of Criminal Procedure, 1991*. Ed. Hugh Maddox. Charlottesville, Va.: Michie, 1990.

American Legion Department of Alabama. *A History of the American Legion and American Legion Auxiliary in Alabama, 1948–1975*. Birmingham: Birmingham Publishing Co., 1978.

Barnes, Margaret Anne. *The Tragedy and the Triumph of Phenix City, Alabama*. Macon, Ga.: Mercer University Press, 1998.

Cater, Douglas. "The Wide-Open Town on the Chattahoochee." *Reporter*, February 24, 1955, 22–27.

"Claude S. Prier Is New Executive Director." *Alabama Police Journal*, Spring 1979, 17.

Coulter, Harold S. *A People Courageous: A History of Phenix City, Alabama*. Columbus, Ga.: Howard Printing Co., 1976.

"Crime—Politics, Incorporated." *Alabama: The News Magazine of the Deep South*, June 25, 1954, 4.

"Crime: The Odds Were Right," *Time*, June 28, 1954, 22.

Gilliam, Thomas Jasper. "The Second Folsom Administration: The Destruction of Alabama Liberalism, 1954–1958." Ph.D. diss., Auburn University, 1975.

Heard, Alexander, and Donald G. Strong. *Southern Primaries and Elections, 1920–1949*. Tuscaloosa: University of Alabama Press, 1950.

Hillyer, Katharine, and Katharine Best. "The Angry Women of Phenix City." *McCall's*, September 1955, 52ff.

Key, V. O., Jr. *Southern Politics in State and Nation*. New York: Vintage Books, 1949.

MacLean, William Campbell, IV. "From the Ashes: Phenix City, Alabama, and Its Struggle with Memory." Master's thesis, Emory University, 1995.

Martin, David L. *Alabama's State and Local Governments*. Tuscaloosa: University of Alabama Press, 1975.

McGlasson, W. D. "Phenix City 1954: Putting Out the Flames of Corruption." *National Guard*, June 1981, 8–13, 29.

Patterson, John. *Messages and Addresses of John Patterson, Governor of Alabama, 1959–1963; Attorney General of Alabama, 1955–1959*. Montgomery: Brown Printing Co., 1963.

Patterson, John, with Furman Bisher. "I'll Get the Gangs That Killed My Father!" *Saturday Evening Post*, November 27, 1954, 20–21, 60–64.

Perry, Emmett. "The Story behind Phenix City: The Struggle for Law in a Modern Sodom." *American Bar Association Journal* 42 (December 1956): 1146–49, 1178–79.

Rumore, Pat Boyd. *Lawyers in a New South City: A History of the Legal Profession in Alabama*. Birmingham: Associated Publishing Co., 2000.

Russell County Historical Commission. *History of Russell County*. Dallas: National Sharegraphics, 1982.

Sentell, J. O. "Roderick Beddow of the Birmingham Bar." *Alabama Lawyer* 31, no. 3 (1970): 342–62.

Sims, George E. *The Little Man's Big Friend: James E. Folsom in Alabama Politics, 1946–1958*. Tuscaloosa: University of Alabama Press, 1985.

Strickland, Edwin, and Gene Wortsman. *Phenix City: The Wickedest City in America*. Birmingham: Vulcan Press, 1955.

Taylor, Sandra Baxley. *Faulkner: Jimmy, That Is*. Huntsville, Ala.: Strode Publishers, 1984.

Index